SUBSTANCE ABUSE PREVENTION ACTIVITIES FOR SECONDARY STUDENTS

Ready-to-Use Lessons, Fact Sheets, and Resources for Grades 7-12

Patricia J. Gerne, R.N., C.A.C.
and
Timothy A. Gerne, Jr., Ed.D.

illustrated by Eileen Gerne Ciavarella

PRENTICE HALL
Englewood Cliffs, New Jersey 07632

Prentice-Hall International, Inc., *London*
Prentice-Hall of Australia, Pty. Ltd., *Sydney*
Prentice-Hall Canada, Inc., *Toronto*
Prentice-Hall of India Private Ltd., *New Delhi*
Prentice-Hall of Japan, Inc., *Tokyo*
Prentice-Hall of Southeast Asia Pte. Ltd., *Singapore*
Editora Prentice-Hall do Brasil Ltda., *Rio de Janeiro*
Prentice-Hall Hispanoamericana, S.A., *Mexico*

6 7 8 9 10

Library of Congress Cataloging-in-Publication Data

Gerne, Patricia J.
Substance abuse prevention activities for secondary students: ready-to-use lessons, fact sheets, and resources for grades 7–12 / Patricia J. Gerne and Timothy A. Gerne; illustrated by Eileen Gerne Ciavarella.
p. cm.
ISBN 0-13-876707-6
1. Drug abuse—United States—Prevention—Problems, exercises, etc. 2. Alcoholism—United States—Prevention—Problems, exercises, etc. 3. Smoking—United States—Prevention—Problems, exercises, etc. 4. Life skills—United States—Problems, exercises, etc. I. Gerne, Timothy A. II. Title.
HV5808.G47 1991
362.29'17'071173—dc20 91-19746
CIP

ISBN 0-13-876707-6

PRENTICE HALL
Business Information Publishing Division
Englewood Cliffs, NJ 07632

Simon & Schuster

PRINTED IN THE UNITED STATES OF AMERICA

Dedicated . . . .

TO OUR PARENTS

Bill & Millie Griffin Tim & Pet Gerne

for their love and support during *our* adolescence.

TO OUR CHILDREN

Mary, Tim, Jean, Eileen, Kathy, Margaret, Donna, Danny, Rose & Michael for all they taught us about the beauty and fragility of this period of growth during *their* adolescence.

TO THEIR CHILDREN

Tim, Megan, Gina, Daniel, John Michael, David, Nicki, Maggie, John Paul, Elizabeth, Jessica, Sarah, Cassandra, Christopher to whom we give our love and our hope for courage and joy as they successfully negotiate passage through *their* adolescence.

ABOUT THE AUTHORS

TIMOTHY A. GERNE, Ed.D., has worked as an educator for over 30 years. He is a professor in the School of Education's Department of Curriculum and Instruction at The William Paterson College of New Jersey in Wayne. Dr. Gerne is Vice-Chairperson of the Professional Advisory Committee, as well as Chairperson of the Education Committee for the Passaic County Division of Alcoholism, Drug Abuse and Addiction Services.

PATRICIA J. GERNE is a Registered Nurse and a Certified Alcoholism Counselor (C.A.C.), with an extensive background in the field of addiction treatment and prevention. Her involvement during the last 17 years has included using her skills in long- and short-term in-patient addiction rehabilitation programs, a detoxification unit, as well as employment as a Family Counselor in an out-patient addiction treatment facility. Presently, Mrs. Gerne is a Consultant to the Center for Family Resources, Inc. of Wanaque, New Jersey. She also meets with families affected by chemical dependency.

DR. AND MRS. GERNE are co-directors of the William Paterson College two-day residential Peer Counseling Institute and the Annual Youth Day Conference, "Reach Out", for high school students throughout Passaic County, which they founded in 1985. They lecture and present workshops on substance abuse prevention for grades K-12. The parents of ten children, Dr. and Mrs. Gerne are also the authors of *Substance Abuse Prevention Activities for Elementary Children* (Englewood Cliffs, N.J.: Prentice Hall, 1986), a unique collection of ready-to-use classroom activities to develop children's knowledge of the facts about substance abuse as well as their positive self-image, decision-making, coping strategies, and personal values.

About This Book

Substance Abuse Prevention Activities for Secondary Students give teachers and counselors in grades 7-12 a store of easy-to-use instructional material to help students become aware of the causes and dangers of substance abuse, and to prepare them with the knowledge, skills, and confidence to make healthy personal and social choices for a drug-free lifestyle. It includes 61 detailed lessons accompanied by over 130 reproducible Fact Sheets and Activity Sheets that can be copied right from the book for immediate classroom use. Six special appendices at the end provide helpful notes to the teacher, information about abused drugs and AIDS, descriptions of several community partnerships, and addresses of self-help groups and state government agencies for drug/alcohol information.

The basic premises underlying the lessons and activities in this book are that *prevention* is the best response to alcohol and other substance abuse. We believe that drug prevention efforts must focus on *people* and the *factors that influence their behavior*. Accordingly, the first chapter of the book, "An Overview," begins by examining the scope of an effective drug prevention program and the role of the educator. Next, though we are aware that most readers will have an understanding of adolescence, it provides a brief sketch of the developmental tasks and some of the particular stresses of contemporary society that young people have to negotiate successfully. Included at the end of each developmental task are clear, simply defined goals to assist adolescents along that path.

The body of the book is organized into two main sections:

LIFE SKILLS ACTIVITIES (Chapters 2-7) and DRUG INFORMATION ACTIVITIES (Chapters 8-17). These are designed to give educators information and strategies to help students see themselves as:

(a) *loveable* (I AM. . . .)

INTRAPERSONAL SKILLS	The activities in Chapters 2 and 3 focus on the *intrapersonal skills* needed to deal effectively with self-concept and one's own feelings.

(b) *capable* (I CAN. . .)

INTERPERSONAL SKILLS	The activities in Chapters 5, 6, and 7 focus on the *interpersonal skills* needed in making connections, communicating, problem-solving, and decision-making, including Refusal strategies.

(c) *responsible* (I WILL. . . .)

DRUG INFORMATION	The activities in Chapters 8 through 17 (Part II) focus on *drug information.* They alert the students to the consequences that can result from its use, misuse, and abuse. This information is a necessary component in their decision-making process.

While the main focus of the Drug Activities in Part II is on those drugs taken specifically for their *psychoactive* properties (to alter consciousness and therefore affect behavior), a brief review of over-the-counter and prescription drugs is also included in Chapter 8, "Introduction to Drugs." Many of these drugs have psychoactive effects and can be abused.

"An awareness that the sequence of drug use *begins* with *legal* substances points up the need to encompass the whole phenomenon of drug use, both legal and illegal. . ." (Mills & Noyes, 1984). In Part II, particular attention is given to (1) *Alcohol,* which is still the *most abused* drug; (2) *Tobacco,* since research indicates that cigarette smoking is strongly related to the onset of (3) *Marijuana* use (which is the most abused *illegal* drug); and (4) *Crack/Cocaine,* because of its high addictive quality and the broad negative social consequences resulting from its use.

Drug use is closely linked with the *AIDS* crisis. *Intravenous drug use* is a route of transmission for the AIDS virus. And the use of *mood-altering substances* impairs judgement and lowers inhibitions, increasing the incidence of *sexual activity* (possibly with an infected person). Therefore, the decision was made to place information about AIDS in the appendix (3A-1 to 3A-5), and not relegate it to any one chapter, to be a readily available reference when it would be appropriate and applicable during any activity in this book.

You will find that *Substance Abuse Prevention Activities for Secondary Students* provides a wide range of activities that appeal to many different students.

The activities include numerous opportunities to examine, explore, and discuss issues of importance to adolescents at various levels of development. They can be presented in the given sequence or be used in any order desired to reinforce or extend a particular program or curriculum.

The following are some special features related to the format and use of these materials:

(1) Each chapter topic is accompanied by an information page headed *Spreading the News—Fact Sheet* that provides important information about the subject matter to be explored in the activities that follow. Each lesson presented under the topic heading includes a teacher's information page as well as one or more reproducible activity sheets for the students.

Spreading the News

(2) When the figure of the "Director" appears on the page, it indicates that the activity can be executed in role play, as well as in writing or group discussion. The teacher will decide which is the most appropriate for his or her group. Confucius said centuries ago:
I hear and I forget.
I see and I remember.
I do and I understand.

(3) *Shedding a little light* is included to offer some interesting facts and ideas, or to emphasize or clarify a specific point that might be of value to teachers or their students. This information has been placed at the bottom of the page so that it will not interrupt the flow of the activity.

Saying "No" to drugs is not enough. We must present our young people with the knowledge and skills, the encouragement and support to say "Yes" to life. It is our hope that you will use *Substance Abuse Prevention Activities for Secondary Students* to do just that!

Tim and Pat Gerne

ACKNOWLEDGMENTS

We wish to acknowledge the professional and personal support of our friends and colleagues, especially:

Irene Montella, Ph.D., English Department, Ramapo High School, Franklin Lakes, New Jersey;

Eleanor Chapman, R.N., B.S., School Nurse/Health Educator, Lodi High School, Lodi, New Jersey;

Carolyn Hadge, M.A., C.A.C., District Coordinator for the national award-winning Toms River Schools' Alcohol and Substance Abuse Program, Toms River, New Jersey;

Veronica H. Potter, B.S., R.N., M.S., Marriage and Family Counselor;

Thomas E. Potter, M.D., F.A.A.P., Chairman, Department of Pediatrics, St. Joseph's Hospital and Medical Center, Paterson, New Jersey;

Robert Gerne, B.S., M.A., Guidance Counselor, Wayne Valley High School, Wayne, New Jersey;

Susan Hunt, B.S., C.A.C., junior high school English teacher, Maywood Avenue School, Maywood, New Jersey;

Robert M. Weiler, Ph.D., M.P.H., Department of Health Education, Southern Illinois University at Carbondale, Illinois.

It was a great pleasure to collaborate with our daughter Eileen, who created the artwork for this book.

Contents

I. AN OVERVIEW

Drug Prevention must focus on PEOPLE and the FACTORS that influence their BEHAVIOR.

The scope of an effective drug prevention program; the teacher's role and the classroom environment, as well as the adolescents' developmental needs, will be examined to provide a basis for understanding and using the activities in Chapters 2 through 17.

1

Programs for Drug Prevention

Scare tactics and preaching are the least successful approaches in making significant long-term behavioral changes in young people. Intellectual activity cannot be separated from the "total functioning" of a person. Cognitive or intellectual development is only a part of growth and development. Another major aspect is EFFECTIVE development, which is concerned with the *attitudes, values,* and *feelings* that students will bring to the learning experience.

All behavior has both affective and cognitive aspects. FEELINGS BECOME FACTORS IN DECIDING WHAT TO DO AND WHAT NOT TO DO (see Figure 1-1, Maslow's Hierarchy of Needs). The *affective* domain provides an important link between the *content learned,* and the *behavior* of the student. It is both an aid to internalization, and an aid to processing information into memory. All experiences are stored for future reference. *Therefore, effective drug prevention education is a "Process."* The individual internalizes self-knowledge, makes value judgments, and assumes the responsibility for his or her decisions and behavior toward drug use or non-use. By recognizing this reality, you as the teacher are responsible for creating an atmosphere in which the student can relate to the information *affectively,* from his or her own experiences.

An important fact about the *process approach* is that the skills that are taught are transferrable to other tasks. Process skills are not isolated bits of knowledge but broad skills that can be used for a lifetime.

Figure 1-1

The humanist psychologist Abraham Maslow theorized that basic *needs motivate* human *behavior.* He identified and clarified the interaction between *internal needs* and *external satisfactions.*

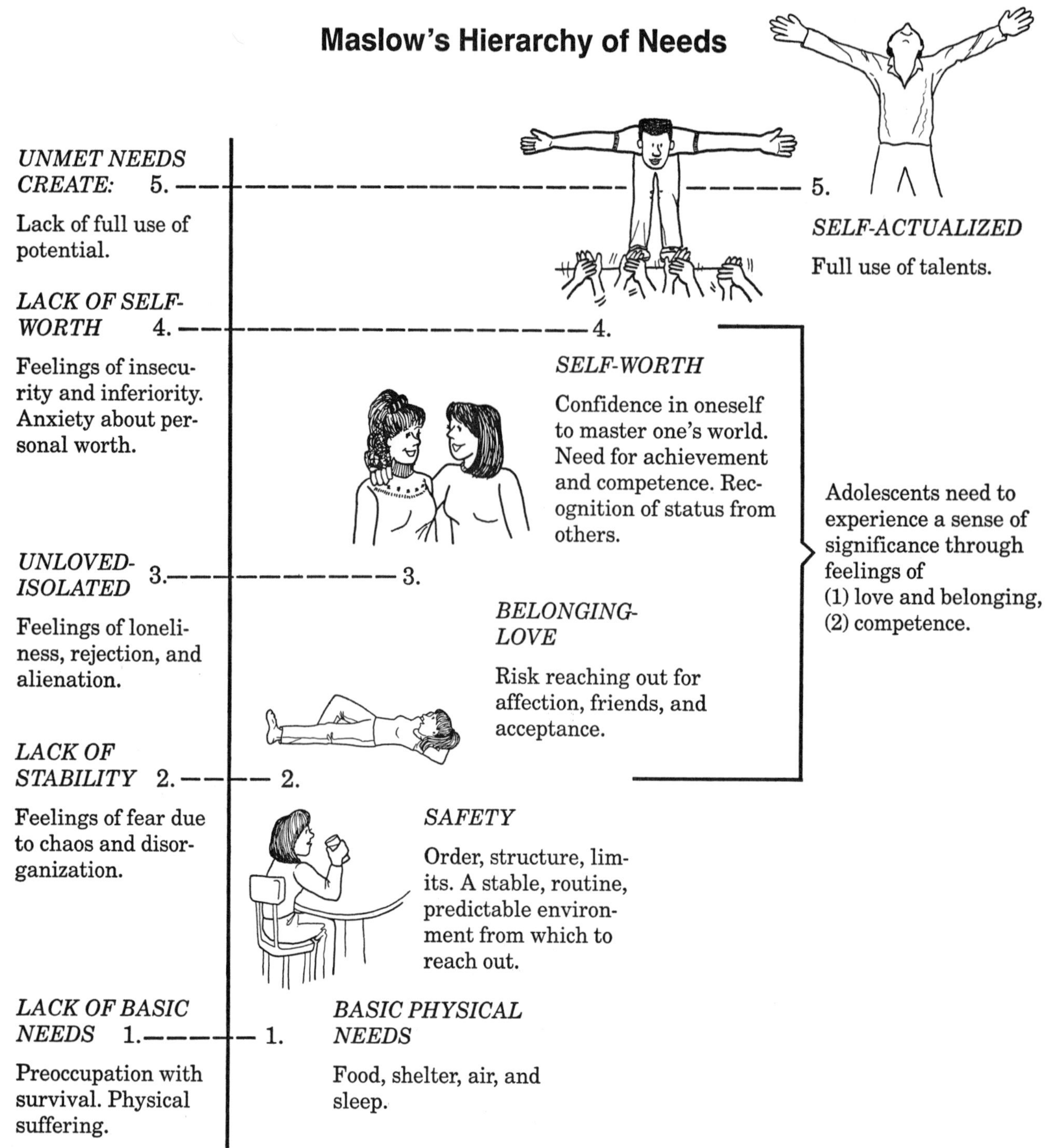

Drug prevention must focus on *people* and the factors that influence their *behavior.* Feelings become factors in what we do—and what we don't do.

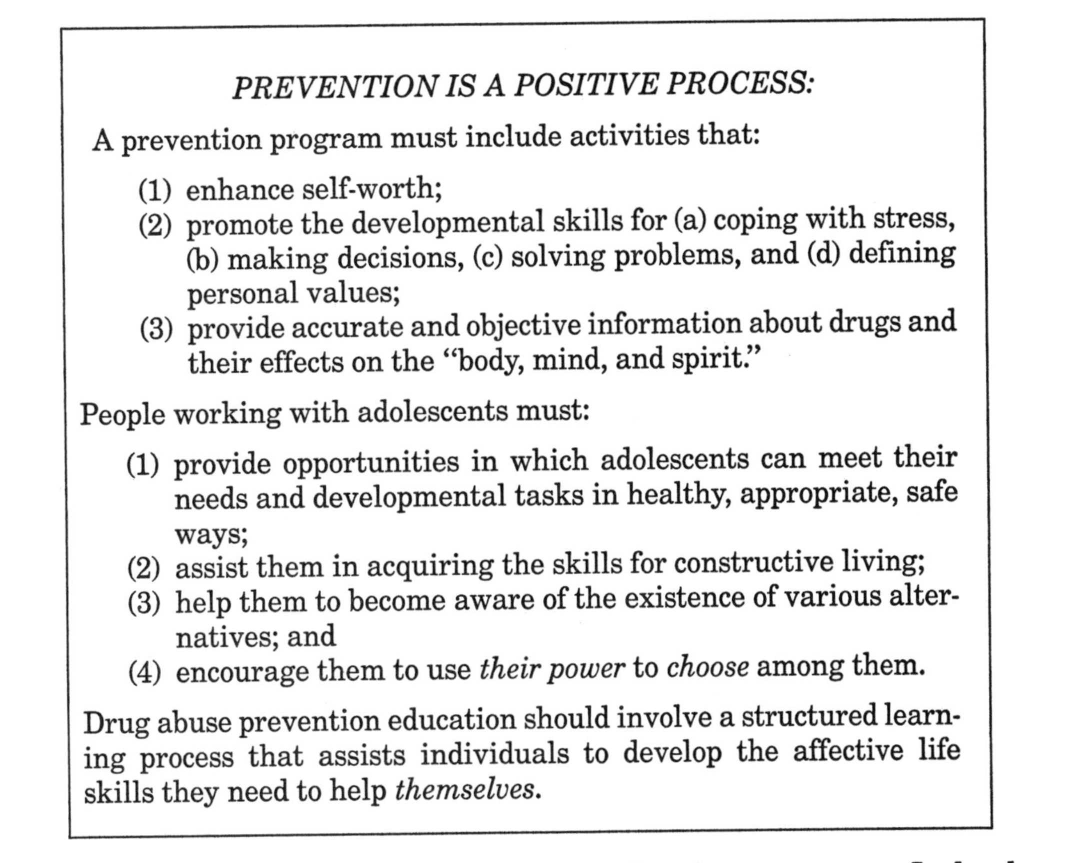

PREVENTION IS A POSITIVE PROCESS:

A prevention program must include activities that:

(1) enhance self-worth;
(2) promote the developmental skills for (a) coping with stress, (b) making decisions, (c) solving problems, and (d) defining personal values;
(3) provide accurate and objective information about drugs and their effects on the "body, mind, and spirit."

People working with adolescents must:

(1) provide opportunities in which adolescents can meet their needs and developmental tasks in healthy, appropriate, safe ways;
(2) assist them in acquiring the skills for constructive living;
(3) help them to become aware of the existence of various alternatives; and
(4) encourage them to use *their power* to *choose* among them.

Drug abuse prevention education should involve a structured learning process that assists individuals to develop the affective life skills they need to help *themselves.*

Education flourishes in an *environment* rather than a program. In developing a theory of human behavior and motivation, Maslow (1968) stated that there are several basic needs that must be met before an individual can function effectively within an environment, and move in the direction of learning and growth. Two of the needs that Maslow defines as basic, relate directly to the adolescent's need to experience *a sense of significance.* Maslow notes that individuals have a need for feelings of: (1) *love and belonging.* They need to receive support from significant others. And, educators, counselors, and parents working with adolescents should examine their interactions to see if they are responding to the young peoples' needs for (2) *a sense of competence,* by providing them with opportunities to be involved and to assume responsibility, within a reasonable amount of structure. Positive experiences which are appropriate to the students' needs build confidence. The degree to which each adolescent experiences a sense of significance, is the degree to which their self-image (and behavior) is positively affected.

THE TEACHER

"I touch the future—I teach." Christa McAuliffe

Teachers have an opportunity to spend time with young people who are in the process of making important decisions about their future. A teacher's contribution can be crucial, particularly to a young person whose ideas of the world and of his/her own potential are uncertain. They have perhaps, the greatest opportunity to prevent the sense of isolation and loneliness so common among young people today. The teacher can provide the understanding and guidance the student needs to work through his/her confusion and conflict.

Because a young person's decision to use or not to use alcohol and/or other drugs is frequently derived from the sum of his attitudes toward himself and the world, teachers have potentially a strong role to play in the whole matter of substance abuse by the young. A single interested adult within a school may offer a whole new view of the future to a youngster. Dr. Michael Rutter, a British psychiatrist, in his book (Rutter et al., *Fifteen Thousand Hours: Secondary Schools & Their Effects on Children.* Cambridge: Harvard Press, 1979) indicated that even children from disadvantaged homes can deal positively with adversity, through the interactions provided in a warm and accepting atmosphere of a school with teachers who are open to the students.

There is no question, that students taught by teachers who can establish open, warm relationships within the classroom learn more than students taught by teachers who do not possess these characteristics.

The attitude a teacher conveys makes a deeper, more profound impression on the student than all the factual information in a text. Students work better when they feel their teacher cares about them and where there is substantial use of praise and approval in the classroom setting. *A teacher's opinion of a student often plays a very important part in the student's own opinion of himself!* This message is part of the information from the environment that the student will internalize to create his self-image. Carl Rogers and other humanistic psychologists believe that the most important aspect of personality evaluation is how the person sees himself. Because one's self-esteem is influenced by the manner in which one is treated, the implications for teachers are clear. Assisting a young person to increase his feelings of self-worth will increase his courage to tackle new challenges, as well as encourage him to make constructive decisions. Students achieve more when teachers treat them in ways which emphasize their successes and potential for good, rather than ways which focus on their failings and short-comings. William Glasser (1969) placed a great emphasis on the *quality of the adult-adolescent relationship* and the degree to which the young person sees himself as valued by adults.

Young people learn TO BE what they SEE and EXPERIENCE. Though modeling is not always a conscious act, the students learn more from what they observe in school, in the home, and from peers than they do in formal classroom instruction. They need to experience people who are worthy role models. Adults must provide examples that indicate the struggle to define one's values and role in society is meaningful, attainable, and worthy of effort.

ADOLESCENTS

The Challenges

The young adolescent is like an astronaut on an uncharted journey. . . . as he moves away from the protected and secure world of childhood toward a new, more independent way of life. No longer a child, and not yet an adult, the adolescent will move erratically between these two worlds. For a time he belongs fully to neither. As a result, his behavior is often inconsistent and unpredictable. Physical changes take place. Even the once familiar body seems strange, as face, arms, legs, and genitals change. And, while he must cope with these physical changes, new social tasks emerge, as the primary focus begins shifting from one social group (the family) to another (his peers). As a result, adolescents are generally in a state of ambivalence, until they finally redefine their relationship to the adult world.

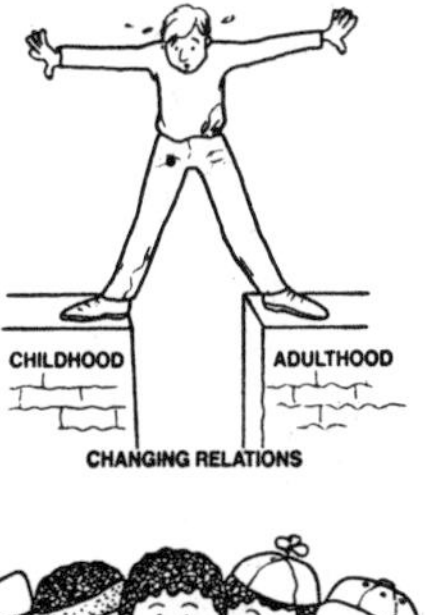

Psychosocial Moratorium

Identity Crisis

The early years of adolescence are often the most confusing. Although a person's identity is continuously modifying throughout the lifecycle, it is in adolescence that a "unique self" will be formed. Over a span of six or seven years, different aspects of the person's identity comes into focus—the sexual self, a sense of confidence or doubt, work or career goals, personal values, and a sense of recognition or isolation. This growing awareness of an inner maturing self is such a profound step in development that young people need a period of time to create a sense of order; and to find their role, their work, and their "place" in an adult society. Eric Erikson, the noted psychiatrist called this period of experimentation a *psychosocial moratorium.* This period serves as a time of freedom when a variety of roles can be explored, prior to adolescents' commitment to their functioning as adults. Gradually, by using their cognitive powers to select and integrate new information and discoveries about themselves, a clear sense of a "unique self" is formed.

Societal Factors

Adolescent behaviors are to some extent a response to the anxiety and confusion experienced while trying out new skills that will be needed to meet these physical and cognitive changes. However, adolescent behaviors are also influenced by many societal factors that intensify these difficulties. Some cultures clearly define the passage from childhood to adulthood. Once the physically mature person has completed the "rite of passage" in his or her culture, he or she is considered a part of the adult community. For those cultures, the passage from childhood to adulthood is abbreviated.

But, not so for our industrial society. The roles of young people have been dramatically affected over the years. The rapid changes in societal structures seem to intensify the conflicts within the developmental tasks facing adolescents.

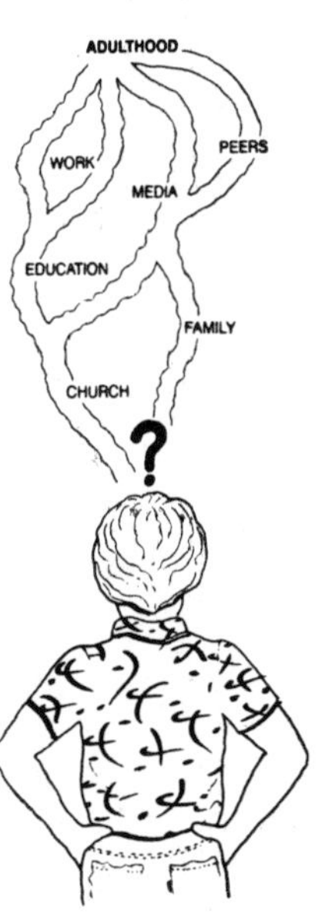

Due to the long period of preparation needed, the complexity of the tasks, and the segregation of the "child's world" from that of adults, our young people are often frustrated in their search for meaning and have difficulty in seeing clearly defined goals worth working toward.

> Since Drug Prevention must focus on *people* and the *factors that influence their behavior*, a clear understanding of adolescence and the challenges our young people face today is of utmost importance. Only then can we give them the help and support they need.

GROWTH SPURT

BODY

Body image is a concept of *physical appearance* and *feelings about it* that is based on the individual's current and past experiences of his or her own body, real and fantasized (Schonfeld, W.A., "The Body and the Body-Image in Adolescents," from H. Caplan et al., Eds., *Adolescence: Psychosocial Perspectives.* New York: Basic-Books, 1969).

Physical Appearance

Adolescents must learn to adjust to rapid physical changes. Within each individual, different body systems grow at different rates. It seems at times to be haphazard and chaotic. Feet and hands undergo a growth spurt before legs and arms lengthen; the nose reaches its adult length before the jaw thickens; and so on. In puberty, as hormones are activated, secondary sexual characteristics appear which help to distinguish males from females and indicate physiological maturity.

"AM I NORMAL?"

Emotional Status

Clothes that were comfortable no longer fit; spaces that once accommodate them are cramped and inadequate. The adolescent questions: "*Am I Normal?*" Each physical change evokes an *emotional reaction.* The degree of the reaction varies from one adolescent to another. Although the body may have changed dramatically during adolescence, the *present* picture may still be influenced by the *old* body image. There is also the fear that the physical characteristics he suddenly is presented with are not up to "acceptable standards." There is a great need to see oneself, and to be seen as "normal." There are many factors that make this a difficult task:

1. the differences in the timing of maturity,
2. the unrealistic expectations that one is *either* "perfect" *or* "unacceptable,"
3. the hormonal changes with their unpredictable impact,
4. the narrow presentation by the television media of what one "should" look like.

It's tough feeling "on stage" all the time

Since these physical changes occur at the same time that adolescents' cognitive skills are developing, there is an intense self-consciousness created. This new self-awareness and sensitivity tends to cause the young person to feel "different." He or she feels his/her situation is unique.

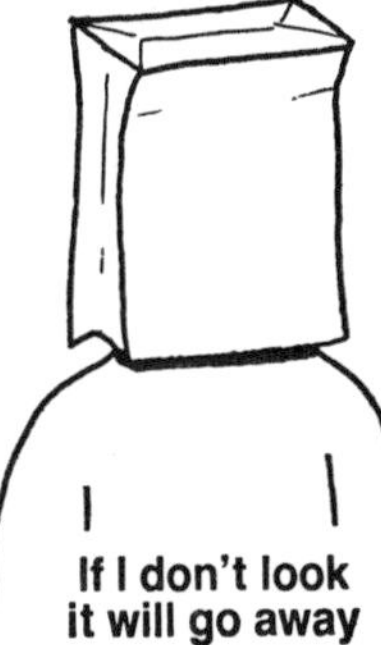

> Adolescents want to be attractive and to "fit in." The assessments by others are particularly crucial. The opinions of parents, teachers, other adults, and their peers, are very important. They need to receive positive statements and to be reassured.

Sexual Identity

Sexual identity is an important part of the overall sense of individual identity that develops during teenage years. As adolescents become sexually mature on the *physical* level, they must deal with the meaning of sexual identity on the *social* level. This is brought about by: (1) the experience of socializing with the opposite sex, (2) feeling desirable or undesirable, and (3) processing the experiences that involve sexual arousal.

While some of these stresses are common to adolescents in all societies, they become more pronounced in modern societies. In our culture, the time between puberty (physical maturity) and adult responsibility (social maturity) is almost as great as the period between birth and puberty. This can create tension for our youth, as social maturity lags so far behind biological maturity. How do they deal constructively with this reality? The adolescent would get different answers from a wide spectrum of adults. People, institutions, their peers, their church or synagogue, and the media (especially TV) give conflicting messages. This increases the anxiety of the adolescent.

> Our young people need accurate, factual information about their physically maturing selves, as well as the consequences of their choices. They need responsible, caring adults to *actively listen to them* and provide the support and respect each young person needs to work through his/her confusion and conflict.

> **Shedding a Little Light:**
> A small percentage of young people experience confusion about their sexual orientation. This issue, left unresolved, appears to lead to a disproportionate amount of addiction to alcohol and other drugs.

Redefining Relationships

Adolescence begins with physical changes but ultimately the young person must make changes in social understanding, and relationships. Relationships with family and friends are redefined. Participation in the family is no longer adequate for developing a full identity. Establishing healthy, satisfying peer relationships is a major developmental task for adolescents. Early adolescence (11 to

15 years of age) is a time of increasing attachment to the peer group. They need to be accepted and sustained by a small group of friends. Young adolescents tend to share their friends' attitudes, clothes, music, activities (shopping, team participation, etc.).

BUDDING INTIMACY

In later adolescence (15 to 18 years of age), friendships mature into fuller, more secure, and loyal commitments.

The peer group provides the setting for help in creating a personal identity. The peer group is used by the adolescent to: (1) try out new roles, (2) be a safe and available source of support, (3) broaden one's exposure to a larger world beyond the family, (4) obtain feedback, and (5) practice forming intimate relationships.

Risks of intimacy in relationships consist of opportunities for success, which results in acceptance; and for failure, which results in rejection. Adolescents must be able to handle both of these results in order to be considered mature.

> They need to be provided with activities for healthy interaction with members of the same sex, and members of the opposite sex. These activities can include sport teams, celebrations, and service groups.

MIND

My "Place" in the world

Cognitive development: Earlier thinking was *concrete*. Elementary grade children learn by doing, by acting out, by handling objects, by seeing pictures, and by hearing stories. Therefore, information must be presented in this concrete form in order for them to absorb it, process it, and assimilate it.

In adolescence, the thought process goes through dramatic changes. The development of *formal operational thinking* now permits abstract thought. Formal operations allow one to think *logically*, and to begin using *symbolic reasoning*. "Children with concrete operational thinking are able to discuss the world as it is; formal operational thought allows adolescents and adults to discuss the world as it *might become*."[1]

This increase in the ability to think abstractly allows adolescents to reflect on, and make judgments about their experiences. The flexibility of formal thought allows them to figure out their "place" in the world. This "new thinking" allows a greater ability to evaluate the *immediate* and *long-range consequences* of their actions. The egocentrism (self-centeredness) of adolescence changes as they expand their awareness and acquire a different view of their world. It is a time of anxiety and challenge.

> Young people must be provided with opportunities to be involved in making decisions in the areas that affect their lives, and to assume the responsibility for those decisions.

---

[1] Clarke-Stewart, Alison, Susan Friedman, and Joanne Koch, *Child Development Approach*, John Wiley & Sons, Inc., New York, 1985.

SPIRIT

In early adolescence, moral decisions are made on the basis of logic, rather than motivated by spiritual values. Kohlberg describes this stage as "Law and Order." Young adolescents, therefore, will tend to accept laws and rules if they appear to be reasonable.

As adolescents acquire more sophisticated cognitive skills, they begin to question a "law and order" morality. With their new capacity to think abstractly and explore alternatives, they may consider changing rules that do not "serve" them, or which appear unreasonable. A more abstract, *personalized* value system begins to develop.

There is much confusion facing today's youth as they struggle to sort out the values that influence their lives. The noted anthropologist, Margaret Mead, observed that in societies characterized by relatively stable customs and values, there is less turmoil in adolescence. In modern society, conflict is intensified by the rapid changes of once reliable structures. Even today's families are often different from their traditional form. As young adolescents work to belong to their peer group, they still desire and need the support of the family. This task is made more difficult by the increasing breakdown of the once traditional family structure. Stress produced by frequent mobility, the distress resulting from divorces, the creation of single parent families as well as blended families, require developing new solutions and networks to deal with the results of these changes.

The "flood" of information that is readily available through the communication media (especially TV), almost "drowns" the adolescent in a "sea" of ideas and choices. They need to learn how to *filter, interpret,* and *understand* the flood of information.

> Young people need worthy role models. They need adults who will provide the TIME and space for discussions and sharing of ideas to encourage and support them towards shaping their character and values. Adolescents need more emotional support and guidance than ever before.

Shedding a Little Light:

(1) Development is a continuous process.
(2) Growth and development vary among individuals.
(3) While general patterns of development are predictable, each person has a *unique personal* pattern.

II. LIFE SKILLS ACTIVITIES

The six chapters in this section of the book provide information and activities relating to:

- Self-Concept *(Chapter 2)*
- Naming and Claiming Feelings *(Chapter 3)*
- Taming and Aiming Feelings *(Chapter 4)*
- Making Connections *(Chapter 5)*
- Communication Skills *(Chapter 6)*
- Problem Solving and Decision Making *(Chapter 7)*

> "I like to think of myself as an artist, and my life is my greatest work of art. Every moment is a moment of creation, and each moment of creation contains infinite possibilities. I can do things the way I've always done them, or I can look at all the different alternatives, and try something new and different and potentially more rewarding. Every moment presents a new opportunity and a new decision.
>
> What a wonderful game we are all playing, and what a magnificent art form. . . ." (Excerpted from *Creative Visualization* by Shakti Gawain. Copyright 1978 Shakti Gawain. Reprinted with permission by New World Library, San Rafael, California.)

The following activities are designed to show a ______________________ Original.
Name

2

Self-Concept

Self-Concept or self-image is the set of *beliefs* and *mental pictures* that we all have about the kind of person we are.

Fact Sheet 1	Self-Concept
Fact Sheet 2	My Declaration of Self-Esteem by Virginia Satir
Activity Title	**Objectives**
2-1 I Am One of a Kind	To encourage self-acceptance
2-2 I'm O.K.	To increase self-awareness
2-3 A Look into the Future	To understand that how we see ourselves affects the decisions we make and the goals we set
2-4 For the Record	To recognize the beliefs and mental pictures we hold about us
2-5 A Vision	To identify one's good qualities
2-6 Choosing the View	To recognize that our expectations affect the outcome of our performance

A positive self-image is the necessary "cornerstone" for us to build a happy life.

Self-Concept

- *Self-Concept* or self-image is the set of *beliefs* and *mental pictures* that we all have about the kind of person we are. As a matter of fact, the quality of our life depends on the self-image *we accept.*
- Without exception, everything about us is a reflection of our self-image. Our mental, physical, and emotional well-being is included.
- Our self-image will affect the *relationships* we have, the *decisions* we make, and the *goals* we set for ourselves.

- Everyone is born with specific physical characteristics, as well as undiscovered capabilities and talents. Our full potential is not yet visible or complete. We are a "work in progress."
- However, we are *not* born with our *self-image.*
- Our beliefs about ourself are *learned*, and can be *unlearned.* The expectations and responses of other people influence how we see ourselves.

- Our *self-esteem* (*feelings* about ourself) is our *response* to our beliefs about ourself.
- It is an indication of how much we like and approve of our self-image.
- *Self-esteem* is the "*reputation* we have with ourself."

- A positive self-image is the necessary "cornerstone" for us to build a successful, happy life.
- *Improving our self-image can change our life.*

EXPECTATIONS

MY DECLARATION OF SELF-ESTEEM

I AM ME

IN ALL THE WORLD, THERE IS NO ONE ELSE EXACTLY LIKE ME
EVERYTHING THAT COMES OUT OF ME IS AUTHENTICALLY MINE
BECAUSE I ALONE CHOSE IT — I OWN EVERYTHING ABOUT ME
MY BODY, MY FEELINGS, MY MOUTH, MY VOICE, ALL MY ACTIONS,
WHETHER THEY BE TO OTHERS OR TO MYSELF – I OWN MY FANTASIES,
MY DREAMS, MY HOPES, MY FEARS — I OWN ALL MY TRIUMPHS AND
SUCCESSES, ALL MY FAILURES AND MISTAKES BECAUSE I OWN ALL OF
ME, I CAN BECOME INTIMATELY ACQUAINTED WITH ME — BY SO DOING
I CAN LOVE ME AND BE FRIENDLY WITH ME IN ALL MY PARTS — I KNOW
THERE ARE ASPECTS ABOUT MYSELF THAT PUZZLE ME, AND OTHER
ASPECTS THAT I DO NOT KNOW – BUT AS LONG AS I AM
FRIENDLY AND LOVING TO MYSELF, I CAN COURAGEOUSLY
AND HOPEFULLY LOOK FOR SOLUTIONS TO THE PUZZLES
AND FOR WAYS TO FIND OUT MORE ABOUT ME HOWEVER I
LOOK AND SOUND, WHATEVER I SAY AND DO, AND WHATEVER
I THINK AND FEEL AT A GIVEN MOMENT IN TIME IS AUTHENTICALLY
ME - IF LATER SOME PARTS OF HOW I LOOKED, SOUNDED, THOUGHT
AND FELT TURN OUT TO BE UNFITTING, I CAN DISCARD THAT WHICH IS
UNFITTING, KEEP THE REST, AND INVENT SOMETHING NEW FOR THAT
WHICH I DISCARDED — I CAN SEE, HEAR, FEEL, THINK, SAY, AND DO
I HAVE THE TOOLS TO SURVIVE, TO BE CLOSE TO OTHERS, TO BE PROD
UCTIVE, AND TO MAKE SENSE AND ORDER OUT OF THE WORLD OF
PEOPLE AND THINGS OUTSIDE OF ME — I OWN ME, AND THEREFORE
I CAN ENGINEER ME — I AM ME AND

I AM OKAY

Virginia Satir

Reprinted from the poster "I AM ME" © 1974 from the book *Self Esteem*, published by Celestial Arts, Berkeley, California.

I AM ONE OF A KIND 2-1

Objectives:

- To recognize one's uniqueness
- To encourage the students to accept themselves as they are

NOTE: We are each unique. There are no two people who are exactly the same. Therefore, we should not compare ourselves with anyone else.

Activities:

1. Ask a member of a medical laboratory or police department to talk about the uniqueness of fingerprints, voice sounds, and/or footprints.

   Note that babies' footprints are taken after they are born in a hospital—to be a source for a permanent positive identification.

   EACH OF US IS TRULY ONE OF A KIND!

2. To demonstrate the foolishness of making comparisons, have the students compare each of the following:

   2 colors   2 fruits   2 ice cream flavors
   2 songs   2 sports   2 seasons

   a. Discuss: (1) How are they the same? (2) How are they different? (3) Take a vote on each item to see which item each person in the class preferred. (It is probable that each item will receive some votes.)
   b. Help the students to recognize that each item was voted for *because* it was either *one* or the *other*. EACH is unique, with its own desirable characteristics and its own limitations.

c. Remind them that not *everyone* will like *us*, but *some* people will like us—just as we are.

3. Have the students complete Activity 2-1A, "I Can. . .,"to focus on their capabilities and accomplishments—including those things that we all may take for granted. For example:
   (1) I can play sports and dance. [The student can appreciate what their *legs* can *do*, even if they don't like the *shape* of their legs.]
   (2) I can smell the flowers, good cooking, perfume [even if they reject the *shape* of their noses].
   (3) I am a good listener, I can enjoy sunsets, paint, help others, etc.

   a. Instruct them to do the assignment over a period of a day or two, adding information as they think of it.
   b. Then, have the students break up into small groups. Each student will take a turn telling the group about one capability. How does it affect his/her life? How does it affect other people?
   (If any student hears of an accomplishment or a capability from one of the group members that they did not include on his/her paper, it can be added to the list now.)
   c. They can keep the list and refer to it when they need a boost.

Shedding a Little Light:
Feelings of gratitude have a positive effect on our self-image and our outlook on life.

Name ______________________________

Date ______________________________

I Can . . .

List the things that you *CAN* do. Be generous with yourself. Include those things we all may take for granted. Do not stop until you have at least *20* items on the list. You may explain or make a comment after each item.

1. ______________________________
2. ______________________________
3. ______________________________
4. ______________________________
5. ______________________________
6. ______________________________
7. ______________________________
8. ______________________________
9. ______________________________
10. ______________________________
11. ______________________________
12. ______________________________
13. ______________________________
14. ______________________________
15. ______________________________
16. ______________________________
17. ______________________________
18. ______________________________
19. ______________________________
20. ______________________________

Select one capability and tell how it affects your life. How does it affect the lives of others?

I'M O.K. 2-2

Objective:

To increase self-awareness
To increase self-acceptance

Activities:

1. Have the students complete Activity 2-2A, "My Diary." (*Optional*: The students can be divided into pairs. Each partner will talk for 2 minutes about an item in the diary that he/she would be comfortable sharing.) The students may share their general impressions about the activity with the class.
2. Ask the students to write a letter to someone from another planet, describing themselves. Include the physical characteristics, intellectual ability, and outstanding personality traits, etc. Remember, this "alien" needs things explained!
   a. Ask the students to create one strong positive statement about themselves, using the information from this activity.
   Example: "I am ____________. I know this because ______________."
   (*Optional*: Volunteers may acknowledge that a student, indeed, possesses that quality: "Mary is ____________. I know that because ________________" —that student will add his/her own validation of Mary's positive quality.)
   b. When the activity is completed, volunteers may be called upon to attempt naming each student and the quality he/she mentioned, to further reinforce and validate hearing the information.
3. Ask the students to bring an object to class that describes something about his/her personality. For example:
   an eraser = forgiving
   a light bulb = bright
   a rock = solid as a rock
   a seed or a small plant = in the process of growing, etc.
   (The remainder of this activity can be written, processed in a small group, or processed with the class.) The students can explain the object and how it relates to his/her personality.
4. Have the students complete Activity 2-2B, "The California Earthquake," to explore personal values.

Shedding a Little Light:
Improving one's self-image can change one's life, but no changes can take place until one *first* becomes aware of the self-image *he/she accepts.*

Name ______________________

Date ______________________

My Diary

Some people keep a diary. It can help them to know and understand themselves better. It can also be a record of how they grow and change. Fill in the spaces below in this "diary." Write a brief explanation after your answer in each category.

The one thing I've done that I am most proud of is ______________________

____

____

The bravest thing I've ever done is ______________________

____

____

Three things that scare me are ______________________

____

____

____

____

____

____

My most embarrassing moment was ______________________

____

____

____

The place I feel the happiest is ______________________

____

Continued

The thing that annoys me the most is

The person I am most comfortable talking with is

I worry sometimes that

In this school

My family

The only thing I would not do is

Continued

Something that I have not done yet that I would like to try is ______________________

____

____

____

I wish ______________________

Name ____________________________

Date ____________________________

The California Earthquake

1. Presume that you are a resident of San Francisco during the earthquake of October 1989. Many homes were destroyed. Some were damaged. You have just received word that because of the weakened structure of your home, you have been issued a green card. This means you have only 5 minutes to go inside your house to take out what you wish to save. What would you save? Explain why.

____

____

____

____

____

____

____

____

2. Your friend lives in the East, and you want to tell him or her about one of the things you lost in the earthquake that you miss the most. Explain why.

____

____

____

____

____

____

____

____

____

A LOOK INTO THE FUTURE 2-3

Objective:

- To inform the students that how we see ourselves affects the decisions we make and the goals we set

Activities:

Each of us has a "story to tell." Our life is a tale of discovery, adventure, decision-making, and special relationships.

1. Have the students each write a message about him/herself (about 20 lines), which is expected to be placed in a "Time Capsule," Activity 2-3A. It will be opened in the year 2500.

   What would you like to be remembered about yourself in that far distant future? Instruct the students to be specific, and write as much as necessary to clarify the message. Remember, it may be difficult to understand the people of today when viewed hundreds of years from now!

2. Have the students complete Activity 2-3B, "Now Playing......." Direct them to think about how they would like to see their lives become in the future. Have them place the title of their "ideal" life story in the marquee. Then ask them to write a brief script of their ideal life:
   a. What characters are important in it?
   b. What is the role you play?
   c. How would you like to see the play end?

3. The students can presume that their autobiography has been accepted by a major publishing company. Ask the students to use Activity 2-3C, "Sell It," to:
   a. Design a book jacket, and choose a title for their "autobiography." (Use a book jacket of a published book for a model. Encourage the students to be as "professional" as they can be. Remember that they pay people in the publishing business to *sell* the story through the book jacket.)
   b. Add a chapter about themselves as they think their lives would appear 4 years from now, using Activity 2-3D, "This Is Your Life."

Shedding a Little Light:
- These activities encourage the students to take a look at where they *are*, and where they are *going*.
- It is important to use our imagination to envision possibilities for our lives.

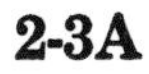

Name ____________________________________

Date ____________________________________

Time Capsule
To be opened in the year 2500

Write a message about yourself that will be placed in a Time Capsule to be opened in the year 2500. How would you like to be remembered? Be specific. Write as much as is necessary to clarify your message. Remember, it may be difficult to understand the people of today when viewed hundreds of years from now.

Name ______________________________

Date ______________________________

Now Playing . . .

1. The Marquee

NEW FEATURE

COMING SOON...

____

____

2. The Script:

Once upon a time ______________________________

THE END

Name ______________________________

Date ______________________________

Sell It

Be creative to "sell" your autobiography through the book jacket.

LAYOUT

______________ Author's Name HEALING PUBLICATIONS	FRONT COVER SPACE	ABOUT THE AUTHOR

Name ______________________________

Date ______________________________

This Is Your Life

Add a chapter to your life story. Write about yourself as you think your life may be 4 years from now. Use the present tense, as though it was a reality.

CHAPTER 15

It is 4 years later now, and I ______________________________

FOR THE RECORD 2-4

Objective:

- To help the students to recognize the "pictures" they have of themselves
- To encourage self-acceptance

Activities

1. Have the students complete Activity 2-4A, "Checklist." (It may be given for a homework assignment to allow time for thoughtful responses.)
   a. Then, have the students each choose a partner, or form a small group.
   b. Ask them to select one positive trait and discuss how it enhances their lives. Tell them to be specific about it.
   c. Ask them to select one negative trait that they want to "leave behind," and tell why.

> NOTE: *NO ONE IS PERFECT.* Everyone has strengths and weaknesses. Encourage the students to see their "weaknesses" as an *opportunity to grow.*

2. Have the students create a record album cover that tells something about themselves. They may use construction paper, a 12″ by 12″ piece of cardboard, or poster board as a base for their cover. They may use magazines to cut out words and pictures that help represent their ideas. They may put a photo of themselves somewhere on the cover. (Or, you can direct them to omit their picture and the class can guess the owner of the record album from the information presented.)

   a. The students can create a "Rap Song" to go with the record album cover.
   b. The albums can be put on display, so classmates can spend more time to learn about each other.
   c. Select a day to review the albums and share the rap song.

Name ________________________________

Date ________________________________

Checklist

Life is like a continuous journey. "Check your list" to prepare for the trip. Circle the words telling what you want to take with you. Cross out the words that tell what you want to leave behind. Underline those words that tell of the qualities you want to acquire, to bring with you. Add your own words to the list.

gentle	crabby	loud	petite	heavy	skinny
slim	polite	artistic	prudish	mean	mature
unique	outspoken	smart	thoughtful	quiet	committed
worldly	attractive	good-natured	lazy	nervous	two-faced
spiteful	hard worker	concerned	vain	stout	friendly
pretty	talented	competitive	reckless	cautious	moody
talkatve	shy	studious	well-built	fat	poised
conceited	short	stubborn	rebellious	angry	tall
clumsy	spiritual	selfish	unselfish	honest	dependent
naive	impatient	sensitive	bossy	dedicated	clever
strong	loyal	athletic	sad	charming	nagging
fearful	responsible	direct	generous	respectful	accepting
in a rut	creative	forgetful	lonely	aggressive	timid
anxious	prejudiced	withdrawn	proud	greedy	wise
defeated	energetic	trusting	peaceful	wasted	dishonest

A VISION 2-5

Objective:

- To assist the students to identify good qualities about themselves that will affect their self-image

> NOTE: POSITIVE IMAGINING CAN BE AS MUCH A HELP TOWARD DEVELOPING POSITIVE ATTITUDES AS REHEARSALS ARE TO THE PRESENTATION OF A STAGE PLAY.

Activities:

Plan this activity around the school schedule to minimize distractions.

1. Prepare the students for this activity of guided imagery. Instruct them to sit quietly, close their eyes, and begin to relax. Use the progressive relaxation technique: Speak softly and slowly as you direct the students to "relax your forehead, then the muscles around your eyes, your jaw, your neck, your shoulders," etc.—all the way down to their toes.
   a. When they appear comfortable and at rest, instruct the students to envision themselves being alone in a room. Continue by saying:
      —"After a second or two, another person arrives whom you like or love. Think of who it is; be very specific about what they are wearing and how they look. Observe them closely. Then, tell the person *three* things that you like about them. Explain why (give them time for this process). Thank him or her for stopping by. Then, watch the person leave the room.
      —"Almost immediately, a second person you like comes into the room where you are alone. Follow the same process of identifying the person, observe them closely, and then tell the person *three* things that you like about them, and why (give them time for this process). Thank him or her for stopping by. Watch the person leave the room.
      —"Now, a third person arrives. It is *you*—visualizing *yourself* coming into the room. Look at 'yourself.' Observe yourself closely. Be specific about what you are wearing. Become aware of some of your feelings now. Then, tell the image *three* things you like about the person you see, and why. (Be very specific. Give the class time for this process.) Say 'thank you' to your image. Watch the image leave the room."
   b. Give the young people a few seconds to remain quiet.
   c. Tell them that when they are ready they can open their eyes slowly.

d. They may now either write about their experiences and feelings; or they can break up into small groups to talk about the *three good things* they told their *own* image, and how it made them feel.

NOTE: We are often more critical of ourselves than we are of others. Making positive comments to the first two images prepares the students to focus more realistically on their own image. LEARNING TO FOCUS ON SUCCESS WILL INCREASE OUR CONFIDENCE AND OUR SENSE OF COMPETENCE.

2. A variation of this activity may be accomplished by videotaping students presenting speeches during the school term. Near the middle of the term, have a student critique three students' presentations, finding three good points about each presentation. (The third video will be the presentation by *the student giving the critique.*) Since the student has already been focusing on the good qualities of the other speakers, finding the good points of their own presentation will be easier.

Shedding a Little Light:
Many of us need *permission* and *practice* to focus on our good points.

* * *

When I see myself in the image I choose, doing what I want —I become an "actor" in my life, instead of a "reactor."

CHOOSING THE VIEW 2-6

Objective:

- To recognize that our expectations affect the outcome of our performance
- To identify negative messages
- To change negative messages

Activities:

1. Have the students brainstorm the following questions. Write their responses on a chalkboard or a flip chart.
   a. What is your definition of failure?
   b. How do you react to "failure"?
   c. What is your definition of success?
   d. How does being successful make you feel?
   e. Do you think it is a permanent state of affairs? (i.e. "I *am* a failure" or "I *am* a success." Discuss the *behavior* vs. the *person.*)
2. Reproduce Activity 2-6A, "Are You Easily Discouraged?" Pass it out to each student, allowing them time to study it.
   a. Ask them to discuss how it might feel to them if those things happen in their lives. (Accept their feelings, which are *always O.K.*) Ask: What would you do?
   b. Now inform the class that the activity sheet is describing Abraham Lincoln, who was elected President of the United States in 1860.
3. Have the students do research on people who were handicapped, limited or "different," but who made a contribution to society in spite of their limitations. (*Examples:* Helen Keller; Ted Kennedy, Jr.; Terry Fox.) Ask what personal ideas and *attitudes* do you think they had to develop. (Note how they turned their lives around.)
4. Inform the students that we sometimes give ourselves negative messages—which affect our expectations—and influence the outcome of our performance (our behavior).
   a. Brainstorm some negative messages people tell themselves. List them on the chalkboard.
   b. Then ask the students to select a *positive message* to replace the negative one. Write it next to the message you wish to replace. As you do that, *cross out* the negative message. The more responses to choose from, the better!

Example:

Negative Messages

a. ~~You can't do *anything* right.~~
b. It's all your fault.
c. You're a loser.
d. Boys don't cry.
e. Girls can't do math.

Positive Messages

a. "I *can* help others, listen well, do well in Spanish, etc." or "I am growing and changing."
b. I am a worthwhile person.
c. It takes courage to try.
d. All feelings are O.K.
e. There are no limits to what I can do.

5. Have the students complete Activity 2-6B, "I Can Choose What I Think."
   a. When they have completed the written assignment, direct them to cut the paper along the dotted line. Then ask them to read the negative message once—then *crumple the paper* (rigorously) and *throw it away.* (You can be creative about how to *get rid of the old message.*)
   b. Tell the students to keep the piece of paper with the *new positive* messages. They may carry it with them, or put it in a prominent place at home. Remind them to look at the new message frequently and repeat it—so it will become their new way of thinking.

6. Have the students complete Activity 2-6C, "I Can Be My Own Best Friend," to practice being gentle with oneself. (The students can make up their own scenarios—and role-play them.)
7. On a separate piece of paper, have the students respond to the following statement: "On a scale of 1 to 10, I am a ________." Ask them to explain their answers.

Shedding a Little Light:
- Listen to what you say to yourself.
- You can change the messages you give yourself.
- *Positive* attitudes, *positively* influence our performance.

ARE YOU EASILY DISCOURAGED?

HERE'S A MAN WHO –

Failed in Business '31

Defeated for the Legislature '32

Again Failed in Business '34

Sweetheart Died '35

Had Nervous Breakdown '36

Defeated in Election '38

Defeated for Congress '43

Defeated for Congress '46

Defeated for Congress '48

Defeated for Senate '55

Defeated for Vice-President '56

Defeated for Senate '58

Name ______________________________

Date ______________________________

I Can Choose What I Think

Below, write two negative messages you have heard others say about you—and now sometimes *you* say it to *yourself.*

1. ____

____

____

2. ____

____

____

Below, write a *positive* message to replace the negative message. PRINT the message clearly in large letters. Be specific.

1.

2.

Now, cut along the dotted lines. The teacher will give you directions on how to *get rid of the old messages.* Keep the *new* messages, and repeat them to yourself frequently!

Name ____________________

Date ____________________

I Can Be My Own Best Friend

List some qualities you look for in a friend.

____

____

____

Read the problems that follow. Respond to each of the statements as if he/she was one of your friends.

1. Dan missed an important appointment with the coach. He is very upset. ____________________

   ____

2. Gina lost her temper. She is embarrassed. ____________________

   ____

3. Chris borrowed a radio from his friend, and broke it by accident. ____________________

   ____

4. Timothy studied hard but failed the test anyway. ____________________

   ____

5. Debbie has gained some weight lately and doesn't want to go to the dance. ____________________

   ____

We are sometimes kinder to others than we are to ourselves. Practice being kind to yourself. Write about a time you did something that upset you, and you "put yourself down." Now, re-write the script. What could you say to give yourself comfort and support?

One time I ______________________________

____

____

____

3

Naming and Claiming

FEELINGS

> Feelings are the "directional signals" that alert us to the state of our physical and emotional health.

Fact Sheet 3 .... Naming and Claiming Feelings
Fact Sheet 4 .... Feeling Stress

Activity Title	Objectives
3-1 Owning My Feelings..........	To identify one's own feelings
3-2 Body Language..............	To identify one's own feelings and the feelings of others by observing non-verbal body clues
3-3 Viva la Difference............	To recognize that people may use *different* ways to express the *same* emotion
3-4 That's My Perception	To understand that how we interpret an event influences our feelings
3-5 Internal Dialogue	To become aware of our *internal* dialogue

> It is important to our overall health and sense of well-being to learn to *name* (identify) and *claim* (accept) *all* of our feelings *before* we can express them in a safe and healthy manner.

Naming and Claiming Feelings

ALL FEELINGS ARE O.K.

- *Emotion* is the general term which encompasses the *feeling tone*, the *biophysiological state*, and includes the *chemical changes* which underlie the sensations we experience.
- *Feeling* is our *subjective awareness* of our own emotional state.
- Feelings are then, *directional signals* essential for human life.
- They are neither right nor wrong.
- They alert us to information about the state of our physical needs (hunger, thirst, etc.) and our psychological needs (love, belonging, competency).
- Emotions and feelings arise from the *interaction* between what is going on around us and *our response* to it. (The event + our thought or perception of it = feelings experienced.)
- It is not the event or the experience that accounts for the feeling, but the *meaning, value, or interpretation* we place on it.

SIGN LANGUAGE

Giving Direction . . .

Feeling Stress

Chemical Changes:

- Our reactions to an event can *cause feelings of stress.*
- Stress is the physical, mental, and chemical reaction to circumstances that cause fear, excitement, irritation, or endangerment. These attitudes affect our bodies with a variety of chemical changes, which in turn produce other dramatic physical and mental changes. *The mind and the body are inseparable.*
  Some immediate changes in our body that may be apparent to us can include:

Heart palpitations
Stomachaches
Rapid breathing
Excess sweating

Tight muscles
Cold hands
Dry mouth
Dilated pupils

"WORN OUT"

OR slower breathing
decreased heartrate
slowed physical activity
increased digestive function

- Prolonged stress can be dangerous, and cause serious consequences.
- But, stress is good for us—most of the time.
- Most types of stress arise from the things that make life interesting, excite us, or force us to excel and grow.
  For example: trying out for the school play
  meeting a new boyfriend or girlfriend
  competing in a sport, etc.
- It is therefore important to our overall health and sense of well-being to learn to *name* (identify) and *claim* (accept) *all* of our feelings, *before* we can express them in a safe and healthy manner.

OWNING MY FEELINGS 3-1

Objectives:

- To help the students identify their own feelings
- To encourage the students to accept *all* feelings as O.K.

> NOTE: Carl Rogers described the fully functioning person as one who is able to live totally in and with each and all of one's feelings and reactions.
> - Learning to accept *all* our feelings makes life more enriching, exciting, rewarding, challenging, and meaningful.

Activities:

1. Have the students name the *four feelings* (mad, sad, glad, scared) and write them on the chalkboard or a flip chart.
   a. Ask the students to describe specific body sensations that they have been aware of when they experienced any of the four major feelings. List them under the appropriate space on the board or chart. For example:
      (1) glad: full of energy, smiling, tingly, etc.
      (2) scared: weak, rigid, breathless, etc.
      (3) sad: tired, heaviness, etc.
      (4) mad: tight muscles, clenched teeth, etc.
   b. Allow enough time for many personal examples to be given.
2. To increase their "feeling" vocabulary, ask the students to (a) write one of the feeling words that they think would best "fit" in the space next to the words in Activity 3-1A, "Zero In." Then, (b) on a separate piece of paper, use 10 words from the lists in a sentence that shows you understand its meaning. The class may review their answers in "Zero In." (Allow for a wide range of responses.)
3. Have the students complete the open-ended sentences in Activity 3-1B, "Describing Emotions," to help the students explore the meaning of the words they use to tell about their feelings.
4. Direct the students to complete the open-ended sentences in Activity 3-1C, "Calling Them Names," to focus on their feelings in a variety of situations.

5. We all experience the four feelings. Some feelings we are more comfortable acknowledging and accepting than others.
   a. Have the students identify the emotion that is the most difficult for them to deal with, and write it at the top of a piece of looseleaf paper.
   b. Draw a straight line in the top quarter of the page, and label each end as illustrated in the example below:

Overcontrolled ———————————————————— Completely Spontaneous

   c. Mark an X on the line to show how they see themselves dealing with the emotion.
   d. Use the rest of the page to explain their answers. (They can include a recent incident in which they experienced that emotion.)

NOTE: Reinforce the idea that *all feelings are O.K.*

6. Have the students read the directions and complete Activity 3-1D, "Attention," to become aware of their feelings during the course of an ordinary day.

Shedding a Little Light:
- It is important to be able to clearly and accurately identify what and how we are feeling.
- Unidentified feelings lead to physical ills and ineffective interpersonal relationships.

Name ____________________________________

Date ____________________________________

Zero In

To increase your "feeling" vocabulary, select ten words from each of the three columns below. On the line next to the word, write one of the four feeling words (mad, glad, sad, scared) that you think matches that word.

__________ Anxious
__________ Appreciated
__________ Ashamed
__________ Astonished
__________ Attacked
__________ Belittled
__________ Betrayed
__________ Blamed
__________ Concerned
__________ Confident
__________ Confused
__________ Content
__________ Desperate
__________ Disappointed
__________ Discounted
__________ Discouraged
__________ Dissatisfied
__________ Disturbed
__________ Isolated
__________ Joyful
__________ Resentful
__________ Threatened
__________ Uncertain
__________ Upset

__________ Angry
__________ Annoyed
__________ Elated
__________ Encouraged
__________ Enthusiastic
__________ Envious
__________ Frantic
__________ Frustrated
__________ Furious
__________ Grateful
__________ Guilty
__________ Hateful
__________ Humbled
__________ Hysterical
__________ Important
__________ Incensed
__________ Indignant
__________ Irritated
__________ Jealous
__________ Patronized
__________ Tempted
__________ Uncomfortable
__________ Wanted
__________ Worried

__________ Affectionate
__________ Embarrassed
__________ Hopeful
__________ Hurt
__________ Ignored
__________ Intimidated
__________ Marvelous
__________ Misunderstood
__________ Naughty
__________ Outraged
__________ Overwhelmed
__________ Pleased
__________ Protected
__________ Put-down
__________ Rejected
__________ Relieved
__________ Ridiculous
__________ Satisfied
__________ Surprised
__________ Suspicious
__________ Terrified
__________ Understood
__________ Unimportant
__________ Willing

Name ______________________________

Date ______________________________

Describing Emotions

Write your own endings to complete the sentences below. Be creative.

1. Love is ______________________________
2. Courage is ______________________________
3. Happiness is ______________________________
4. Sadness is ______________________________
5. Loneliness is ______________________________
6. Hope is ______________________________
7. Peaceful is ______________________________
8. Understood is ______________________________
9. Confident is ______________________________
10. Obnoxious is ______________________________
11. Embarrassed is ______________________________
12. Daring is ______________________________
13. Miserable is ______________________________
14. Depressed is ______________________________
15. Relieved is ______________________________
16. Confused is ______________________________
17. Worried is ______________________________
18. Challenged is ______________________________
19. Delighted is ______________________________
20. Frustrated is ______________________________
21. Elated is ______________________________
22. Accepted is ______________________________
23. Furious is ______________________________
24. Hurt is ______________________________
25. Betrayed is ______________________________
26. Neglected is ______________________________

Name ______________________________

Date ______________________________

Calling Them Names

Complete the open-ended sentences to help you focus on your feelings in a variety of situations. (Make comments if you wish.)

1. I feel important when ______________________________
2. I feel lonely when ______________________________
3. When people yell at me, I feel ______________________________
4. When someone ignores me, I feel ______________________________
5. If I knew that my parents would be coming to visit my school, I would feel ______________________________
6. When I forget an appointment or "mess up" in any other way, I feel ______________________________
7. I get mad at myself when ______________________________
8. I make myself depressed by ______________________________
9. I sometimes feel sorry for myself when ______________________________
10. At this moment I resent ______________________________
11. Right now I am feeling guilty about ______________________________
12. When I get tickets to my favorite group's concert, I feel ______________________________
13. When I look in the mirror, I feel ______________________________
14. When I think of the future, I feel ______________________________
15. When I start a project and I finish it, I feel ______________________________
16. On Spring Break, I feel ______________________________

Name ________________________________ 3-1D

Date ________________________________

Attention!

Feelings are an important part of your personality. They are neither right nor wrong. They can be friendly "sign posts" to know more about yourself. (1) Pay attention to how you feel for this day. (2) Be alert to any strong feelings that you become aware of. (3) Use the key at the bottom of the page.

TIME	HAPPY	MAD	GLAD	SAD
a.m. 8:00				

Key—You may also choose a key of four different colors or signs; for example:

glad- ↑ sad- ↓ mad- scared- ■

At the end of the day, hold the chart away from you. What emotion appears the most often? Would you like to talk to someone about your feelings? Who could you choose?

If few spaces are marked, you might think about "checking in to your feeling zone" more often.

How honest are you with yourself?

BODY LANGUAGE 3-2

Objective:

- To identify one's feelings and the feelings of others by observing nonverbal body clues

> NOTE: Messages can be sent by means of *body language,* which provides clues to one's feelings and emotions. Nonverbal clues can be given by one's *manner of dress, posture, facial expression,* degree of *eye contact, tone of voice, hand gestures, spatial distance,* and *touch.*
> - Nonverbal clues are being given continuously.

Activities:

1. Write a list of the four feeling words (mad, sad, scared, glad) on the chalkboard or a flip chart.

   a. Have a student volunteer to choose one of the words from the board or chart and nonverbally act out that feeling. Allow a minute or two to complete each performance.
   b. After each emotion is acted out, ask the class to *describe* the facial expressions, the body posture, hand gestures, etc. What idea was expressed?
   c. To complete the exercise, give the "actors" a "task" to do while they are *still role-playing* the emotions.
   Examples: waiting for an elevator
   opening the door for another person
   cleaning one's room
   getting dressed to go to a dance
   babysitting for a young child, etc.
   d. Ask: Do our feelings affect the way we behave?
   (Continue asking for volunteers until all the feeling words have been acted out.)

2. Have the class play a game of charades to show body language with fun and humor.

3. As a homework assignment, ask the students to watch a television program.
   a. Tell them to *turn off the sound* while watching.
   b. Instruct them to observe the body clues, and write down the emotions/feelings that they think are being expressed. Include the specific body language that helped them to come to their conclusion.
   c. Discuss the homework assignment with the class.

4. Ask the students to come to class prepared to tell a 2- to 3-minute story that is funny, exciting or otherwise emotionally charged.
   a. In class, direct the students to form small groups.
   b. Each student will take a turn telling a story *without* using *any* body language.
   c. The other group members are to *observe* and note *any* body language used during the presentation.
   d. When the presentation is complete, allow the students time to talk about their observations.
   e. They may discuss the following questions:
      (1) Do you think that we are *always* communicating through body language?
      (2) Was the performing student aware of changing his/her voice tone, facial expressions, hand gestures, etc., at any time during the presentation?
      (3) What effect do you think these messages may have on a relationship, especially if we are not aware of them?
      (4) If there was in fact *NO* body language, ask the "actor" what it felt like to communicate an emotional issue *without* letting some of the feelings "out" through body movement.

Shedding a Little Light:
Studies have shown that the inability to read nonverbal messages, leads to failure in mastering basic social skills that mar relationships.
See Chapter 5, Making Connections and
Chapter 6, Communication Skills.

VIVA LA DIFFERENCE 3-3

Objectives:

- To note that people may use different ways to express the same emotions
- To recognize how our feelings influence our relationships and the decisions we make

Activities:

1. Our feelings influence how we respond to others. To illustrate, select four students to participate in this activity. Give each of the students a card with one of the four feelings (mad, scared, glad, sad) on it.
   a. Tell each of the students to respond to the sentence "*I need help*!" as if they heard it while in the feeling state listed on their card.
   b. Ask the other students to observe the difference in their responses.
2. Select students to say the words or statements in the box below. Each student will say it as though he/she was either mad, sad, scared, or glad.

1. No	4. Please	7. Here
2. Never mind	5. O.K.	8. What
3. I'll do it	6. Stop that	9. Wow

   a. Have the other students share their observations.
   b. Ask: How might your responses affect your relationships?
   c. Ask: When we are in different moods, may we choose *different* solutions to the *same* problem?
3. Write the four feelings on the chalkboard or flip chart. Give each a number from one to four (1. mad, 2. glad, 3. sad, 4. scared).
   a. Write the *number* of each of the emotions on small pieces of paper. Make enough for each student in the class. (Mark more papers with the numbers for *mad* and *scared*, as these emotions are most often misinterpreted.) Fold the papers to conceal the numbers. Place the papers in a container, and have each student select one of the papers. (Maintain secrecy!)
   b. Then, have each student act out (non-verbally) the emotion listed on his/her paper. The class will guess the "feeling" being acted out. (Keep track of how many incorrect guesses there were. Keep track of which emotions the students had the most difficulty guessing. Often, *mad* and *sad* feelings are not identified easily.)
   c. When each student has participated, discuss the *different expressions* by the students of the *same emotion.*
   d. Discuss the effect on a relationship if emotions are misinterpreted.

THAT'S MY PERCEPTION 3-4

Objective:

- To become aware that how we interpret an event influences our feelings

NOTE: It is important to understand that:
(1) perception of an event is a personal (subjective) experience
(2) that each interpretation seems correct to the viewer
(3) we give the *meaning* to a *neutral* event

Activities:

1. To reinforce the ideas mentioned above, fill a glass *exactly* halfway with water. Ask several students if the glass is half full or half empty. Discuss the students' interpretation (perception) of the water in the glass.
2. To support the ideas that how we *think* of an event (our perception) determines how we *feel*, ask the students to describe a *thought* and then a *feeling* that each person might experience during each of the following situations:
   a. A HEAVY SNOW FALL:

   Example:

Person	Thought	Feeling
• an old person	I may fall.	fear
	I enjoy my warm house.	happy
• a child	I may have to stay in the house.	sad
	School is cancelled.	happy
• a sanitation worker	There is too much work to do.	mad
	I can make extra money.	glad

   b. AN AUTOMOBILE ACCIDENT: (1) the driver of the car, (2) a passenger in the car, (3) a witness to the accident, (4) the police officer, (5) a person viewing the TV news report of the accident.
   c. A SOLD-OUT ROCK CONCERT: (1) a young fan, (2) the janitor, (3) the security guard, (4) the entertainer.
   d. SMOKING TOBACCO CIGARETTES: (1) The Surgeon General, (2) an advertising agent, (3) a heavy smoker, (4) a person with lung cancer, (5) the president of a cigarette company.

3. Have the class complete Activity 3-4A, "It's All in My Head."
   a. They may share their responses in small groups to see how others interpreted the situation.
   b. The class can then discuss their impression after completing their small-group experience.
4. To help the students become aware of their personal belief system and the ways in which it will affect their thinking, have them study Activity 3-4B, "Stinking' Thinkin'." Discuss the material with the class.
5. Direct the students to complete Activity 3-4C, "A Head Trip."

Name ____________________

Date ____________________

It's All in My Head

Read each of the situations below. Write down what your first *thought* was when you read it, and how it would make you *feel.*

1. My new friend passed me in the hall without saying hello to me. (Thought) ____________________

   (Feeling) ____________________

2. Your friends said they would meet you at 6 P.M. You rush through dinner to get there on time. When you arrive at exactly 6 P.M., they are not there. (Thought) ____________________

   (Feeling) ____________________

3. When you ask a girl (or boy) to the school dance, they say they will have to check their calendar and get back to you. (Thought) ____________________

   (Feeling) ____________________

4. They ask you to be a peer tutor. You are teaching history to a student in a lower grade. Today, she spends a lot of your time together with her head down on the desk during the session. (Thought) ____________________

   (Feeling) ____________________

5. You are expected to come right home after school today so your mother can take you shopping. She is not there when you arrive. (Thought) ____________________

   (Feeling) ____________________

Name ____________________

Date ____________________

"Stinkin' Thinkin'"

Our beliefs are learned. They can be self-fulfilling prophecies. If our beliefs are no longer appropriate or helpful, *they can be changed.*

Study the following examples of how our belief system influences our thoughts, then our feelings, and finally our behavior.

Distorted Thought	Description	Example
1. Exaggeration/ Magnification	See a single event as conclusive evidence.	A pimple = acne. Failing a test = failing the course.
2. Mind Reading	Are sure you know what the other person thinks?	She doesn't like me. When I did that he must have thought . . .
3. Jumping to Conclusions	Make judgment or decision with incomplete or inaccurate information.	John didn't come to the game. I guess he doesn't like basketball.
4. Shoulds	Living up to another's expectations.	I should never make a mistake. I should be happy all the time.
5. Generalizations	Presumptions and assumptions.	Fat people are . . . Men are . . . Dogs hate me.
6. All or Nothing	Either/Or.	Perfect -or- Failure Pretty -or- Ugly Smart -or- Stupid
7. Focus on Your Dents	Only see the negative.	Even though I got an A on the test, I missed one answer.
8. Magical Thinking	It will be O.K.	Even though I didn't study and I heard the test is hard, I'll pass.

Name ____________________ Date ____________________

A Head Trip

Fill in the missing information in # 2 and 3. Then, give other examples of distorted thinking and its effects to complete # 4 and 5.

Situation	Distorted Thought	Feeling	Corrected Thinking
1. Gail wants to be an accountant but doesn't think she'll make it because girls really don't do well in math.	Generalization	discouraged (sad or scared)	If I apply myself, I can do anything I want to do.
2. I should have known that last answer on the test because I read the book.	Shoulds/Expectations		
3. No one will look at me because of the way my hair looks.			
4.			
5.			

INTERNAL DIALOGUE 3-5

Objectives:

- To become more aware of our *internal* dialogue
- To understand how thoughts affect feelings, which in turn affect our behavior

Activity:

This activity may be divided into two sessions. One session can be used to make the Feeling Cube. Another session can be used to do the Feeling Cube Activity.

1. Make a "Feeling Cube" by following the directions given in Activity 3-5A.
2. Explain to the students that they will use the Feeling Cube to become aware of the large amount of mental and emotional activity that goes on within us at all times.
   a. This activity can be initiated during a routine lesson. *Or,* you may want to have the students discuss a controversial issue for this period to allow more emotional responses.
   b. Tell the students to have a piece of paper available to keep a log.
   c. Tell the students:
      (1) Place the Feeling Cube on your desks at the beginning of the period. (Proceed with the day's regular classroom work.)
      (2) As you become aware of your mood or feelings changing, (without talking) quietly rotate the "face" on the cube that reflects that feeling outward to the class.
      (3) Write in your log report anything that happened in the classroom that changed how you felt. *And* a *thought* of a person, event, or thing which made your feeling change? (*You* may choose to acknowledge, or question, some of the students as they change the position of their Feeling Cubes.)
   d. Ask: Would thinking about something that is *not* happening *right now* change your mood? Discuss.
      (*Example:* While sitting in English class, you think of the concert you will attend on the weekend.....)

e. Ask: How would *not* being in touch with our thoughts and feelings affect our relationships and the decisions we make? Discuss.

> NOTE: • *You* may also make a Feeling Cube and place it on *your* desk to share some of your feelings with the students. Your role-modeling, by identifying and sharing some of your feelings, will assist the students to be more comfortable with their own personal sharing.
> • It would not be surprising if they help *you* to identify some of the feelings they observe from you *before* you reach for your Feeling Cube.

Making a "Feeling Cube"

Materials Needed:

- 14″ × 17″ oaktag or lightweight cardboard
- scissors
- adhesive tape
- marker
- decorations (optional)

Directions:

1. Cut a piece of oaktag or cardboard into a T shape following the measurements in the illustration.
   a. Mark off 4-inch sections as indicated.
   b. Fold the oaktag along these lines to create a box shape.
   c. Tuck the tabs inside the box form.
   d. Use adhesive tape to fasten the sides together.
2. Draw a different feeling face (mad, glad, sad, scared) on each of the four sides of the cube with a marker.
3. Make the box as elaborate as you wish. Use ribbons, earrings, bow ties, etc.

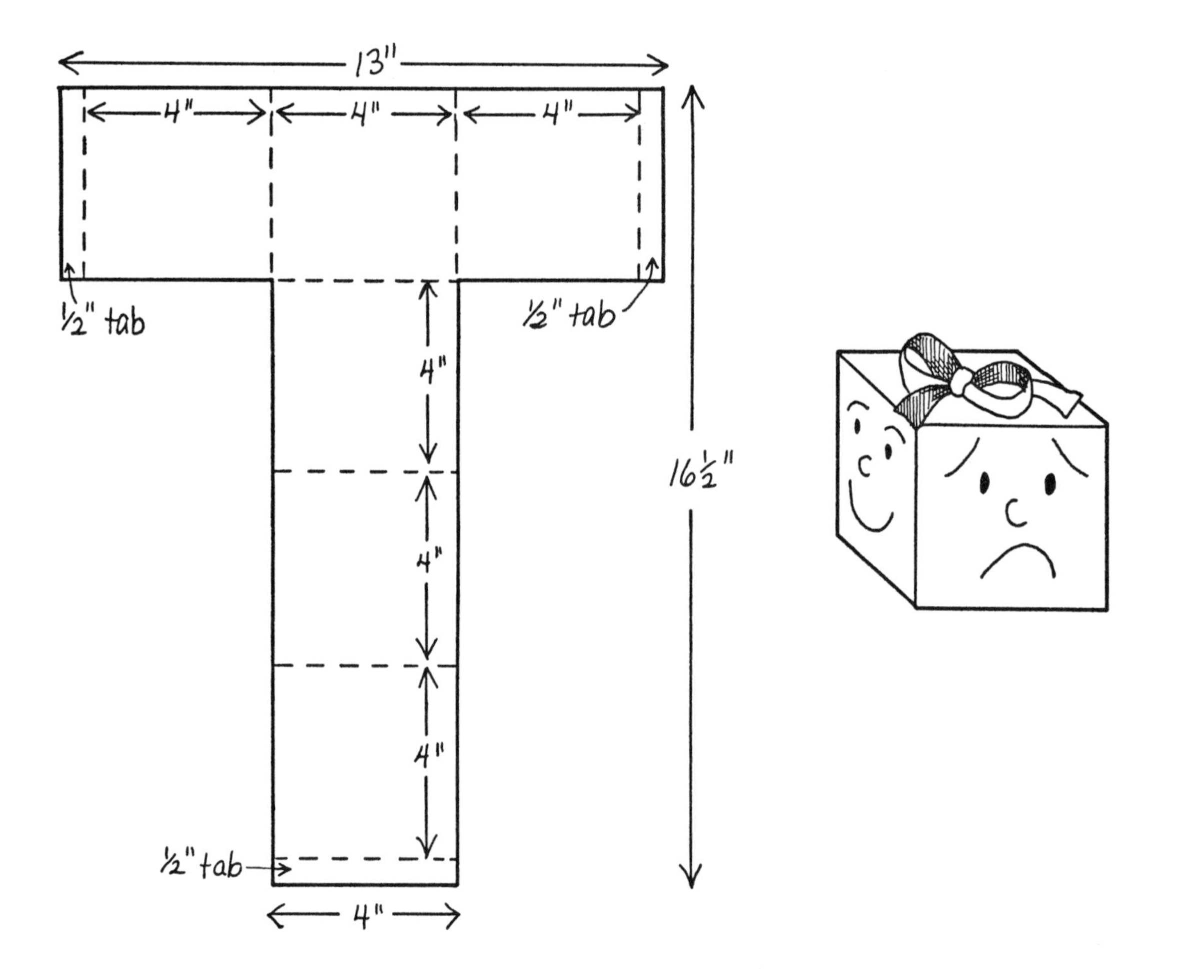

4

Taming and Aiming

FEELINGS

Feelings are a *means* to an *end.*

We can experience problems in our lives *not* because feelings are present, but because we do not *use them constructively.*

Taming and Aiming Feelings

- Feelings are a *means* to an *end.*
- They alert us to conditions that call us to:
  - solve our problems,
  - meet our needs,
  - find ways to restore ourselves to a sense of balance.
- Without *awareness* of our feelings, we cannot *express* them in a way that will lead to our emotional growth, state of comfort, and feelings of satisfaction.
- Allowing strong emotional feelings to remain unaddressed leads to physical and emotional "dis-ease."

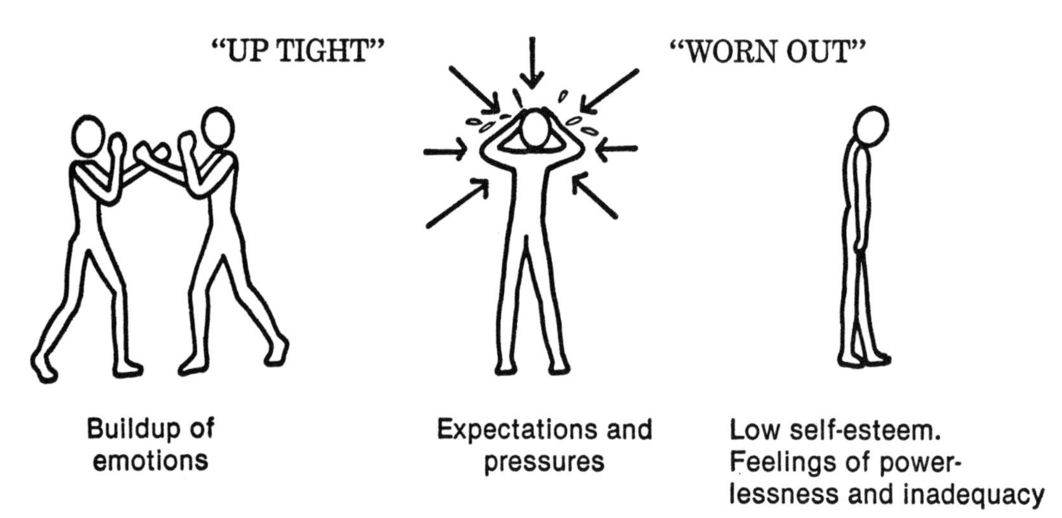

- When there is no *outlet* for the expression of the *physical energy* caused by prolonged stress, severe illness can result.
  Examples are:
  ....high blood pressure.... allergies ....ulcers.....
  ....heart disease....depression.....headaches.
- During the teen years, with their important and rapid physical and mental changes, feelings may seem even more turbulent, confusing, and powerful than ever.
  (Perhaps alcohol, tobacco, and other drugs might be used to attain some level of comfort during times of stress. This response can begin an *unhealthy pattern of coping behavior.*)

- It is important, then, to learn and practice ways to *reduce* the intensity of the feelings (tame) and to express feelings in a safe and healthy manner (aim) in order to:
  - — know and understand ourselves,
  - — reduce stress,
  - — refresh our spirit,
  - — to communicate successfully with others.
- Everyone carries with them readily available and easy to use *Drug-Free Remedies* that relieve tension, improve self-image, and provide personal satisfaction by creating opportunities:
  - — for TIME OUT,
  - — to WORK OUT,
  - — to REACH OUT.

  (The activities in this chapter offer some examples.)
- We can experience problems in our life *not* because emotions and feelings are present but because we do not *use them constructively*.
- Feelings *influence* our behavior, but they *do not control it.* We can choose!

DEAL WITH THE FEELINGS 4-1

Objectives:

- To demonstrate the importance of releasing pent-up energy
- To understand the need to find outlets for expressing feelings constructively

Activities:

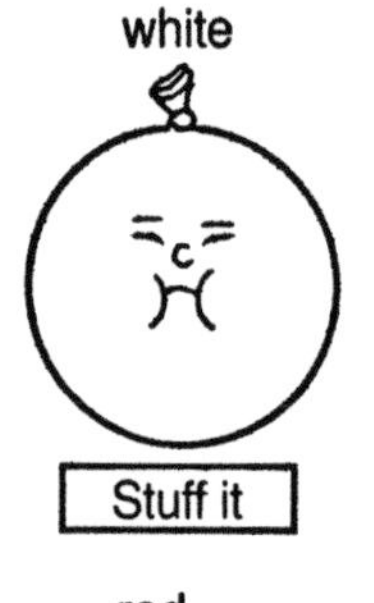

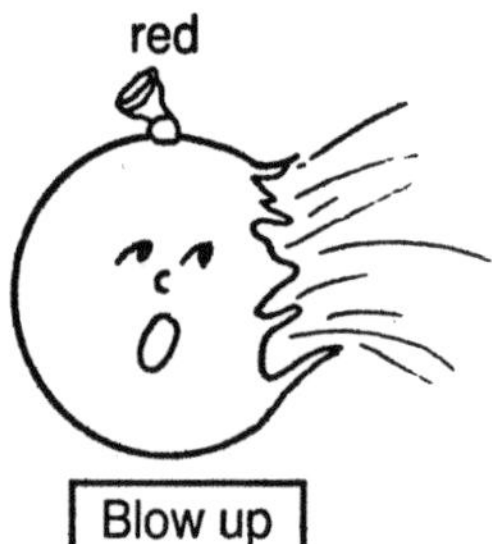

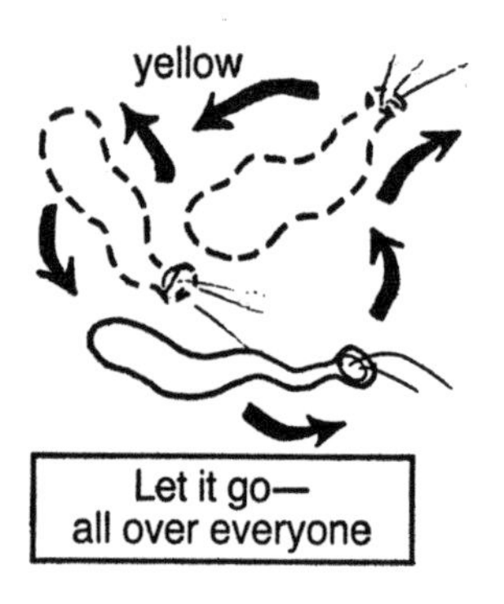

1. Our reactions to an event can cause feelings of stress. (Stress is the physical, mental, and chemical reaction to circumstances that cause fear, excitement, irritation, or endangerment.) If the energy produced in the body is not released, the energy *build-up continues* and can cause problems for us, and for others.
   a. To *demonstrate* what can happen at different levels of physical arousal with pent-up energy, follow the directions below. Use four different-colored balloons (white, red, yellow, and blue) for this activity.
      (1) Blow the white balloon up *fully*. Tie it off. (Be careful not to let it break.) Discuss some of its qualities. (It's nice to look at. It can be used for a decoration. It needs to be *handled with care* so it won't "pop," etc.)
      (2) Blow the red balloon up "too much" *until* it pops. Describe what happened and why. (It exploded. It blew up. It came apart, etc.)
      (3) Blow the yellow balloon up fully, then *pinch it off* at the top with your fingers and hold it for a few seconds. Now take your fingers off the top of the balloon and *let it go*. Discuss what happened and why. (It went *all over the place*. I was no longer in control of it. It took me by surprise, etc.)
      (4) Blow the blue balloon up. Do not overfill. It should have some elasticity. (If it is too full, you can let a little air out.) Tie it off. Now, toss it around with a few of the students. Discuss what happened and why. (It is more flexible, more resilient. It is less likely to explode when it is tossed about, etc.) Ask: What is your style? Discuss.

2. Now have the students brainstorm words that tell the degree of escalating feelings that might indicate an increase of stress. Write them on a chalkboard or flip chart. For example:

	1. →	2. →	3. →	4. →	5.
Mad —	irritated,	annoyed,	angry,	furious,	enraged
Glad —	pleased,	happy,	delighted,	elated,	ecstatic
Sad —	feeling low,	feeling blue,	down,	depressed,	devastated
Scared —	nervous,	anxious,	worried,	afraid,	terrified

Have the students discuss feelings and pressures they have experienced, which they can relate to the different-colored balloons. (Reinforce that it is important to deal with our feelings before the level of stress and pent-up energy build up.)

> NOTE: You may wish to review Fact Sheet #3: Naming and Claiming Feelings, #4: Feeling Stress, and #5: Taming and Aiming Feelings, for further information about feeling stress.

BLOCK OUT 4-2

Objectives:

- To reinforce that *all* feelings are acceptable
- To identify some of the reasons for stress build-up
- To demonstrate some of the negative consequences of denying our feelings

Activities:

1. Explain to the students that physical and emotional tensions *build up* when:
   a. we do not *recognize* the symptoms of stress,
   b. we have not *learned how to reduce* the stressful feelings,
   c. there is no immediate *outlet* for *discharging the energy,*
   d. we deny or ignore the feeling and *do not act on it.*

2. On a separate piece of paper, ask the students to use the format below to indicate, on a scale of 1 to 10, how they think they recognize and express that feeling—and why.
   Example:

   X^1 ____ X^{10}

   Seldom Show Anger   Often Show Anger

   because ____

   Repeat the format for feeling *Sad, Glad,* and *Scared.*

Cover the dominant hand also

3. Brainstorm some reasons a person might not show a feeling—or act on it. (For example: I was taught that men don't cry; nice girls don't get angry; etc. He/she might not like me. I'm afraid I'll lose control. I'll be too vulnerable—I'll leave myself wide open. They'll laugh at me. I can't approach him—I have to wait for him to talk to me first, etc.).

4. To demonstrate that feelings that are denied or ignored can cause problems for us and for others, follow the directions below:
   a. Place a splint on the dominant arm of a student volunteer to immobilize that arm. This student is to *ignore* or *deny* the fact that he/she is wearing the splint and the arm is immobilized! He/she must deal with the results of his/her efforts and interactions in any appropriate way *except* acknowledging his/her situation. (Prepare the class lesson in such a way as to support the demonstration; i.e., give a writing activity; ask the students to help you by holding several items at once; others can ask the student to write on their papers; he/she can pour a glass of water, etc.)

b. Then have the students discuss their observations. Talk about the things this student did to *justify* not being able to participate fully (excuses, blaming, changing the focus, etc.). Ask how it made the other students feel. (Be specific.) Could it interfere with a relationship?
c. Ask the student with the splint to discuss his or her feelings and reactions.
d. Ask for suggestions on how the situation could have been improved. (Suggestions: Explain the situation. Ask for help, etc.)
e. Now have the student with the splint ask for help in removing the splint. Then ask the volunteer how he/she feels now—and would he/she want to do something to release feelings of stress that may remain.
f. Have the class thank the volunteer and give applause to distance him/her from the role.

TIME OUT 4-3

Objectives:

- To recognize that we have *within ourselves* the ability to calm our minds and bodies
- To practice ways to reduce feelings of stress

> NOTE: Taking *TIME OUT* to do any of these simple exercises should (a) reduce the feelings of tension, (b) recharge your "batteries," so to speak, and (c) restore a sense of well-being.
> - The more regularly these exercises are practiced, the greater is the benefit derived.

Activities:

1. *Breathing:*
   Study Activity 4-3A, "Breathing Exercises." Then lead the students in practicing: (a) The Diaphragmatic Breath and (b) The Complete Breath to help create and maintain a state of equilibrium.

2. *Relaxation:*
   The health benefits of using relaxation techniques have been well-documented. Study Activity 4-3B, "Relaxation Exercises." Then lead the students in practicing: (a) Relaxation Response and (b) Progressive Relaxation.

3. *Visualization:*
   The body really cannot tell whether an image the mind holds is real or a fantasy. If the image is *clearly defined,* the body will respond according to *that* image. If the image is peaceful and relaxing, the body and mind will be more able to respond to situations in healthy and constructive ways.

   Lead the students in practicing the exercises in Activity 4-3C, "Creative Visualization": (a) Take a Mini-Vacation and (b) Practice Positive Picture Power.

Shedding a Little Light:
Rest and relaxation restore balance and counteract the increased sympathetic-nervous-system activity that accompanies "fight or flight" arousal.

Breathing Exercises

Breathing provides both a nourishing and a cleansing function for the body. The oxygen brought in to the blood with inhalation is utilized by every cell. The waste product, carbon dioxide, is cleansed from the blood by exhalation. If this task is performed efficiently and effectively, a sense of calm can be created and maintained in the body and the mind.

Two breathing exercises that can be practiced safely by almost everyone are diaphragmatic breathing and the complete breath.

(1) *Diaphragmatic Breathing:*

a. Sit comfortably in a chair.
b. Place your left hand on the upper chest.
Place your right hand on the abdomen.
c. As you inhale, using the diaphragm, the belly will expand. Therefore, you will notice the right hand move. (The left hand should not move at all.)
d. Breathe at a regular rhythm, and keep the breathing effortless as you inhale and exhale.

(If this exercise is done while laying on the floor, you can place a piece of paper on the abdomen. If you are breathing properly with the diaphragm, the paper will rise and fall.)

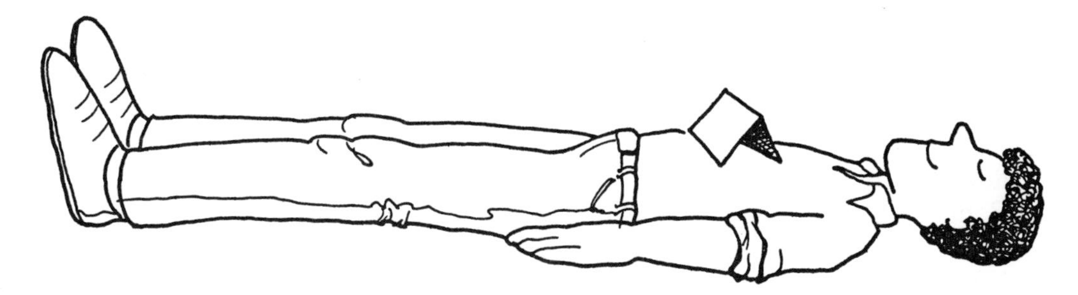

(2) *The Complete Breath:*

a. *Inhale* using the diaphragm. Inhale through your nose.
b. Smoothly and slowly continue the inhalation by letting the chest expand.
c. Continue the inhalation until you cannot comfortably take in more air.

Hold the breath for a few seconds and then . . .

d. *Exhale*: by slowly letting your breath out through the mouth.
e. Continue the exhalation by letting the chest wall and then the belly collapse as the diaphragm moves upward, *pushing the air out of the lungs.*
f. Repeat the process two more times.

Relaxation Exercises

The evidence validating the physical benefits from doing relaxation exercises (reduced blood pressure, slower heart rate) now include the positive effects on the immune system, increasing resistance to illness. It also affords the practitioner a feeling of calmness and a sense of well-being.

(1) *Relaxation Response*:

a. Sit in a comfortable chair, in a quiet environment, with the eyes closed.
b. Take a deep breath and let it out slowly.
c. Now, concentrate on the breath going in and out.
d. When the mind begins to wander and you become aware of any thoughts, gently draw the mind back to the breath.
e. Continue this process for 10 to 20 minutes once or twice a day for maximum benefits.

(2) *Progressive Relaxation*:

a. To become aware of the general feelings of tension in the body, systematically *tense* each major muscle group in the body for five seconds, and then be aware of the feeling as you *release* the tension. Through the systematic tensing and relaxing of the muscle groups, you learn to *recognize* and to *control* the "power on" feeling under stress and the "power off" feeling of being relaxed.
b. Now, sit in a comfortable position in a quiet atmosphere with the eyes closed.
c. Slowly relax each muscle group, beginning at the forehead; i.e., "Relax your forehead until it feels nice and relaxed; now relax your cheeks; slowly relax your chin; let your shoulders relax," and so forth until you have relaxed all the muscles right down to the toes.
d. Remain in the totally relaxed position for several minutes—feeling the peacefulness.
e. When you are ready, slowly open the eyes and sit comfortably for a minute before returning to your normal activities.

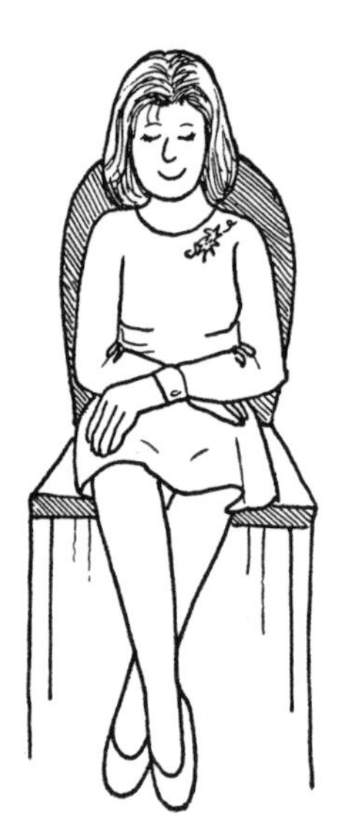

Visualization

The body really cannot tell whether an image the mind holds is real or a fantasy. If the image is clearly defined, the body will respond to *that image.* Practice using this powerful technique by doing the following exercises.

(1) *Take a Mini-Vacation.* Ask the students to:

a. Sit in a quiet place, in a comfortable position, with eyes closed.
b. Begin to relax. Focus on the breath going "in" and "out."
c. Now take a mini-vacation! Visualize yourself in a scene that gives you a feeling of happiness and pleasure. It may be a beach, a mountain scene, lying lazily on your bed, listening to your favorite music group, etc.
d. It is important to be *very specific* about the scene. Notice what your surroundings are like; notice any smells or sounds. Look at what you are wearing. What is the weather like? If it is a beach scene, feel the sand under your feet and hear the ocean sounds. If you are visualizing yourself in your bed listening to the music, feel the mattress under your body and the texture of the bed covers, etc.
e. Stay there for 10 minutes. Enjoy it and feel the peace and happiness.
f. When you are ready, open your eyes slowly.
g. Sit quietly for a minute, and then resume your activities.

(2) *Positive Picture Power:*

a. Positive images add to our feelings of self-mastery and afford us a sense of control in our lives.

Positive picture power

(Jack Nicklaus, the champion golfer, calls his use of this technique "going to the movies." He imagines *each* shot in his mind before he executes it.)

b. Proper mental imagery, then, is really nothing more than learning to use our mental capacities in a positive way by effectively *choosing* positive pictures in minute detail. Remember, clear mental pictures profoundly affect your thoughts and feelings.
c. Now, use your *Positive Picture Power* to recall a time when you felt very successful, won an award, were given special recognition, felt especially loved or appreciated.
d. Sit in a quiet place, in a comfortable position, with your eyes closed.
e. Begin to relax. Focus on the breath "in" and "out."
f. Recreate the scene in your mind: (1) Who else was present; (2) where are you in the scene—note what you are wearing, get in touch with some of your feelings; (3) become aware of sounds; (4) concentrate on your activity, and the feelings of pleasure and success—stay with that image for a few minutes—enjoy your success.
g. When you are ready, open your eyes slowly.
h. Sit quietly for a minute. Then resume your daily activities, enjoying your feelings of renewal and self-appreciation.

A LAUGHING MATTER 4-4

Objectives:

- To allow the students to experience the physical and emotional benefits of laughter
- To reduce stress, improve self-image, and prepare us to respond more constructively to our life's problems

NOTE:
- Humor is useful when faced with events over which we have no control.
- Laughter can take the edge off our tension, reduce our fear, and give us an emotional distance—a perspective on ourselves and our problems.

Activities:

Before any of the following activities are used, stress the idea that the humor should not be offensive to anyone in the group.

1. Ask each student to bring in a joke, a cartoon, or a funny story. (Provide a container for this material.) Select a different student each day to choose something from the container—to present a "stress break."
2. Inform the class that they will create a story. Remember to keep humor in mind as the goal.
   a. One student will begin the story and, after a few sentences, pass it on to the next student, and so forth. Each student will participate.
   b. The last student will complete the story—"The End."

3. Have the students bring in cartoons or other funny material to be placed on a bulletin board.
4. Watch a funny movie together.
5. For a homework assignment, have the students write about the "funniest thing that ever happened to me." They may read their papers in small groups. (It would be expected that the laughter will be contagious.)
6. Play a game in which all participate. The commercial game "Pictionary" or charades may provide opportunities for laughter.
7. What makes people laugh differs from individual to individual. Observe your group and notice what things would help them experience humor—then do it!

Shedding a Little Light:
Some scientists report that with humor the brain is stimulated to produce chemical pain relievers. The oxygen supply is increased in the blood, and the body's production of immune cells increases when we laugh.

"WOW" EXPERIENCES 4-5

Objectives:

- To identify experiences that one can get "high" on naturally
- To recognize that "wow" experiences can happen almost daily in our lives—and we can miss them
- To understand that feelings of joy, wonder, and gratitude reduce our feelings of stress, and restore us to a sense of balance

Activities:

1. Introduce the phrase " 'Wow' experiences."
   a. Ask the students to define it.
   b. Select students to say the phrase in as many different ways as they possibly can (with surprise, softly with awe, loudly with enthusiasm or excitement, etc.). What emotion or emotions do the responses express?
2. We are surrounded by these experiences every day, but we may not take the opportunity to "pay attention" to them because we are "too busy," "too angry," "too sad," "too worried," etc.
   a. Help the students begin to find opportunities to see the "extraordinary" in the ordinary. Instruct them to:
      (1) Take a walk—and notice three things that you may not have noticed before.
      (2) At any time during the day, close your eyes and become aware of the sounds around you.
      (3) Look for a full minute at the face of someone you love without letting your mind wander.
      (4) Hold a flower in your hand and look at it, giving it your *full attention.*
   b. Ask the students to brainstorm some things that they might include in a list of "wow" experiences. (*Examples*: sunsets, sunrises, a new building beginning to be..., a new boyfriend or girlfriend, a first car, my birthday, getting money back you loaned a long time ago—and wrote it off, winning a game, being assertive in an important situation, getting a pet, being sick and getting well, being noticed at something that is important to you, reaching goal weight after dieting, a ride on a roller coaster, receiving recognition over the public address system at school, receiving a surprise compliment, getting hard-to-get tickets for a football game or a rock concert, winning the lottery, and so forth.)
   c. Have the student choose a "wow" experience and write about it.
3. Have the students complete Activity 4-5A, " 'Wow' Memories." This "Time Line" of good experiences will also help the students learn to "tap in" to their good, successful, and pleasant memories as a source that is readily available to them to reduce stressful feelings and return to a sense of equilibrium.

Name ______________________________

Date ______________________________

"Wow" Memories

Our happy, successful "wow" memories are stored in our memory banks—waiting to be recalled for our own pleasure, wonder, and gratitude. Use the format below to open your "bank" and "draw out your treasures." Since the mind does not know whether the picture it holds is real and present—or only an image or memory—you may happily experience some of the pleasant feelings again. Also, since the mind cannot hold *two* pictures at the same time, focusing on pleasant pictures will give you a "mini-vacation" from the pressures of your day. (Start with the earliest "wow" memory you can remember.)

TIME LINE

AGE	First "wow" experience.	Next.....	Recently........
"WOW" MEMORY (Event)			
FEELING			
I NOW KNOW...			
THAT KNOWLEDGE HELPS ME.....			

I CAN RECALL "WOW" MEMORIES ANYTIME I WANT TO FEEL GOOD!

WORK OUT 4-6

Objective:

- To identify activities that provide: (1) an outlet for the physical energy caused by stress, (2) reduce the intensity of strong feelings, and (3) lessen anxiety and depression

Activities:

1. *EXERCISE* is the natural outlet for reducing daily tension.
   a. Have the students talk about some specific exercises that they have done, and how it made them feel.
   Examples:

   b. The students can develop a daily exercise program. They can use the form in Activity 4-6A, "My Exercise Program," to keep a record of their progress. (It is important that they *like* the exercises they will be doing, so they will be *consistent.*)
   c. In a week or two, you may want to follow up by asking for a "progress report," and discussing what the students have noted on their program.
2. Everyone should take time to find an outlet for tension in *PLAY*. Play provides diversion for the mind and lets it change its focus from problems to a chosen, personally satisfying activity; improves body image; and increases confidence that comes from mastering a skill.
   —Have the students talk about those personally satisfying physical "play" activities that reduce tension and leave us *feeling good.*
   Examples:

3. *Optional:* You may bring in a cassette player. The class can choose a high-energy, up-beat music tape to play on the cassette player. If it can be arranged safely and comfortably for everyone concerned, the students can dance to the music.
   —Then, ask the students how they feel physically *and* emotionally. Did it reduce feelings of stress? Was it possible to be thinking of one's problems when you were involved in this activity?

Name ______________________________

Date ______________________________

My Exercise Program

"Letting Off Steam"

DAY	EXERCISE	DATE	TIME	FEELING	COMMENTS
Mon.					
Tues.					
Wed.					
Thurs.					
Fri.					
Sat.					
Sun.					

HOW IS IT GOING?

ACT OUT 4-7

Objectives:

- To identify some healthy and unhealthy ways to act out a feeling
- To recognize that our behavior has consequences
- To understand that we are responsible for our behavior

Activities:

1. Behavior is observable. You see it and so does everyone else who happens to be there. Our emotional responses help others to (a) know what is important to us, and (b) communicates information about the situation to be acted upon.
   a. Copy and distribute Activity 4-7A, "I Have Options!" The students will read the instructions.
   b. Now, have the students brainstorm some things a person might do to act out (show) a feeling. (This includes positive feelings of joy, as well as fear, sadness, and anger.)
   c. *You* can write the suggestions on the chalkboard or flip chart. The *students* will copy the options available to them on Part I of their activity sheet.
   Example:

Clap
stomp the floor

hug someone	pound a pillow	smoke
quit	talk to a friend	yell
exercise	listen to music	cry
overeat	write it out	drink
hide out	keep a diary	bite your nails
get even	use a drug	hit someone
kiss someone	dance	run
clean your room	talk to a friend	sleep
sing	throw things	laugh
overwork	exit (leave)	scream, etc.

jump up & down
Chop wood
dig in a garden

   d. Discuss which options are healthy and which are unhealthy. Talk about some possible consequences for the behaviors.
   e. *Optional:* When the students have completed Part II of Activity 4-7A, about a situation in which they used one of the behaviors mentioned as an outlet for a feeling, you may choose to have them break up into groups of four to discuss their answers; or, they may role-play the situation. (If one of the students has chosen an outlet that produced negative consequences, have the class discuss other possible responses. Remember to concentrate on the *behavior*. Always accept the *feeling* of the student.)

2. Ask the students to tell some ways to discharge the energy and reduce the tension build-up in situations where there is a *limited* opportunity to express their emotions.

   Examples:
   - a library (diaphragmatic breathing)
   - a passenger in a car (visualization)
   - a house of worship (progressive relaxation)
   - visiting someone in a hospital (walk up and down the corridor, visit the chapel)
   - restaurant (breathe completely, leave for the bathroom)

Shedding a Little Light:
To act on a feeling, I CAN also CHANGE:
My Location
My Expectations
My Involvement
My Attitude
My Objectives

Name ________________________________

Date ________________________________

I Have Options

Part I

Behavior is observable. You see it, and so does everyone else who happens to be there. Your emotional responses help others to know what is important to you and tell something about the situation that is affecting you.

It is important to identify some healthy outlets for the emotional expression of our feelings. The class will brainstorm some things people do to act out a feeling. You can write a list of the suggestions for the options available to you in the space below:

Part II

Select one of the options above and, on the back of this sheet, write a paragraph about a situation in which you used that behavior as an outlet for a feeling. Note whether it was effective. What were the results?

TAKE ACTION! 4-8

Objectives:

- To practice using constructive ways to express an emotion
- To understand that we can *choose* our behavior

Activity:

1. Inform the students that they can express an emotion in three different ways: (a) Name it, (b) Describe it, and (c) Tell an urge you feel.

   For example: You have just won the audition for the play.
   a. Name it—"I'm so *happy*!"
   b. Describe it—"I feel like I'm floating on a cloud."
   c. Tell an urge you feel—"I could shout it from the roof tops!" (That might be dangerous) or "I could just kiss you!" (Some people might object).

   Since it may be unacceptable, inappropriate, or impossible to carry out that urge, it is important to identify and practice more ways to express the emotion constructively.

2. Have the students complete Activity 4-8A, "Deal with It!"
   a. They will read the situation and respond to it by expressing the feeling in the three ways. They may also need to "tame" the intensity of a feeling. (For more information, see Activity 4-3, "Time Out," and Activity 4-6, "Work Out.")
   b. Now, they can *choose* an action to deal with the situation that will leave them satisfied and/or comfortable. (See Activity 4-7, "Act Out," to review some options.)
   c. Discuss the responses. You may have a class discussion.
   d. *Optional:* Break up into small groups or do a role play to observe the behavior *selected*. (Remember, one's feelings are always O.K. Concentrate only on the *behavior*.)

Name ______________________________

Date ______________________________

DEAL WITH IT!

Read each of the following scenarios, and then tell how it might make you feel. What could you do to reduce intense feelings? What action would you *choose* to deal with the situation which will leave you feeling comfortable and/or satisfied?

1. You are trying to make a good impression, but you trip as you enter the classroom. Your books drop out of your arms, and spill all over the floor.

Feeling: Name it ________________ Describe it ______________________________

Tell an "urge" ______________________________

Tame it: Reduce the tension ______________________________

Aim it: Choose an action ______________________________

____

2. A good friend tells you, "I was very upset by what you said to me yesterday. It really sounded like a 'put down.' I don't feel I can trust you anymore."

Feeling: Name it ________________ Describe it ______________________________

Tell an "urge" ______________________________

Tame it: Reduce the tension ______________________________

Aim it: Choose an action ______________________________

____

3. You have been waiting on the ticket line for three hours. The manager has just announced that there are only ten more tickets. You are number 13.

Feeling: Name it ________________ Describe it ______________________________

Tell an "urge" ______________________________

Tame it: Reduce the tension ______________________________

Aim it: Choose an action ______________________________

____

Continued

4. Your best friend moved away. You have been keeping in touch by telephone and through the mail. You have just received a call from your friend's mother telling you that he/she is seriously ill.

Feeling: Name it ____________ Describe it ____________

Tell an "urge" ____________

Tame it: Reduce the tension ____________

Aim it: Choose an action ____________

____

5. You are shopping in a busy department store. As you look for your wallet to make a purchase, you realize it is missing. It has all the money you made this week working at the pizza shop. You begin to frantically retrace your steps. As you are ready to give up hope, someone taps you on the arm and says, "I think this is yours. You left it on the counter." There is your wallet with all the money in it!

Feeling: Name it ____________ Describe it ____________

Tell an "urge" ____________

Tame it: Reduce the tension ____________

Aim it: Choose an action ____________

____

Now add one of your own stories.

6. ____________

____

____

____

Feeling: Name it ____________ Describe it ____________

Tell an "urge" ____________

Tame it: Reduce the tension ____________

Aim it: Choose an action ____________

____

REACH OUT 4-9

Probably the most significant way to release tension and restore ourselves to a sense of balance is to *talk* about our feelings.

Talk to a friend

Develop a support system

Build intimacy

Express feelings

For information about "reaching out" see:

Making Connections—Chapter 5
and
Communication Skills—Chapter 6

5

Making Connections

We are social beings whose main goal is to belong.

Fact Sheet 6 .... Making Connections

Activity Titles	Objectives
5-1 My Support System	To help identify the people in one's own support system
5-2 Quality People	To identify the personal qualities and character traits one values in relationships
5-3 Getting Acquainted	To help get to know each other better
5-4 Feedback	To become aware that the responses of other people influence how we see ourselves
5-5 Giving Gifts	To demonstrate, practice, and accept positive "feedback"
5-6 Wearing Labels	To recognize the discouraging effects of negative response from others
5-7 Roots	To become aware of one's heritage through research
5-8 My Family System	To understand that a family is a system in which each person is important
5-9 Family Relations	To focus on positive aspects of one's family

Seeing ourselves as competent, respected, and accepted by others is a basic ingredient in the development of a positive self-image.

Making Connections

- We are social beings. This means we *need* people. We need to belong.
- Our mental health is very closely related to our social health.
- Our self-worth is influenced by the degree to which we believe that we are *liked by* and *important to* people who are important to us.
- This need is met in *relationships* with family, friends, and other groups.

- We perceive ourselves largely in the "feedback" of one another's reactions.
- In order to build close, satisfying personal relationships, the communication of mutual acceptance is essential.
- Mutual acceptance leads to a feeling of safety and security.
- It is only then that we will reach out further to connect with others.
- Seeing ourselves as competent and respected by others is a basic ingredient in the development of a positive self-image.

[1]Donne, John, "Devotions Upon Emergent Occasions," Sermon #17.

MY SUPPORT SYSTEM 5-1

Objectives:

- To help the students to identify the people in their personal support system
- To increase a feeling of security and a sense of belonging

Activity:

There are people in our lives who care about us and to whom we can go for help. To help identify them:

a. Ask the students to think about the people in their lives.
b. Then, have them complete Activity 5-1A, "My Human Resources."
c. Remind them to be specific about the name of the group and the organization to which the person belongs (church, team, neighborhood, family, school, etc.).
d. Encourage them to write a comment in the space provided in the activity. (It might include a feeling or a need that is satisfied by that relationship.)
e. Looking at the completed "picture" of "My Human Resources" will help them see the scope of their social network.
f. You may wish to have the students discuss the information with the class, or in small groups, while they explore the ideas of how they might strengthen their support system.
g. Remind the class that it is up to each of us to create our own network of caring people. We all need to surround ourselves with a "circle of love."

Name ____________________________________

Date ____________________________________

My Human Resources

List the people in your life at this time. Write their name, relationship, group or organization, and a personal comment. Place them in their order of *closeness* to you starting from #1, and working outward.

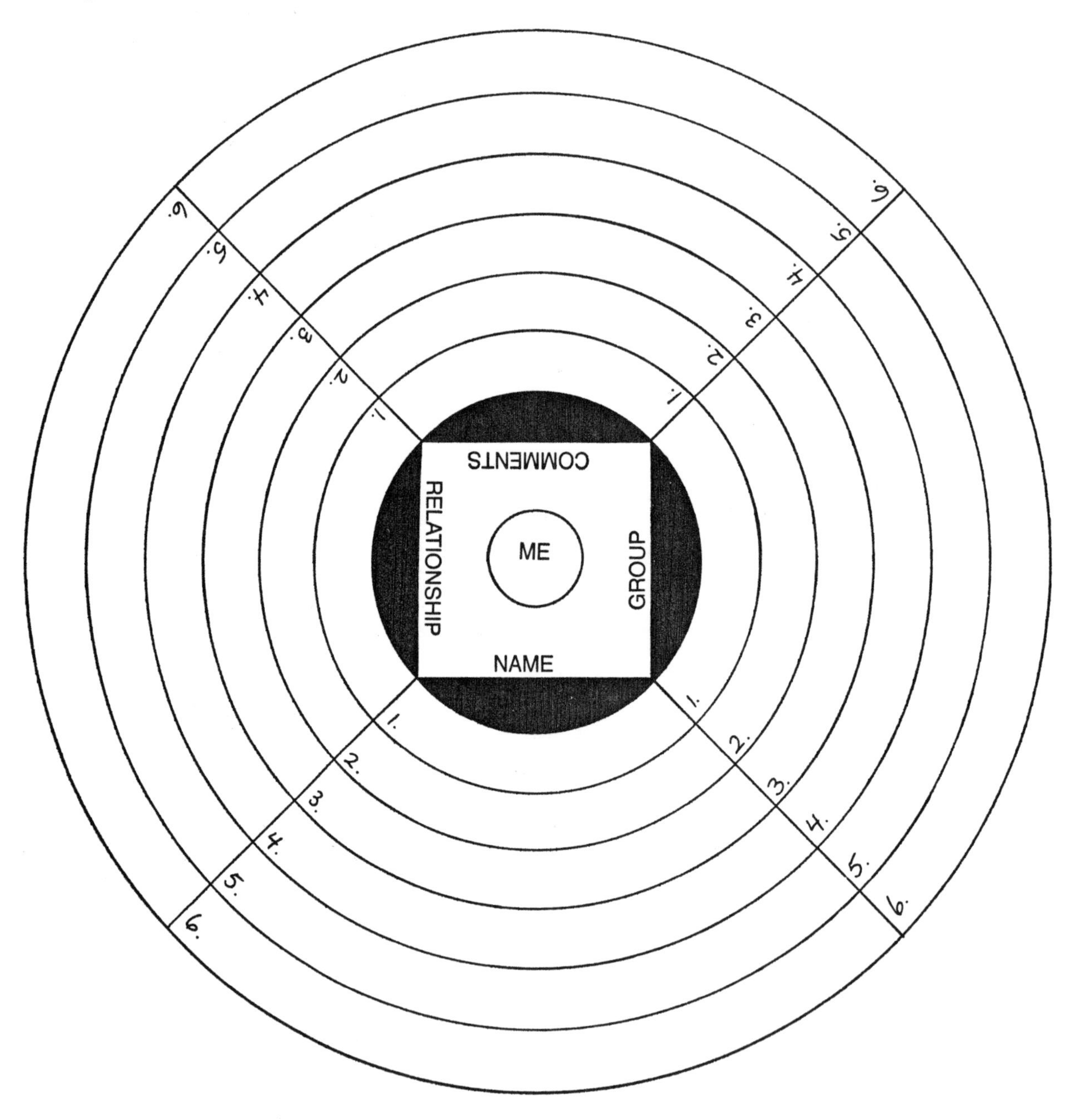

Study your support system. Are you happy with what you see? Do you want to expand your social network? How can you strengthen it?

QUALITY PEOPLE 5-2

Objective:

- To help the students identify the personal qualities and character traits that they value in forming relationships with people

Activities:

1. We are usually attracted to people whose performance, achievements, and/or values we relate to, or to which we aspire. To help the students identify some of these qualities that attract and/or impress them, instruct the class to name and discuss the following:
   a. Who is the one person in the world you most admire? Why?
   b. Name a person from the following categories who has made a deep impression on you. Why?
      - an entertainer
      - an athlete
      - a TV character
      - a family member
      - a political figure
      - a religious figure

> Young people need to recognize that they have people in their *daily lives* who can be considered *heroes*. Ask: who would that be for you? Write about your "everyday" hero.

2. To prepare the students to complete Activity 5-2A, "Wanted: A Friend," have them:
   a. Brainstorm, *briefly,* a list of qualities that they would like in a good friend (i.e., helpful, dependable, etc.).
   b. Then have them complete the "want ad" on the activity page. Encourage them to be creative. (They may write, cut out letters, and use artwork to complete the project.)
   c. The ads and notices in the "personal column" can be exchanged and discussed in small groups.
   d. Encourage the students to take note of any people in the group who exhibit these qualities. They may share the information with them. (Giving positive "strokes" reinforces the *positive behavior.*)
   e. A member of each group may be selected to share the information that was discussed with the rest of the class.

Name ________________________________

Date ________________________________

Wanted: A Friend

Part I

You have just moved to a new school. You want to make new friends. You decide you will use the school newspaper to help you. You are fortunate to be able to afford a 1/4-page ad.

Write an advertisement for "A Friend." Be specific about what you want. You may want to tell them something about yourself also.

Part II

Now, you don't have enough money for a large ad to advertise for a friend, but you can afford a small space in the Personal Column. You have to limit your information to *10 words or less.* Go to it!

PERSONALS

GETTING ACQUAINTED 5-3

Objectives:

- To help the students to get to know each other better
- To provide opportunities for personal sharing

Activities:

Choose any one or more of these activities to practice taking a *risk* in sharing and having some fun.

1. Name-Calling:
   a. Each student in the class will say his/her name and state one quality they have that begins with the first letter of their name; i.e., "My name is *Bob* and I'm *b*right" (or *b*old or *b*ashful, etc.).
   b. Each person must say the names and qualities of all those who have spoken before him/her—and *then* give their own name and quality. It makes it more challenging and more fun as the amount of information each person must remember increases.
   c. After the last person has spoken, talk about the activity: Did you know everyone's name before? Are you more comfortable with the group now?
   d. Now ask a volunteer to do it *one more time*!

2. Changing our perception of a situation can help us to learn new things about ourselves. Have the students:
   a. Complete the activity sheet 5-3A, "Use Your Imagination" on Side I. Now direct them to fold the paper so that their answers are not visible.
   b. Have the students count off numbers 1 to 4. Match all students with odd numbers (1 and 3), and even numbers (2 and 4) to form pairs. (When they pair off, they may greet their partner with the labels they chose in Activity 1, "Name-Calling"; i.e., Hi Bashful Bob, etc.).
   c. They will exchange their papers and complete Side II.
   d. Ask the students to compare their answers. Ask:
      (1) Did the answers tell you something new about yourself?
      (2) Did others see you as you thought they would?

3. Have the students complete Activity 5-3B, "I Am Somebody Who. . . ." (They will need room to move around.)

4. The students will get a chance to know more people when they become involved in the next activity, 5-3C, "Student Search." Allow about 10 or 15 minutes for the search so they will have time to talk about their similarities and interests.

5. This activity is best done later in the term when the students know each other better. Everyone can get involved when you play the guessing game, "Will the *Real* One Please Stand Up."
   a. Have the students write a brief autobiography (about one page).
   b. Instruct them *not* to put their names on their papers. Collect the papers.
   c. Select one of the papers to be read. Choose a student volunteer who will study the paper selected, and then either change *one fact* or add *one false statement* to the paper. (Encourage the student to make it reasonable and believable.) When the student is comfortable with the material on the paper, he/she can read it to the class.
   d. You can call on a student to guess who it is, *but*, they must *also* guess which fact or statement is false. If they are not correct, another student will be selected to guess, and so on.
   e. When the *Real* person is identified, he/she can stand up.
   f. Discuss the feelings, thoughts, and questions that may have occurred during this activity.
   g. Continue the activity so that other students can have their papers read and learn how others perceive them.

> NOTE: Peers can serve as a powerful tool for enhancing self-awareness.

Name ______________________________

Date ______________________________

Use Your Imagination

Directions: Complete Side I of the activity sheet. Fold the paper so that your answers are not visible. Exchange papers with your partner and complete Side II of the paper. Then compare the information.

I

1. What animal would you like to be?

   ____

   Why? ______________________________

   ____

2. What piece of furniture would you be?

   ____

   Why? ______________________________

   ____

3. What color would you be?

   ____

   Why? ______________________________

   ____

4. What kind of sport would you be?

   ____

   Why? ______________________________

   ____

5. What famous person would you be?

   ____

   Why? ______________________________

   ____

II

1. What animal would you like to be?

   ____

   Why? ______________________________

   ____

2. What piece of furniture would you be?

   ____

   Why? ______________________________

   ____

3. What color would you be?

   ____

   Why? ______________________________

   ____

4. What kind of sport would you be?

   ____

   Why? ______________________________

   ____

5. What famous person would you be?

   ____

   Why? ______________________________

   ____

Continued

6. What song tells something about you?

____

Why? ______________________________

____

Write four lines of the song that will explain your choice: ______________________________

6. What song tells something about you?

____

Why? ______________________________

____

Write four lines of the song that will explain your choice: ______________________________

Name ________________________________

Date ________________________________

I Am Somebody Who. . .

Directions: Circle the items below that tell something about yourself.

has a neat room	blushes	can play a musical instrument
likes books	likes to dance	plans to go to college
loves plants	talks a lot on the telephone	watches TV late at night
can wiggle ears	likes to draw	likes to compete in sports
has blonde hair	hates wrestling	has a pet
skips breakfast	likes to sing	is an only child
wants to do things by self	has a boyfriend	has a brother
has two grandmothers living nearby	worries all the time	can speak another language
is left-handed	has been in an airplane	cares about people
hates to speak first in a group	loves to listen to music	uses a video tape to do exercise
trusts most people	cries easily	likes to daydream
loses temper *often*	bites nails	just got a haircut
jogs every day	has a tooth missing	has a birthday in October
has own phone	is shy	has two sisters
likes the color red	won a trophy	always arrives on time!
borrows clothes	hates to wear a tie	is the oldest child

1. Now, slowly read the items you have circled.
2. Select one of the items you have circled. Look for a person in the class who circled the same one. Talk briefly about the similarities.
3. Look for someone in the group who has circled TWO of the items you have circled. Talk briefly about the similarities.
4. Can you find someone in the group with THREE or FOUR items that are the same?

Name ______________________________

Date ______________________________

Student Search

Get to know more about yourself and the other students by going on a Student Search. Walk around and try to find others in the room who "fit" with each statement below. Have them write their initials on the line next to the question. Get to work now! Look for:

1. Someone who has been in my class since grammar school ______________
2. Someone with the same color eyes as I have ______________
3. Someone who walks to school ______________
4. Someone who was born in another state ______________
5. Someone who never uses a hair dryer ______________
6. Someone who has the same astrological sign as I do ______________
7. Someone who lives in a house where no one smokes ______________
8. Someone whose last name has six or fewer letters ______________
9. Someone who takes music lessons ______________
10. Someone who doesn't like chocolate ______________
11. Someone who sings in the shower ______________
12. Someone who has season's tickets for sporting games ______________
13. Someone who has the same middle name as I do ______________
14. Someone who is an inch taller than I am ______________
15. Someone who is in three of my classes this term ______________
16. Someone who has seen the same movie at least three times ______________
17. Someone who laughs a lot ______________
18. Someone who is the youngest in their family ______________
19. Someone whose mother has a job outside the home ______________
20. Someone who has six or more people in their family ______________

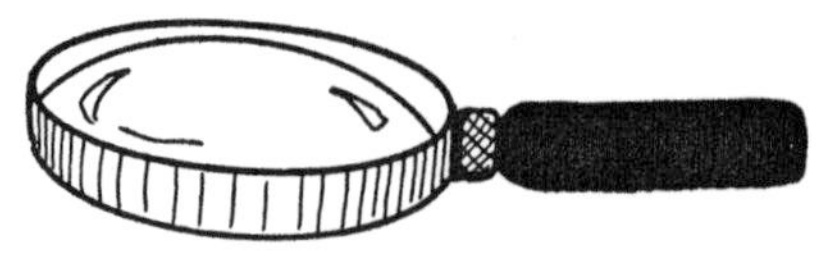

FEEDBACK 5-4

Objectives

- To help the students to become aware that the responses of other people influence how we see ourselves
- To define and explore "feedback"

Activities:

NOTE: Adolescents are *highly sensitive* to, and powerfully influenced by, feedback from others.

1. Ask the students: "What Is Feedback?" (It is verbal or non-verbal responses from others that:
   a. gives the person information about how he/she affects others,
   b. helps to reinforce or extinguish specific behaviors and attitudes,
   c. helps one define and create a personal identity.) Others help shape us.
2. Copy Activity #5-4A, "*Reflections,*" and give a copy to each student.
   a. Provide a mirror for the students to use.
   b. Have the students use the mirror to read the message.
   c. Help the students to recognize that the message remained hidden until it was *reflected back* in the mirror (feedback).
   d. Emphasize that we act as mirrors for each other as we come to know ourselves better in the responses of others.
3. To demonstrate how feedback can affect us:
   a. Have a lump of clay available.
   b. Remind the students that a lump of clay cannot form itself. It is molded (affected) by others.
   c. Have several students poke a finger into the clay. Note the *impressions* that were made. Does it appear different than it was before?
   d. Note that when it is acted upon by others, a new and different form comes into being. Have two or three people make something together. Consider how each one helps shape the finished product.
4. Have the students complete this assignment before the class meets again. They are to:
   a. *smile* at three strangers in a friendly, approving way,
   b. say something nice to two people you know,
   c. log all of the responses,
   d. discuss the experience with the group.

Shedding a Little Light:
I cannot interact with you without either a *positive* or *negative* contribution to your self-image.

Reflections

You reflect back to me parts of myself
that I cannot see –
Like the reflections in this mirror.

You smile – you like me! It gives me courage.
Now, I can tell you more.

You turn away – and I am afraid – to be
different; to be alone.

I need <u>you</u> to know more about <u>myself</u>—
to be all I can be!

Be there for me – please.

P.G.

GIVING GIFTS 5-5

Positive Feedback

Objectives:

- To help the students demonstrate, practice, and accept positive feedback
- To recognize the encouraging effects of *positive* peer pressure
- To increase feelings of self-worth
- To promote a climate of trust

Activities:

Help the students give each other "gifts" of praise.

a. Pass out small strips of paper.
b. Direct each student to write his/her name on the piece of paper.
c. Fold it and put it in a container. Shake the container.
d. Have each student pick a piece of paper out of the container.
e. Tell them that during the course of the week they will observe the student whose name was on the paper they selected. *The objective will be to "catch" that person doing something good!*
f. They are to keep a secret log of their observations.
g. At the end of the week, have each student compose a letter to the person they have been observing. (If it is possible, have them write it on gift-wrapping paper, to reinforce that positive messages give a person the same feelings of joy and acceptance that receiving a gift might.) When it is completed, it can be folded and tied with a ribbon.
h. Give the *gift* to the student chosen.
i. Allow time for the students to (privately) read their positive feedback—or they may take it home to allow more time for processing the information.
j. Then, discuss how it felt to receive positive information about oneself. (They may wish to express their thanks directly to the person from whom they received the "gift.")

Shedding a Little Light:
People who show us our value help free us to be all we can be.

WEARING "LABELS" 5-6

Objectives:

- To identify that the expectations and responses of others influence how we see ourselves
- To recognize the discouraging effects of negative "feedback"
- To have students experience peer pressure

Activities:

1. Have the class discuss the use of labels to identify things.
   a. Name some things that have labels on them (i.e., canned food, designer jeans, medicine bottles, etc.).
   b. Ask: What do labels tell us? Do we usually believe what the labels tell us without checking it out? (*Example:* Calvin Klein™ jeans are ______ because the ad told us so.) Why?
2. Ask the students to think of groups of people to whom some others unjustly give a "label." *You* can write the list on the chalkboard as they give you the information.
   Example: All ______________ are ______________

   because ______________________________.

   All young men who wear earrings or have long hair

   are ______________________________.

   All ______________ are the best ______________.
   a. If the class participation is vigorous, it may help the students to be aware of the fact that they do have prejudices and "label" people. Inform them that the first step toward changing beliefs and behaviors is by becoming *aware* of them.
   b. After you have finished writing the list, ask the students to give an example of someone from each group who does *not* fit the "label." Write the examples on the chalkboard next to the "label."
   c. Discuss the problems caused by stereotyping.
3. Ask the students to think about some words that people use to "label" other people (stupid, a jock, smart, a nerd, etc.). Does the label affect how we treat the person? Discuss.

4. Help the students recognize that "labels" are often arbitrarily given. To illustrate, select any one of the following qualities as being *unacceptable:* People who have:
    - brown shoes
    - blue eyes
    - striped shirts
    - a June birthday
    - rose-colored nail polish
    - size 5 shoes
    - a first name beginning with R
    - haircut with bangs on the forehead

    a. Have the students who fit into the "unacceptable" category identify themselves to the rest of the class.

    b. Direct the other students to give negative non-verbal messages when they are involved with the "labeled" students during the class activities.

5. OR, you could use another scenario to illustrate that "labels" are arbitrarily given. This time select people who have the things that will identify them as *different*—i.e., brown shoes, a first name beginning with R, etc. Only, this group will *now* be "labeled" as the *privileged* group, and the rest of the class will be *denied* their privileges. Remember, this "special" group has not *earned* these privileges!

    a. Have the "privileged" students identify themselves to the rest of the class.

    b. *They* will be the *only* students in the class who may either: (1) chew gum during the class, (2) leave the class first when the bell rings, (3) be excused from this night's homework, or (4) be given a snack during the class which *you* will provide.

6. Whichever scenario you have chosen, discuss the experience at the end of the class. (If you chose to have the "privileged" students leave early or be excused from homework, you may have to process the following questions at the next class meeting.) Ask:
    - How did it feel to be rejected, left out, or denied approval?
    - How did it feel to be the "in" group?
    - Could it affect how you see yourself—the relationships you choose—or the decisions you make?

    (Help the students recognize that if the *unacceptable* category was changed tomorrow, they could be "it.")

    Talk about decisions that the person who was "left out" might make to belong *somewhere.*

NOTE: Be sure to have time for those selected to be *labeled* to leave their role. Let other students give affirmative statements to them. The class can give them applause for their "performances"!

ROOTS 5-7

Objectives:

- To have the students research their heritage to become aware of their roots
- To increase their sense of belonging and security
- To encourage a sense of pride and understanding

Activities:

1. Define "genealogy." (The science or study of tracing a person or family through several generations, to explore one's family roots.)
2. The class will use the genogram to research their family history. Discuss why one might want to know that information.
   a. Define "Genogram." (It is an instrument, in the style of a diagram, which visually shows your family history.)
   b. Have the students study the genogram information in Activity 5-7A, "The Historical Genogram" and 5-7B, "Genogram Symbols."
   c. Then, direct the students to complete the genogram for their family in Activity 5-7C, "My Family Map."
   d. Tell the students to keep their genogram so they can add other facts as they collect more information.
3. Ask the students to do a more in-depth interview with their grandparents (or the oldest member of their family). The interviewee may write the information down or use a tape recorder to collect the material. Include:
   a. Place of birth, year of birth, family structure.
   b. What was life like when they were growing up? Discuss the history during that time. Include descriptions and stories about the clothes, politics, entertainment, diseases and remedies, transportation, songs, dance crazes, educational opportunities, etc. Talk about how they coped with some problems they might have had.
   c. Look at family pictures of their grandparents' youth. (More information can be obtained at this time.)
4. Write reports on the countries, states, and cities of origin mentioned in the interviews. (Include costumes, customs, and both past and present lifestyles. Note some of their favorite recipes that were passed down through the families.)

NOTE: If families are separated by great distances, encourage communication by telephone or through the mail to explore the students' heritage. Supporting a sense of continuity and communication between generations enriches each life, and increases feelings of security.

Name ___________________________________

Date ___________________________________

The Historical Genogram

A genogram is a diagram of a family over several generations. This basic genogram tells WHO, HOW, and WHEN. WHO makes up your family; HOW they got to be family (birth, marriage, adoption); and WHEN they arrived (birthdate, birth order, marriage dates, etc.) and WHEN they left the family (through death, divorce, or separation).

You need page 5-7C, a pencil, an eraser, and a ruler. The symbols you need are listed on page 5-7B. Study the information on pages 5-7A and 5-7B before you begin your own genogram. (You can add any additional information you wish, such as hobbies, education, etc. You might also extend the genogram to the fourth generation and beyond, if possible.)

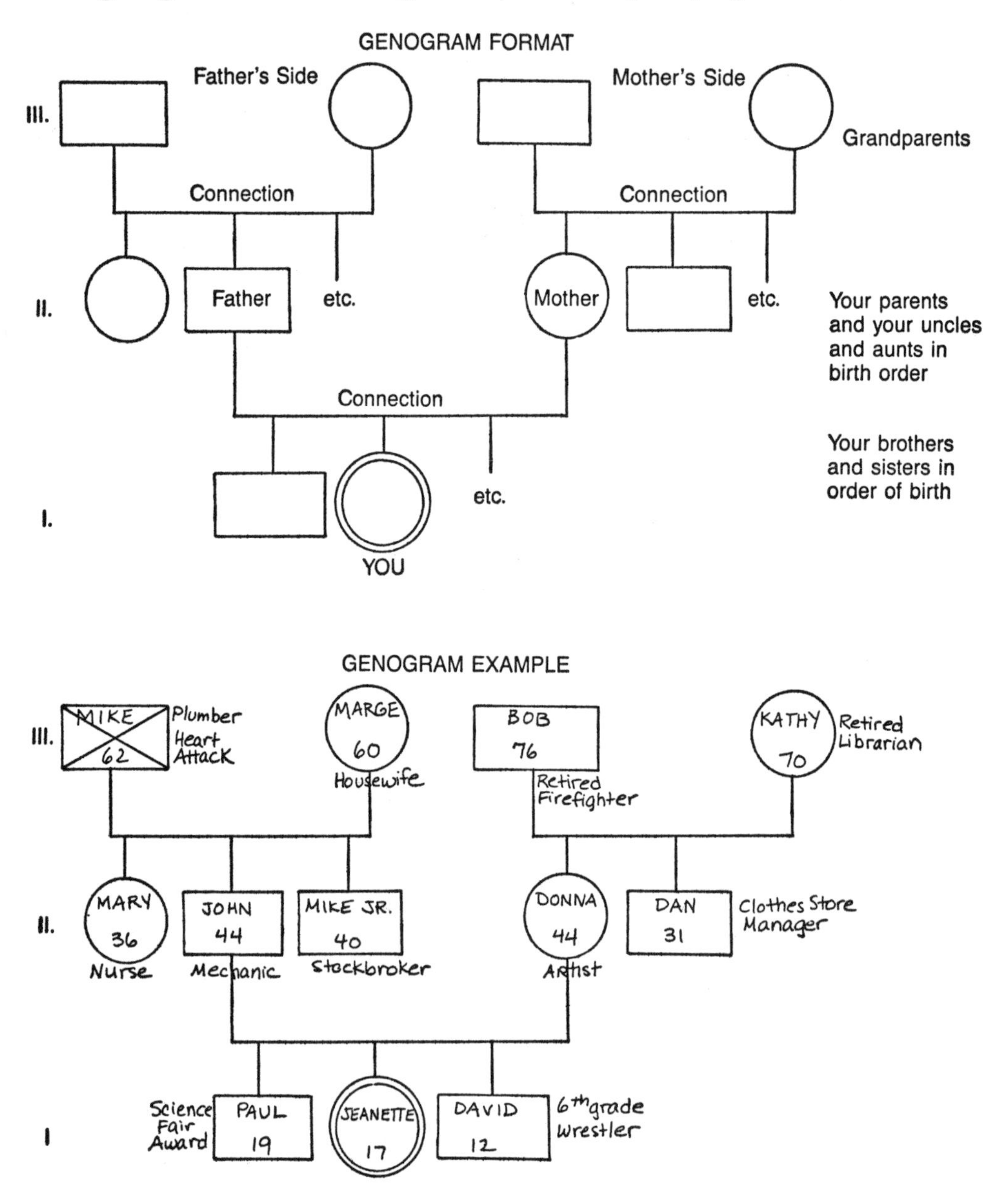

Genogram Symbols

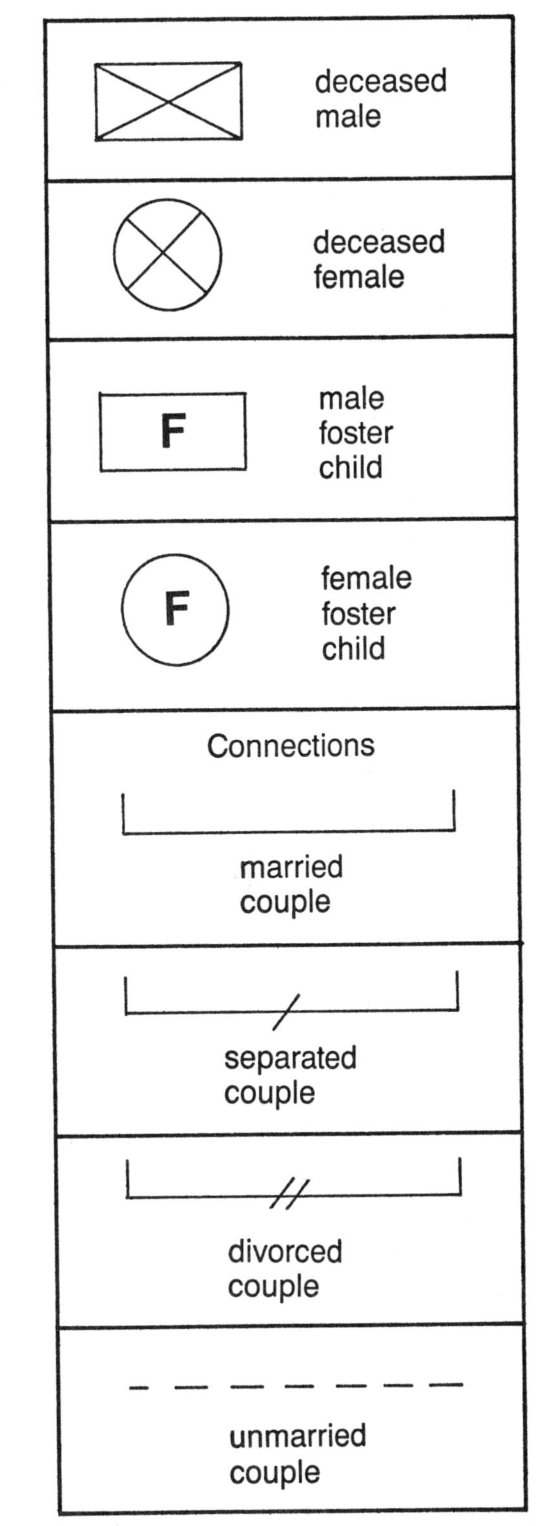

My Family Map

All families have roots. We are here today because roots were "planted." You are who you are partially because you are a member of this particular family. People have kept track of their family histories for centuries. You will learn about your family by doing this basic historical genogram. Keep the genogram and add new facts as you learn them.

MY FAMILY SYSTEM 5-8

Improving Relationships

Objectives:

- To help the students understand that a family is a system in which each member is important
- To recognize that each member affects all other members in their relationships

Activities:

1. Have the students define "system." (A set or arrangement of things *so related* or *connected* so as *to form a unity or* organic *whole. Webster's New World Dictionary of the American Language, College Edition.)* Briefly talk about systems: solar system, irrigation system, the human body's circulatory and digestive systems, etc. (Note that *each* part is important to that system. They *all* have to work together for the system to be effective.)
2. Ask the students to watch a TV family to begin to recognize "how the system works." (*Examples:* "All in the Family," "The Cosby Show," "Roseanne," "Dallas," "Family Matters," etc.)
   a. Then discuss in class what they observed. (What was the family structure? How did they talk to each other—father to mother, parents to children, children to children? And so forth.)
   b. Ask the students to think of a family motto that would "fit" that family.

> NOTE: After collecting information by watching the TV families, it should be clear that there are many types of families (traditional, blended, single, step, and more). Each of these families will develop its own system to be effective.

3. Now that the students are aware of the important role they have in affecting other family members, they can take a look at their own special family. See "FAMILY RELATIONS," Activity 5-9.

FAMILY RELATIONS 5-9

Objectives:

- To recognize that each family member has an effect on all other family members
- To encourage them to focus on positive aspects of their family to improve family relationships

> NOTE: Review "My Family System," Activity 5-8, for background information.

Activities:

1. All families have *rules*, both spoken and unspoken. To help the students to become aware of some important messages in their family, ask them to create a Family Crest and a Family Motto.

   a. They can draw the crest on the front of a page, and place the motto at the bottom of that page.
   b. The students can write on the back of the page to explain the crest and the motto.

2. Complete Activity 5-9A, "Getting to Know You." Tell the students to: (a) Fill in Side Ia of activity. (b) Fold the paper so that your answers are not visible. (c) Ask one of your family members to fill in Side IIa. (d) When the written work has been completed, talk about your answers with each other. How many answers were the same? Did you talk about the new things you learned about each other? (e) Discuss the experience with the class or in small groups, or write a one-page summary of the experience. (f) Repeat the exercise again, but this time have the *family member* fill in Side Ib. (g) After they have completed their answers and folded the paper so the answers are not visible, *you* fill in Side IIb. (The students can report on their experience doing the activity.) (h) The students can select one piece of information from Activity 5-9A to help them choose a thoughtful "gift" for their family member. For example: Compliment what they are wearing, buy a tape of their favorite music, change the station on the radio to where they will hear their favorite music, make their favorite dessert, *stop* and talk about something that you now know they find interesting. Discuss the results of the activity.

3. We all need encouragement and recognition.
   a. Have the students complete Activity 5-9B, "Picking Positive Points."
   b. Encourage the students to find opportunities during the course of the week to recognize and comment to their parents about those qualities they had identified in Activity 5-9B. Or, they can choose to write an "appreciation letter" to their parents (noting these qualities) for no special occasion. It would be nice to send it through the mail.

> NOTE: It is important to know that the *only* person we can change is *ourselves*. But, by changing *our* responses, we can make changes in our relationships in the family (system).

(The students can write a paper about their feelings and the responses from their family members, to complete any of the above activities.)

4. Have the students complete Activity 5-9C, "From Generation to Generation."

Name ________________________________

Date ________________________________

Getting to Know You

Directions: You fill in the information on Side Ia. Fold the paper so your answers are not visible. Ask a parent or other family member to answer what they think you would have answered using Side Ib. Compare answers.

SIDE Ia	SIDE Ib
My favorite:	Your favorite:
food is ____________	food is ____________
dessert is ____________	dessert is ____________
musician is ____________	musician is ____________
sport is ____________	sport is ____________
friend is ____________	friend is ____________
color is ____________	color is ____________
TV program is ____________	TV program is ____________
school subject is ____________	school subject is ____________
way to relax is ____________	way to relax is ____________
The thing that most annoys me is ________ ____________________	The thing that most annoys me is ________ ____________________

Now, Your parent or other family member will fill in the information on Side IIa. *You* will now fill in Side IIb without looking at their answers. Compare the lists.

SIDE IIa	SIDE IIb
My favorite:	Your favorite:
food is ____________	food is ____________
dessert is ____________	dessert is ____________
musician is ____________	musician is ____________
sport is ____________	sport is ____________
friend is ____________	friend is ____________
color is ____________	color is ____________
TV program is ____________	TV program is ____________
school subject is ____________	school subject is ____________
way to relax is ____________	way to relax is ____________
The thing that most annoys me is ______ ____________	The thing that most annoys me is ______ ____________

Name ______________________________

Date ______________________________

Picking Positive Points

Part I
Everyone has seen an advertisement created to sell a *house*. You probably have noticed that it focuses on all of the good qualities to make the house more appealing to the buyer.

- Well, *we all* have good qualities, too. When we want to feel good about ourselves, we focus on them. If we want to appreciate others, we will notice some of their assets and good points.
- Now, imagine that you have been commissioned to create a "For Sale" advertisement for one of your parents. Pick out some positive points. What information would you include?

FOR SALE:

Part II
Select one of your parents to include in this activity.

- Develop a job application for that "position" on a separate piece of paper.
- Include:

Name: ______________________________

Position: ______________________________

Job Description: ______________________________

____

Qualifications: ______________________________

References: ______________________________

(Consider yourself one of the references, and write a letter to recommend him/her for that position.)

Name ______________________________

Date ______________________________

From Generation to Generation

Complete the following sentences.

1. Three things I particularly like about my family are ______________________________

____

____

____

2. Two things I would like to change about my family are ______________________________

____

____

____

3. The best time I ever had with my family was ______________________________

____

____

____

4. Two customs that we have in our family that I especially like are ______________________________

____

____

____

5. The one lesson I learned in my family that I would like to pass on to my children is ________

____

____

____

____

____

____

6

Communication Skills

All human progress has been achieved through cooperative action, which depends upon effective communication.

Fact Sheet 7 . . . . Communication Skills

Activity Titles	**Objectives**
6-1 Self-disclosure	To understand and practice appropriate self-disclosure
6-2 The Communication Process	To provide an overview
6-3 Sending Messages	To learn and practice skills to effectively express thoughts, feelings, needs, and wants
6-4 Listening	To understand and practice effective listening
6-5 Hearing the Message	To learn and practice *active* listening skills

"....Communication is the greatest single factor affecting a person's health and relationships with others."—*Virginia Satir.*

Communication Skills

- There is no single factor that has more potential for expressing concern and respect for others than the way in which people *speak* and *listen* to each other.
- We are not born with these skills. They must be learned!
- The value of learning and using effective communication skills cannot be overemphasized.
- *Good communication skills* help us to: (1) *share* thoughts, feelings, and behavior about what is presently happening, in an *open* and *honest* way; and (2) *confirm* by our responses *the other person's worth and value.*
- The *inability* to read and send such messages adeptly is a *major social handicap* which leads to feelings of low self-worth.
- Our ability to communicate is basic to everything we do.

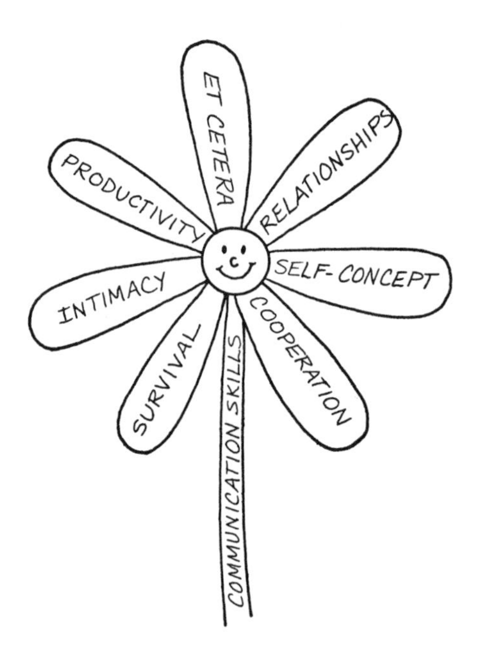

- All human progress has been achieved through cooperative action, which depends upon effective communication!

SELF-DISCLOSURE 6-1

Objectives:

- To help the students recognize the importance of appropriate self-disclosure
- To provide an opportunity for the students to practice sharing information about themselves

> NOTE: 1. Healthy relationships are built on self-disclosure.
> 2. Being self-disclosing means being "real."
> 3. It is important to be sincere and honest.

Activities:

1. Review the Johari Window in Activity 6-1A. (This visual concept was developed by Joseph Luft and Harry Ingram to illustrate that by combining information about ourselves that only *we* know, with an awareness of how *others* perceive us, we may begin to see ourselves in a sharper perspective.) Reinforce the idea that building a relationship involves letting others get to know you (i.e., "opening your window" so that others can "see in").
2. Ask the students to:
   a. Describe specific actions or behaviors that other people do to make it *easier* to share information about ourselves (i.e., "appear to be paying attention to me," "I know they won't laugh at me," "They don't gossip," "They share back with me.").
   b. Then, ask about actions and behaviors from others that make it *difficult* for people to self-disclose (i.e., "They talk about others behind their back." "They always look like they are bored when I talk to them," "They have a smirk on their face—I think they must think I'm stupid.").
3. There are two basic elements to develop trust in a relationship: (1) One person takes a risk by sharing (self-disclosing); (2) The second person involved responds with acceptance and support. To offer the students an opportunity to practice these skills, have them create a booklet about themselves for a homework assignment. Tell the students:

   a. On the outside cover, put information that represents aspects about yourself that you have shared or would be comfortable sharing with others. (Write words, draw pictures, cut out words and pictures from magazines, or use any other material to illustrate your point.)
   b. In the pages of the book, use the same technique to illustrate the information about yourself that you usually do *not* share with others. (The

students will be informed that they *need not share* the information *inside* the book.) We can call that part of your life "a closed book."

c. When the assignment has been completed, have the students form small groups. Allow about five minutes for each person to talk about the *cover* of his/her book. They may choose/or *not choose* to share a piece of information in the *closed* part of the book. *Respect privacy*!

d. After each person has had a turn to talk in the group, ask them to return to their seats and discuss the activity.

e. Have the students keep the books and continue to work on it for their own growth and enjoyment. The better we know each other, the more self-disclosing we can be. The more self-disclosing we are, the more we get to know each other, and so on. (As the students share "inside information" they can cut out the symbol and paste it on the cover of their booklet.)

f. Later, you may want to do a follow-up to ask the students how their booklets are progressing. Do more symbols appear on the cover? Are they more able or willing to share with others?

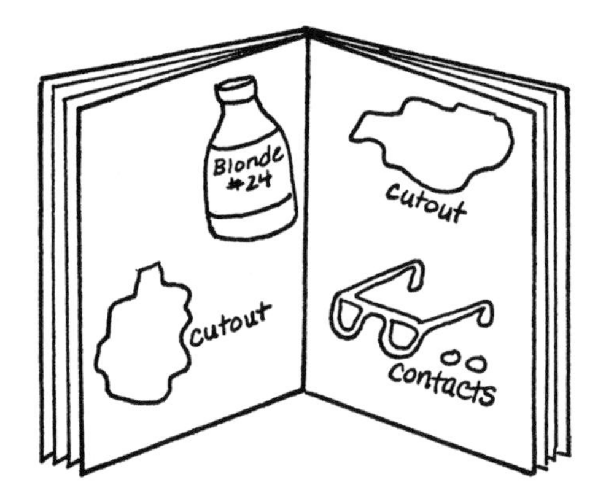

The Johari Window

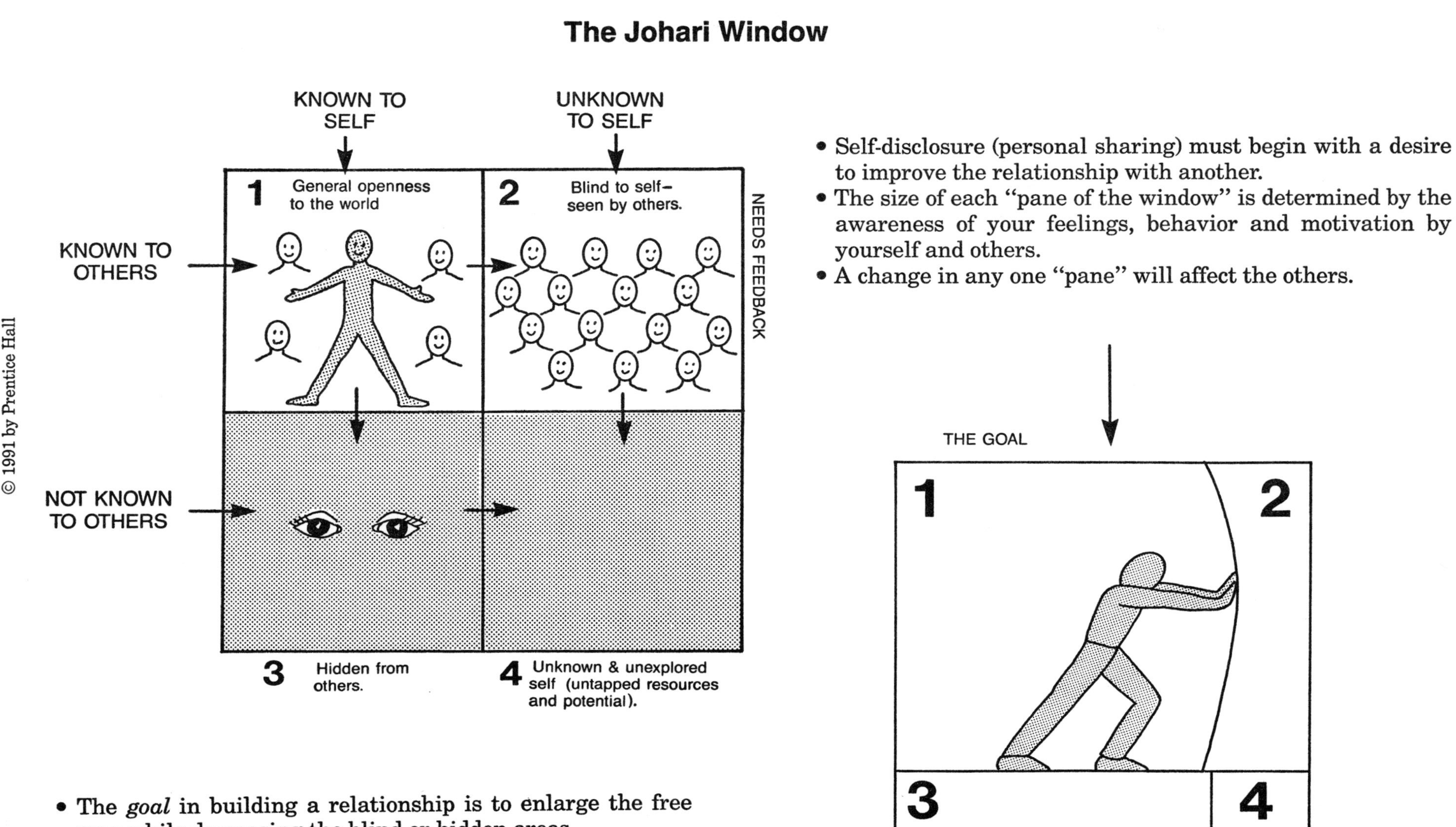

- Self-disclosure (personal sharing) must begin with a desire to improve the relationship with another.
- The size of each "pane of the window" is determined by the awareness of your feelings, behavior and motivation by yourself and others.
- A change in any one "pane" will affect the others.

- The *goal* in building a relationship is to enlarge the free area while decreasing the blind or hidden areas.
- Relationships are built gradually.

Name ______________________________

Date ______________________________

The Communication Process
An Overview

Our ability to communicate is basic to everything we do. We can learn the skills necessary to communicate effectively. Study the model of the communication process below:

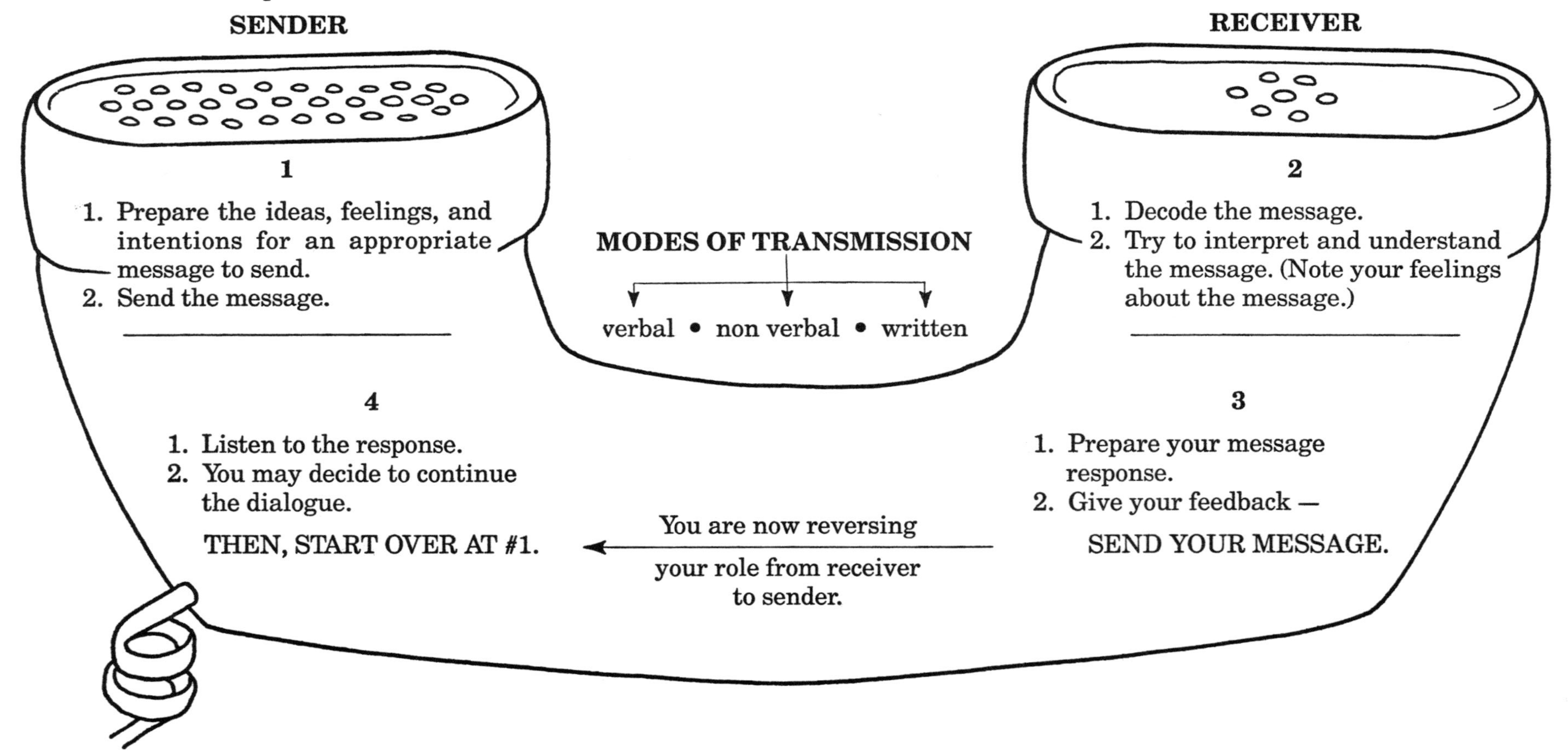

SENDING MESSAGES **6-3**

Objectives:

- To have the students learn and practice skills to effectively express thoughts, feelings, needs, and wants
- To have the students take responsibility for how they feel and how they communicate that to others

NOTE: Review "The Communication Process: An Overview," in Activity 6-2.

Activities:

1. Study the diagram below for good sending skills.

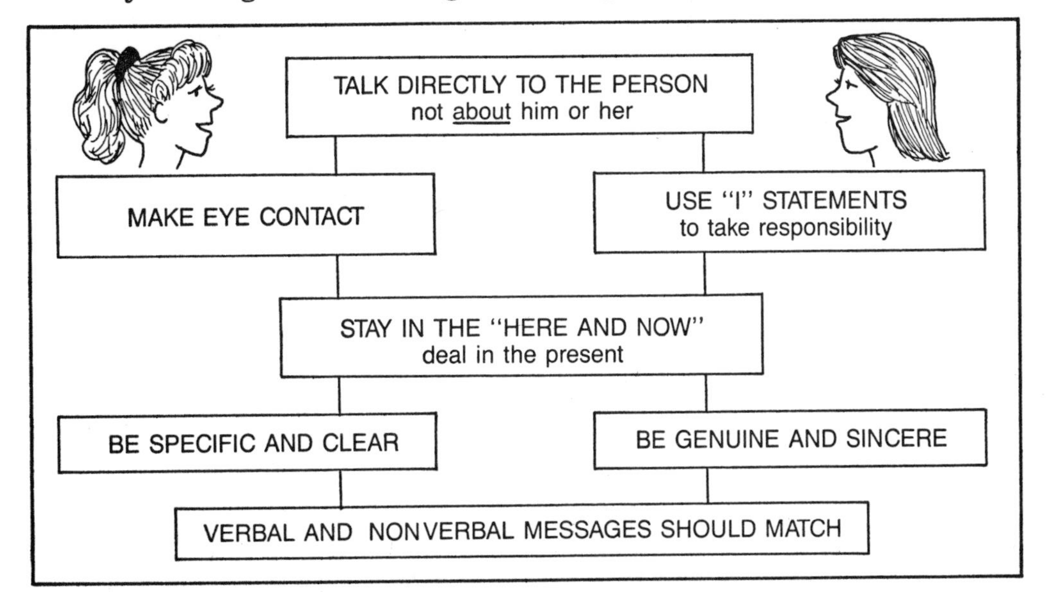

2. Have the students form into groups of six people. Explain to them that they are going to practice making *eye contact.* Select one student to demonstrate the activity. Each student in the group will have a turn.
   a. Direct the designated student to stand in front of each member of the group. He/She may choose the distance that is comfortable.
   b. No words are to be spoken. (Encourage the students to be respectful and cooperative.)
   c. Have the student make *eye contact* with each student and maintain it for approximately 10 seconds, and then move on to the next person in the group, and so on.
   d. Ask each group to discuss how the experience affected them. The group leaders may then share the information with the class.

3. Review the information about "I" messages with the students.

Describe the Behavior	Share Your Feelings	Tell Why	What You Want
Separate the deed from the doer. Focus on the behavior *not* on the person.	Label or describe your feeling about the behavior (See Chapter 3, "Naming and Claiming Feelings!)	State the reason you have the feeling.	Name a specific action or idea you would like done to change the situation.

Example:
The music is too loud. *I feel* angry *because* I can't study. *Will you please* turn it down.

4. The students can practice creating "I" Messages by using Activity 6-3A, "Owning the Problem." A class discussion can follow to critique the sentences that were constructed.
5. Do Activity 6-3B, "Cease Fire," to illustrate the negative effect of using *blaming* and *criticizing* "You" messages.
6. Have the students complete Activity 6-3C, "Sending 'I' Messages." You can have the students report the results of this skill in the personal situations they listed. They need not go into detail about the problem or the other people involved, just the outcome of the encounter.
7. Have the students *role-play* situations in which they use "I" messages. They may create new ones or act out those examples that appear in Activity 6-3A, "Owning the Problem."

Shedding a Little Light:
My feedback responses should be:
1. descriptive rather than evaluative (how it makes me feel),
2. specific rather than general (observable behaviors),
3. focusing on something the receiver *can* change,
4. delivered at the earliest opportunity,
5. to identify what others do that I like or do not like.

Name ______________________________

Date ______________________________

Owning the Problem

Directions: Read each problem, examine the "You Message" in the second column, and then write an "I Message" in the third column.

Problem	"You Message"	"I Message"
1. Your brother is playing music so loud that it is interfering with your telephone conversation in the next room.	Why do you play that music so loud? Don't you think of anyone else but yourself? You are so inconsiderate.	
2. Bob promised to buy a cake early in the day for a family party. Less than an hour before the party, he has not shopped.	Your promise means nothing. No one can depend on you for anything. You only think of yourself.	
3. Kay borrowed the family car and promised to be back at a certain time. The car is returned two hours later.	You stupid girl, can't you tell time? You can't be trusted with the family car.	
4. Your sister has borrowed a special item of clothing from you to wear. She promised to return it at a certain time, but does not.	You are irresponsible. You have no respect for me. I'll never lend anything to you again. You are so selfish.	
5. Sue forgets to show up for a date to a school function. You stand alone as all your classmates pass by.	You made a fool out of me in front of the whole school. I'll never meet you anywhere again. You never think about anyone but yourself.	

Continued

Owning the Problem

Problem	"You Message"	"I Message"
6. Joe borrowed a book from you which you took out of the library. He lost the book.	You got me in trouble with the library. You can never be trusted again. You are so careless.	________________ ________________ ________________
7. Your friend promised to dress casually for a movie date, but she comes in all "dressed up."	You are a liar. You are trying to make me look foolish. I'll never believe you again.	________________ ________________ ________________
8. Everyone was asked to bring a particular snack for the party. Your friend arrives without bringing the snack promised.	You care only about yourself. You spoiled the party. You embarrassed me to tears.	________________ ________________ ________________
9. YOU ARE THE TEACHER IN THIS SITUATION. RESPOND AS THE TEACHER.		
One of your students has not handed in his homework assignment.	You are lazy, inattentive, and useless in this class. You'll never make much of yourself in this life.	________________ ________________ ________________
10. YOU ARE THE PARENT NOW. RESPOND AS THE PARENT.		
Your child is late getting up for school.	You're lazy. You'll never be able to hold a job. You'll never amount to anything.	________________ ________________ ________________

CEASE-FIRE

Teacher Directions:

In this activity, the students will use role-play to see the negative effects that "attacking" or "you messages" have on relationships and problem resolution.

1. Have the class create a problem that might be caused by someone's behavior. (For example: Tim told Cindy that he would meet her outside the gym with her ticket for the basketball game. All her friends are already inside watching the game as it begins. Tim never showed up.)
   a. Then have them brainstorm a list of "You Messages," which you can write on a chalkboard or flip chart. (For example: "You made me look like a fool," "You made me miss the game," "You embarrassed me," "You made me a laughingstock last night.")
   b. Next, ask a student to copy the "You Messages" on individual pieces of paper.

2. Choose the two actors for the role-play.
   a. Give Actor #1 the papers which have the "You Messages" written on them to hold.

   b. Actor #1 will prepare to talk about "the problem" in his/her own words. He/she should get into the *feelings* evoked by the problem. Have the actor make clear why he/she is so upset. (They can try for the Academy Award with their performances!)
   c. Actor #2 will remain oblivious to the needs or desires of Actor #1, and continue with his/her problematic behavior.
   d. Finally, in exasperation, Actor #1 will be instructed to deliver the "You Messages," loudly and repeatedly from the papers he/she is holding. *As the message is being delivered verbally, the actor will crumple up each paper and throw it at Actor #2.*
   e. If Actor #2 sees the paper coming at him/her, which is the *visible* sign of the "attacking" message, it is probable that this actor *will assume a position of defense.* If not the first time, certainly he/she will prepare to defend him/herself the next time.
   f. It is also possible that Actor #2 will begin tossing some papers back to Actor #1, and use a few "You messages" of his/her own—or leave the scene, etc.)

3. Ask: What happened when Actor #2 was attacked? Did Actor #1 get across the message he/she wanted the other actor to hear? What was accomplished?
   a. Have the actors discuss how it felt to be in their roles.
   b. Have the students discuss the effect of this communication on a relationship.

4. You may want to do another role-play. (You may want to choose new actors, or have the *same* actors *exchange* roles.)

Name ____________________ 6-3C

Date ____________________

Sending "I" Messages

1. Write an "I" message for this situation. You are walking home with your friend. You are trying to tell her a story. Every time you begin to speak, she interrupts you.

   When you ____________________

   I feel ____________________

   Because ____________________

   I would like (Will you please) ____________________

   ____

2. Write about a situation at home that has become a problem for *you*. Then write an "I" message that you can use to deal with the situation during this week.

   Situation: ____________________

   ____

   ____

   When you ____________________

   I feel ____________________

   Because ____________________

   I would like (Will you please) ____________________

   ____

3. Is there a difficulty that *you* are having at school with one of your friends or a teacher? Describe the situation below, and then construct an "I" message that you may use.

   Situation: ____________________

   ____

   ____

   When you ____________________

   I feel ____________________

   Because ____________________

   I would like (Will you please) ____________________

   ____

LISTENING 6-4

Objective:

- To have the students recognize and practice effective listening

Activities:

1. Have the students list things that help them to know when people are listening to them.
   a. Write their responses on the chalkboard (e.g., looks at me; lets me finish what I am saying; isn't distracted with other things; etc.).
   b. *You* will model good listening skills as *you* receive their information.
   c. When there are no further responses, ask the students if they had observed *you* doing any of those things as you were taking information from them. Ask them to be specific.
   d. Ask: How did it make you feel? (e.g., more open to sharing, squelched or discouraged from further involvement, helpful, etc.).
2. The following activity will help the students practice *listening* in a *one-way* communication (e.g., lectures, TV programs, receiving directions or instructions).
   a. Ask for a volunteer from the group. *Privately*, inform the volunteer that he/she will instruct the group to draw one or more figures found in Activity 6-4A, "Communication 'Creations.'" The volunteer will turn his/her back to the group so as not to accidentally reveal the design or give nonverbal clues.)
   b. When the volunteer has familiarized him/herself with the drawing, the group will be informed that they will listen to the instructions from the volunteer on how to draw the particular creation. They will take out paper and pencil.
   c. They will also be advised that they are to *REMAIN SILENT* throughout the activity as they complete the drawing.
   d. Have the class discuss any feelings and thoughts they had during the activity.
   e. Then, have the students explore the possible consequences of poor listening if: (1) you needed directions to a new history class; (2) you were listening to a lecture that you would be tested on; (3) you were receiving instructions from the salesperson on how to operate your new stereo; or (4) you were listening to a TV advertisement on how to order tickets to your favorite rock concert.
3. This part of the activity will bring out the value of *dialogue* (two-way conversation).
   a. Make copies of Activity-6-4A, "Communication 'Creations.'" Fold the copies in half so the design is not visible.

b. Assign a partner for each student. Give one of the folded pages to *one* of the partners in each set.
c. Ask that these students *privately* study the design and describe it to their partner in sufficient detail so that it can be drawn from the description.
d. During the instruction of this drawing, the other partners *may ask questions* to clarify the directions they are receiving.
e. When the drawing is completed, they can compare it to the original picture held by their partners.
f. Discuss the experience. Ask:
   (1) Was it easier to follow the directions accurately when you could ask questions?
   (2) Are there times you are confused and do not know how to proceed, simply because you have not risked the questions you need to ask to get more information or to clarify what you heard?

Name ______________________________

Date ______________________________

Communication "Creations"

HEARING THE MESSAGE 6-5

Objectives:

- To learn and practice active listening skills
- To confirm, by your responses, the other person's worth and value

Activities:

1. The class will practice paying attention to the *speaker* and the *message.* Ask a student to prepare two sentences to say to the class using *verbal* and *nonverbal* information. (*Example:* "I'm late!"—places both hands on top of head. "They will be so mad at me."—wringing hands and wincing.)
   a. Another student will volunteer to *mimic* the nonverbal signs and repeat *verbatim* the verbal message that was delivered.
   b. Repeat the above activity with several other volunteers to reinforce the importance of paying attention to the speaker and the message.
2. Review the information in the diagram "Active Listening" on Activity 6-5A. Emphasize the need for the total involvement of the listener. *Hearing* is not the same as *listening.* Active listening requires one to *hear the message* and the *feeling* behind the words.
   a. Have the students break up into groups of six.
   b. Let the group choose a topic that can evoke some emotional reaction (i.e. lengthening the school day, curfews, women firefighters, etc.).
   c. Each person in the group can speak *only after* he/she has *restated the idea and feeling* of the previous speaker. Everyone in the group should take a turn. One person at a time will speak for one minute. After the first person has spoken, and *before* the second person can express his/her point of view on the subject, #2 must repeat, to the satisfaction of #1, a *summary* of his/her thoughts and feelings—and so on.....).
   d. Discuss the experience of the group.
3. Have the students form groups of four (a listener, a speaker, and two observers).
   a. The speakers will talk on a topic of interest to themselves for approximately 2 minutes.
   b. The listener will use good listening skills as noted in Activity 6-5A, Section I. They may use some of the words and phrases from Section II of that activity to encourage the speaker.

c. After the speaker has finished talking, the listener will summarize the message and the feelings presented by the speaker. They can begin their summary using phrases in Section III. For example: "Let me see if I'm hearing you correctly, etc....."

d. The two observers will then report on their observations using the "Observer's Check List Form," Activity 6-5B. The recommendations or prescriptions can be discussed and given to the participants.

e. Within several days, follow up to see how the students have improved in using the active listening skills.

Name ________________________________

Date ________________________________

Tools for Active Listening

Active listening involves *MOBILIZING THE TOTAL SELF:* mind, senses, feelings, intuition, experience, sensitivity, and a receptive frame of mind.

Section I GIVE FULL ATTENTION

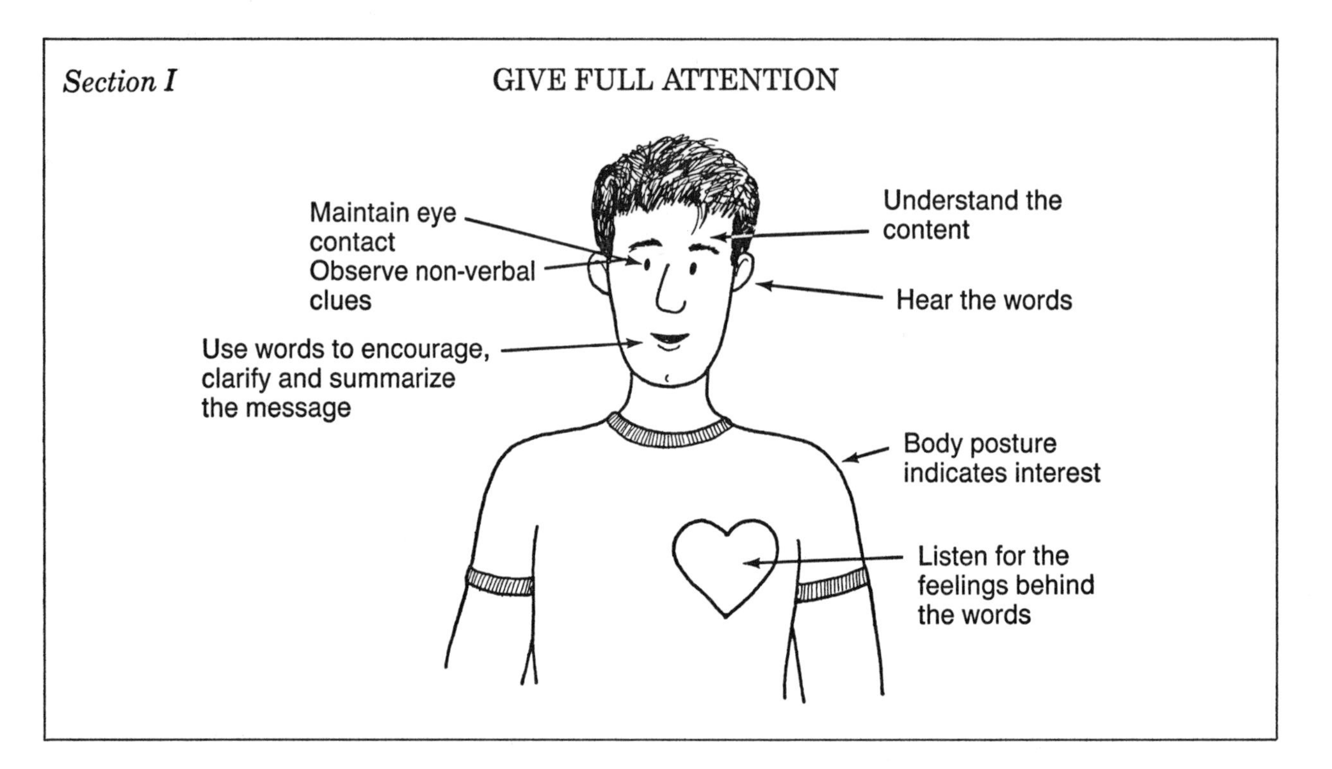

Section II **Words and body language to encourage the speaker**	*Section III* **Phrases to help *clarify* and/or to preface your interpretation of the message**
Uh huh Oh my.... Tell me more..... Right..... I see.... nodding affirmatively smiling	Maybe you feel..... It seems that you........ Could it be that........ Do I understand you correctly... You seem to be feeling..... Let me see if I'm hearing you correctly....

Section IV. Restate the message in your own words. Identify the feeling beyond the words.

> Active listening is an attempt to view the ideas and feelings of another person from *his or her* point of view.

Observer's Check List

The observer will assess the skills of both the listener and the speaker. Rate the performance of the communication skills using the scale below. The scale is one to five: one = excellent, two = good, three = fair, four = poor, and five = not at all.

Scale

Person	1 excellent	2 good	3 fair	4 poor	5 not at all
LISTENER					
1. Good eye contact					
2. Body posture (showed interest)					
3. Identified the speaker's feelings					
4. Understood the content of the talk					

SPEAKER					
1. Good eye contact					
2. Verbal and nonverbal messages match					
3. Used "I" statements					
4. Was clear and specific					

Comments and Recommendations:

To improve the listener's skills ____________________

____

____

To improve the speaker's skills ____________________

____

____

As the observer I learned ____________________

____

____

____

____

____

Observer's Name Date

7

Problem-Solving and Decision-Making

Problems are a fact of life!

Fact Sheet 8	Coping
Activity Titles	**Objectives**
7-1 A Value Judgment	To identify and clarify our values
7-2 Creative Solutions	To know that we have *within* us the ability to generate new perspectives
7-3 Recognizing Conflict	To identify the physical and emotional feelings of conflict
7-4 Resolving Conflict	To use decision-making skills to resolve conflict and problem-solve
7-5 Carrying Out My Decision (Feeling Peer Pressure)	To demonstrate how peer pressure can influence the decisions we make
7-6 Carrying Out My Decision (Refusal Strategies)	To prepare students to resist peer pressure
7-7 My Family Decisions	To learn and use the Family Meeting format

We are capable of making choices that decide our future. Feelings become guides to that choice. We are not passive responders.

Spreading the News

Coping by
Problem-Solving and Decision-Making

- *Problems are a fact of life!*
- Running away, denying the problem exists, or avoiding problems by any means (including the use of chemicals), keeps us from personal growth and destroys the opportunity to make the changes that will improve our situation.

TAKE CHARGE

- The ability to deal with life's problems effectively depends upon:

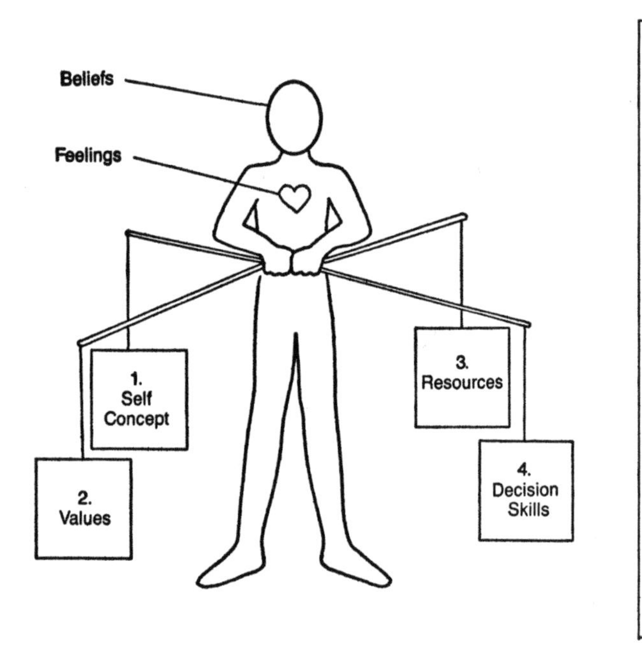

1. A *Positive Self-Concept* allows us to believe in our capability to overcome obstacles.
2. *Values* and beliefs form the framework for our lives.
   - Beliefs are those ideas about reality which we hold to be true.
   - Values are those things which we consider *important.*
   - They give meaning to our lives.
   - They strongly influence the *choices* we make.
   - These choices determine the direction our future will take.
3. Identifying and using appropriate *resources.*
4. The *skills* necessary to make effective *decisions* when we are faced with a *problem,* can be learned.

FACE IT!

State the Problem ____________________

SKILL FORMAT

C	*C*ollect information
O	*O*rganize and analyze the data
P	*P*icture all the alternatives
I	*I*dentify the consequence
N	*N*ame your choices
G	*G*o to it!

- Choices have unavoidable consequences that affect our lives and the lives of others.
- Problem-solving and decision-making are dynamic, ongoing processes.
- By practicing problem-solving and decision-making, we know that:
  a. more than one choice is available,
  b. each choice has positive and negative consequences,
  c. we are responsible for our choices.

A VALUE JUDGMENT 7-1

Objectives:

- To help students understand that we are not always conscious of our value judgments
- To have students identify and clarify some ideas and things that are important to them

Activities:

1. Decision-making has been described as *using what you have to get what you want.* The difficulty is that many of us do not know what we want. To help the students identify some of the things they value: (a) write the following list on the chalkboard, (b) ask the students to put them in the order of their importance to them, on a separate piece of paper:

    Security   Pleasure
    Popularity   Health
    Power   Service
    Independence   Education

    You may choose to have them write or discuss why they choose the first three items on their list in that particular order.

2. Notify the class that they have each won the lottery for a different state in the United States. They are to receive the money only after they tell the state lottery official the answers to the following—With my money:
    —the one thing I will do for the world is...
    —the one thing I will do for myself is...
    —the one thing I will do for my school is...

    The class may form small groups to discuss their answers. (It is possible that someone may have identified a common value in his/her answers.)
    Example: a. World—get rid of illiteracy; b. self—attend the best college; c. school—restock the library. = Value: Learning is important to me.

3. Have the students complete Activity 7-1A, "FIND MY PLACE," to help them identify personal interests and skills that are important to them.
4. After the students have completed Activity 7-1A, they can discuss their choices and their comments. What type of future work might appeal to them using that interest and/or talent?
5. Ask how they might feel if they had to spend the night with one of the groups they had *not* chosen. Why?

NOTE: Group I — might indicate an interest in "hands-on" activities.
Group II — might indicate an interest in working with people—maybe even on a grand scale, as a leader.
Group III — could be detail-oriented and enjoy problem-solving situations.
Group IV — are creative people who are willing to find new perspectives.
Group V — shows some people displaying some of the qualities of "helpers" in their concern for others.

Shedding a Little Light:
Decision-making is *using what you have to get what you want,* when you know *what it is.*

Name ______________________________

Date ______________________________

Find My Place

You have moved to a new town. You are invited to a giant celebration for the entire student body on the first day of school. It is to be held in the new gym. When you arrive, you notice how cheerfully the gym is decorated. What a turnout of students! You feel a little uneasy because you don't as yet know anyone. You know it is going to be a *long* night. You don't want to get "stuck," so you walk around the gym to see where you fit in. You notice that students with similar interests and skills have formed their own groups.

A. After you have listened to each group for awhile, decide with which group you will pick to spend time. Why?

Group I Tools, tools, tools! Everyone knows how to do something. This one could fix a car, that one built his own closet, she could wire a lamp...	*Group 4* This seems to be quite a creative and imaginative group. One of them was talking about his "invention" that could shut off his alarm without his having to get out of bed. The tall one plays the drums, the other one paints...
Group 2 Some of these students sure know how to get things done! They seemed to know just how to influence the others and get them to work together.	*Group 5* Everyone seems to be listening to the one student explain the new math problems to them. She does a good job of it. When the shortest girl in the group keeps coughing, the young guy on the left offers her a glass of water.
Group 3 Such attention to detail! Such patience. They just hang in there until they figure it out.	

B. If that group disbanded and left, which group would you chose next? Why?

____

____

____

____

____

CREATIVE SOLUTIONS 7-2

Objectives:

- To help the students become aware that they have *within themselves* the ability to generate new perspectives
- To practice creative techniques that can increase problem-solving abilities

> NOTE: "*A creative solution is a problem-solving act*, and, in particular, it is the solution to an ill-defined problem" (John R. Hayes, *Cognitive Psychologist*).
> - Making up alternatives is the creative aspect of decision making.

Activities:

1. At the early stages of problem-solving and decision-making, a person must generate many possibilities by using creative thinking skills. To facilitate creativity, it is necessary to increase a sense of security by providing a supportive environment. Therefore, inform the students that:
   (1) There are no right or wrong answers.
   (2) They can s t r e t c h their imaginations and include even ideas that seem ridiculous or "silly."
   (3) *All* ideas are to be accepted without criticism.
   a. To "loosen" their minds, name an object and have each student, in turn, respond immediately with the first word that comes to his/her mind. (*Example:* bird—fly, badminton, feathers, red, etc.) Note that it is important to be open and accepting to the ideas that come to us!
   b. It is important to see the extraordinary in the ordinary. To practice seeing new perspectives: (1) select an object, (2) think of new ways the object can be used and (3) list on the board *all* of the students' responses. (*Example:* a tin can—to hold food, as a pencil holder, with string as a walkie-talkie, a flower pot, to bake bread.)
   c. Have each student take out a piece of paper and place three dots anywhere on the paper. *After* they have complied with that direction, then ask them to create a picture incorporating the three dots and create a brief story to go with the picture. The students may share their stories with the class. Note the diversity of the student's creative products arising out of the same instructions. GOOD FOR THEM!
   d. Alex Osborne's technique of *Brainstorming* requires a group to identify as many solutions to a problem as possible (no matter how apparently silly or foolish the answers may seem) in the hopes that some of the ideas might turn out to be productive. Have the students describe

on a piece of paper a problem of interest to them, which they may be experiencing now or in the future, and place their problems in a container.

(1) Now, select a problem from the box.
(2) Choose a secretary to write on the chalkboard the problems and the list of solutions that are offered. (ALL solutions will be accepted without comment.)
(3) When all the solutions have been received, begin to explore each solution with the class for its positive and negative consequences.
(4) Have the class vote on two or three solutions that they think would be the most helpful. (Remember, everyone will have to accept the responsibility for *whatever* decision they will make.)

Some examples include:

- I want to go to college, but I don't have enough money to pay for tuition.
- I want to give a party. I don't plan to have alcohol. What can I do if someone else brings alcohol to the party?
- A group of seniors keep harassing this new freshman at school. He's from another country. I don't think it's fair. What can I do to help without making enemies for myself?

RECOGNIZING CONFLICTS 7-3

Objective:

- To help the students identify the physical and emotional feelings associated with conflict

> NOTE: Tension is caused by a need to strike a delicate balance between conflicting wants, needs, goals, and duties.

Activities:

1. Have the students:
   a. Define the word "conflict." (being pulled in two directions, as in a tug of war; a struggle.)
   b. Describe some of the physical symptoms from the struggle (tight muscles, headache, stomachache, itching, etc.).
   c. Describe some emotional symptoms (irritability, distraction, preoccupation, short-tempered, etc.).
   d. Give some examples of conflicts:
      study ⟷ play eat ⟷ diet drink ⟷ abstain
      hoard ⟷ share tell ⟷ refrain face it ⟷ avoid it
2. Have the students give some examples of conflict situations they have dealt with in the past.

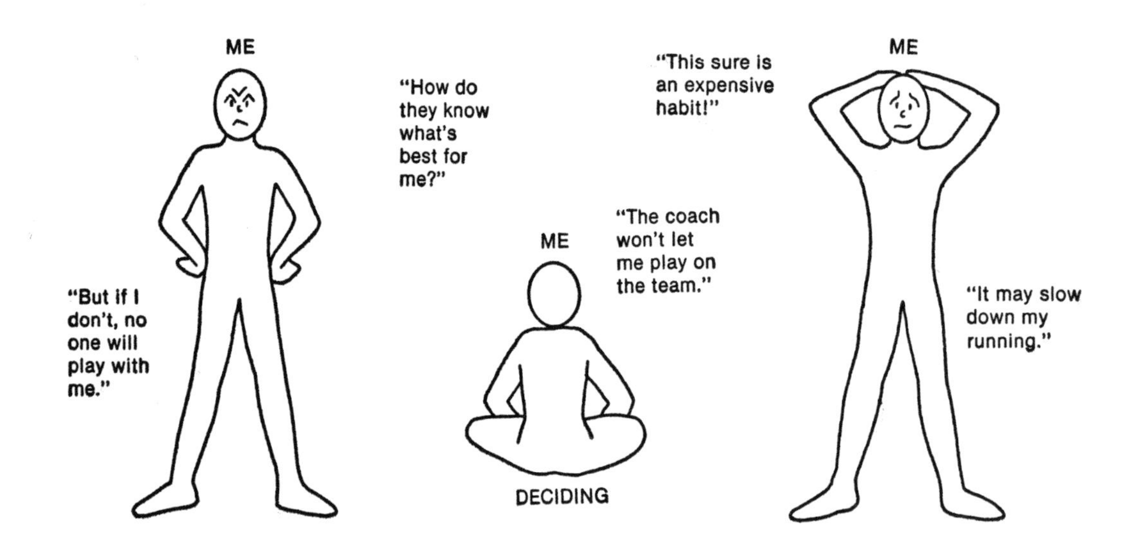

3. To help the students identify internal tension, ask volunteers to role-play what is going on *inside* a person.

   a. The volunteers will prepare by choosing a topic that might cause a conflict. (If they need suggestions, you might offer those mentioned in #1d.)
   b. Actors 1 and 2 will each take one side of the conflict, and try to convince Actor 3 that his/her view is *right.*
   c. Actor 3 will sit *in the middle* and "experience" the "tug of war."
   d. After a few minutes, stop the performance and ask all the actors to share their feelings about the activity.

4. It is important to recognize that conflicts are inevitable. And, there are always two sides to a story. Have the students complete Activity 7-3A, "A Conflict in My Life," to give them an opportunity to view a conflict they might be experiencing, from a different perspective. Sometimes seeing the problem from the other person's point of view can increase understanding, reduce tension, and aid in resolving the conflict. (See Activity 7-4, "Resolving Conflicts," and Activity 7-4A, "C.O.P.I.N.G." for further information.)

Shedding a Little Light:
Not to decide *is* to decide!

Name ______________________________

Date ______________________________

A Conflict in My Life

It is important to recognize that conflicts are inevitable, and there are two points-of-view.

- Select a situation in your life that is causing you to be in conflict with a parent, a brother, sister, friend, classmate, teacher, coach, or employer.
- Present the information in the form of newspaper *headlines* that make the problem clear to the reader. Under each headline, write a brief "editorial" comment to support one side and then the other.

The Problem:

THE WAKE-UP MORNING NEWSPAPER

MY SIDE

1. HEADLINES

2. EDITORIAL COMMENTS:

THE OTHER SIDE

1. HEADLINES

2. EDITORIAL COMMENTS:

Sometimes seeing the problem from the other person's point-of-view can increase understanding, reduce tension, and aid in resolving the conflict.

- Do you wish to "rewrite" the headlines now? If so, why? If not, why?

Problem

RESOLVING CONFLICTS 7-4

Objectives:

- To resolve conflicts by using problem-solving and decision-making skills
- To learn how to evaluate the "payoffs" and "costs" involved in making each decision
- To practice these skills

Activities:

1. Review the *C.O.P.I.N.G.* skills for problem-solving and decision-making found in Activity 7-4A.
2. Have the students study how to evaluate the "payoffs" and "costs" involved in making decisions:
   a. Copy and distribute "Evaluating Consequences," in Activity 7-4B.
   b. Together, you will read the information presented in this activity.
   c. Then, have the class brainstorm information they might put in the space for *Long-Term Payoffs.* You will write their suggestions on a chalkboard or flip chart.
   d. Now each student will choose the answers that are "right" for him/her and write it in the space on the paper.
   e. Fill in your number evaluations for each column.
   f. Total the number columns.
   g. Write your decision at the bottom of the activity.
   h. Repeat the same procedure for "Evaluation Consequences," Activity 7-4B (continued).
   i. Discuss the activity.
3. Inform the students that the decisions they make will naturally affect their lives, but it will also affect the lives of others. Have them list several decisions they might make now or in the next year or two. Place them on the chalkboard. Have the students volunteer to name the people in their lives whom the decision would affect, and *how* it would. For example:
   - going away to college — mother = will worry about me
father = feel proud of me
sister = no clothes to borrow
boyfriend = ????? etc.
   - taking a job after school
   - borrowing money
   - starting to take drugs, etc.

4. Have the class choose a problem or a conflict they wish to explore as a group. Use the form in Activity 7-4C, "Continue C.O.P.I.N.G.," to practice their decision-making skills. Additional xeroxed copies can be given to the students to work with in resolving the problem or conflict they may be experiencing now—or in the near future.

Shedding a Little Light:
A person has control over the decision—*not* the outcome!

Name ______________________________

Date ______________________________

C.O.P.I.N.G.
Skills for
Problem-Solving and Decision-Making

Identify the Problem or Conflict: ______________________________

C - Collect Information
from *people* — who have had a similar situation, experts, professionals,
from *places* — libraries, agencies, a site involved,
from *things* — magazines, periodicals, equipment.

O - Organize and Analyze All the Information
identify facts vs. value judgments,
credibility of the source,
relevance or irrelevance of the information.

P - Picture the Alternatives
Thinking up alternatives is the creative aspect of decision-making.
Think of as many alternatives as possible, no matter how foolish some may appear at first.

I - Identify the Consequences
Every choice has a consequence. To evaluate the possible outcomes of choices:

- On one side of a piece of paper, list the short- and long-term payoffs (Pros).
- On the other side of the paper list the short- and long-term costs (Cons). See Activity 7-4B and 7-4B (continued) for examples.
- Are you willing to accept the consequence of your choice?

N - Name Your Choice
Make a decision. After a time, review your choice. If it is not effective, repeat the steps and make another decision.

G - Go for It!
Implement your decision. Take action!

Name ______________________________

Date ______________________________

Evaluating Consequences

Study the model below to understand how to use this format in evaluating the "payoffs" and "costs" involved in making a decision.

1. Brainstorm what might be included in the blank space: *Long-Term Payoff.* Next, choose the answers that are "right" for you, and write them in the empty space.
2. Fill in your number evaluations in each column. (1 = least important; 10 = most important).
3. Total the number columns.
4. Write in your decision.

Jeff has not started to smoke cigarettes. Since he moved to a new school recently, he is feeling some pressure to do that. Most of his new friends smoke, and Jeff is wondering if he will join them.

WILL I SMOKE?

	1-10 Number Evaluation	Payoff (Pro)	Cost (Con)	1-10 Number Evaluation
SHORT-TERM		I will feel more comfortable with the group.	Shortness of breath may interfere with playing sports	________
		It peps me up.	My clothes and breath will smell.	________
		It helps me when I feel nervous.	It can get expensive.	________
		It shows I make my own choices.	My parents will be upset	________
	________	Total	Total	________
LONG-TERM		?	I will be "hooked" on tobacco . .	________
			I won't be able to save that money toward a car or clothes .	________
			I could develop a serious health problem (lung and heart disease).	________
	________	Total	Total	________

MY DECISION ____

Continued

When there are two or more alternatives from which to decide, you will explore the consequences of each. Study the format. Fill in the blank spaces (A. = long-term payoffs, and B. = long-term costs) after brainstorming. Complete your number evaluations and total the columns. What would you decide?

Jessica, a 16-year-old junior, is being pressured by John Paul to go steady.

	1-10 Number Evaluation	Payoff (Pro)	Cost (Con)	1-10 Number Evaluation
A. "Going Steady" SHORT-TERM	______ ______ ______ ______	Always having a date Never being lonely Not having to risk being "turned down" Total	Not meeting new guys Usually doing the same things Not seeing my girlfriends often Total	______ ______ ______ ______
LONG-TERM	______	? Total	Being limited in my social life Worry about the relationship breaking up—and getting back into the dating scene Total	______ ______ ______
B. "*Not* going steady" SHORT-TERM	______ ______ ______ ______ ______	Being free to meet new people Being free to go out with my friends when I want to Developing a hobby with my free time Getting involved in a sport or school group Total	Having to deal with loneliness Having to deal with some rejection Feeling at "loose ends" Total	______ ______ ______ ______
LONG-TERM	______ ______ ______	Being open to new relationships Learning to *handle* feelings of loneliness and rejection. Total	? Total	______

MY DECISION ______________________________

Name ____________________

Date ____________________

Continue C.O.P.I.N.G.

Identify the problem or conflict: ____________________

____

C — Collect Information:

	People	Places	Things
1.			
2.			
3.			
4.			

O — Organize and Analyze All the Information:

P — Picture the Alternatives:

1. ____________________
2. ____________________
3. ____________________
4. ____________________
5. ____________________

Continued

6. ______________________________

7. ______________________________

8. ______________________________

9. ______________________________

10. ______________________________

I — Identify the Consequences:

1-10	Payoff	Cost	1-10
____	Total	Total	____
____	Total	Total	____

N — Name Your Choice: ______________________________

G — Go for It!
Implement your decision. Take action!

CARRYING OUT MY DECISION 7-5

Feeling Peer Pressure

Objective:

- To demonstrate how peer pressure can influence the decisions we make

Activities:

1. It sometimes takes courage and determination to carry out our decision—especially when it will make us unpopular. To demonstrate some feelings we may experience under pressure:
   a. Put a long strip of masking tape on the floor. It will help identify the degree of commitment we will make to a decision.

   (masking tape)

10	5	1
feel strongly *for* the issue		feel strongly *against* the issue

   b. Now, ask a student to "take a stand" on an issue. For example:
      (1) A woman should be able to hold *any* job a man can hold in the workplace.
      (2) Boxing should be outlawed because of the damage it can do to a man.

      The student will stand on that part of the masking tape line that indicates his or her position on the issue.
   c. The rest of the class will try to "pressure" that student to change his/her mind by offering arguments or promises. Encourage them to be persistent.
   d. Discuss the experience when the activity is completed.
      Did the decision-maker change his/her mind?
      How did it feel to be under so much pressure?
      How did those giving the pressure feel?

2. Each student will use the C.O.P.I.N.G. steps detailed in the preceding activities to make his/her own decision on the following situation:
   Your best friend is the student leader who has called a class "walk out" because the lunch hour was shortened. The principal is aware of this, and has declared a three-day suspension for everyone who participates. Your parents will ground you for the weekend if you take part. Your friend will be upset if you don't join in. Take a stand (1 through 10).

a. When the students have each finished making a decision, select one of the students to tell his/her decision to the class.

b. Choose actors to role-play: the best friend student leader, the principal, the parent, and the decision-maker. The decision-maker will stand in the middle as they respond to his/her decision. (The other actors may use some energy—even talking all at once—so the decision-maker can experience some feelings of pressure.)

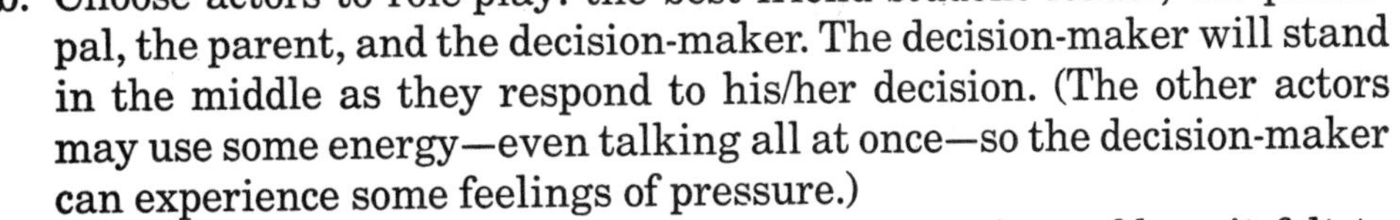

c. Now, have each of the actors give their impressions of how it felt to participate in this scene.

d. Ask:
   How often do you think you do things just because your friends are doing them?
   Do you sometimes change your mind to feel more comfortable in the group, even though you do not agree with your friends?

(Activity 7-6A, "Say NO, Successfully," will present some refusal skill strategies to help the students "take a stand," and say no, successfully.)

CARRYING OUT MY DECISION 7-6

Refusal Strategies

Objectives:

- To learn and practice "taking a stand" on decisions we make
- To help the students to feel more prepared to resist peer pressure and to gain confidence when they want to say "No"

NOTE: These strategies are presented to *Say NO*, and—

Survive
Save face
Stay drug free
Still have friends
Still have fun

Activities:

1. Have the students study some strategies to Say NO, as shown in Activity 7-6A, "Say NO Successfully."
2. The students will practice these strategies by completing Activity 7-6B, "Scene-Stoppers." Volunteers could be asked to role-play some of the scenes presented in this activity—and their responses.
3. Next, each student will think of a scenario to which they would like to say NO, and write it on a slip of paper.
   a. The slips of paper will be folded, collected, and put into a container marked "#1—Scenes."
   b. While they are doing that, *you* can write each of the *strategies* on individual slips of paper, fold them, and put them into a container marked "#2—Strategies."

   c. Now, ask one of the students to pick a paper out of the "#1—Scene" container. He/she will read the scene, and then pick the cast of characters for the role-play. (The student who is to role-play saying NO successfully will pick a paper out of "#2—Strategies" container, and use that strategy in his/her response.)
   d. The selection of "scenes" and "strategies" will continue so the students can practice taking a stand. (Some of the scenes may be repeated, using a *different strategy* to say No.)

Name ______________________________

Date ______________________________

Say "No" Successfully

Following are a list of strategies that can help you to "take a stand" on your decision to say NO successfully. Study them.

SAY NO.......	A = Explanation B = Example(s)
with *DIRECTNESS*	A. Look 'em in the eye, confidently. B. "No, thanks!" (offer no explanation) "No, that's not my thing!"
with *HUMOR*	A. A quick, witty response that ends the conversation. B. When asked to cut class, "Hey guys, I'm not a scissor." "No beer now, thanks, I'm doing brain surgery later."
with *A BUDDY*	A. Plan with a good friend beforehand to stick to the decision agreed upon. B. "I'll pass." (knowing your friend will pass also)
with *AN EXIT* THIS WAY OUT	A. Plan ahead how to physically relocate. B. Go to the next room; go to the bathroom; go home; go for a walk; etc.
with *AN EXCUSE* please excuse Eileen because	A. "Give away" the responsibility. B. "I'm going to the dentist and I don't want my breath to smell of smoke." "No thanks. The coach won't let me play if I do."
with *AN INVITATION* LATER please Come to	A. Leave the door open for future activities. B. "I can't stay now, but come over to my house later and watch MTV."
with *IMAGINATION*	A. Think of ways to change the focus. B. Get sick; cry; etc.

Name ___________________________

Date ___________________________

Scene-Stoppers

Following are situations for you to practice saying NO successfully. Read the situation, and then respond using the strategy indicated.

1. You are sitting with a group of your friends. You notice that you are the only one *not* smoking. Someone offers you a cigarette. You don't want to smoke because you are aware of the health dangers. Respond...

   with AN EXCUSE ___________________________

   ____

   ____

2. There is a very generous person in school who is very helpful and often does things for others. You notice that almost everytime that person has done something for you, there was a string attached. He/she has just offered to help you again. This time you want to say No, but you don't want to hurt him/her. Respond...

   with IMAGINATION ___________________________

   ____

   ____

3. Your friends got together tonight to go to a Major League baseball game at the Stadium in the next town. It was great! Your team won. Everyone is feeling happy—and wants to celebrate. It's 11 P.M. You have a curfew for 12 midnight. It will take at least an hour to get back to town and drop everyone off at their homes. It is your car. You want to keep your curfew. (You have a good relationship with your parents—and you want to keep it that way.) Respond....

   with AN EXCUSE ___________________________

   ____

   ____

Continued

4. Celeste is a good friend of yours. You share a lot of the same interests. Both of you are on the school newspaper. You even went to grammar school together. The only problem you have with Celeste is she always arrives late when you make plans together. Tonight she offered to come by your house at 7 P.M., so you can go together to the Student Council meeting. You know that she will arrive late, and it is important for you to get there on time to present information on a special project. Respond...

   with AN EXIT ______________________________

   ____

   ____

5. There is a member of the school's championship basketball team sitting next to you in your History Class. He's pleasant enough, but he doesn't do any of his school work. Repeatedly, he has asked for your homework and lecture notes. Once he didn't return your notes in time for you to study for a test. He has just asked you again for your notes. Respond...

   with DIRECTNESS ______________________________

   ____

   ____

6. Your sister has asked you to do her chore tonight (wash the dishes), so she can go to the movies with her friends. You two get along pretty well. If you didn't have plans now, you probably would have done it for her. You have to say No now. Respond...

   with HUMOR ______________________________

   ____

   ____

MAKING FAMILY DECISIONS 7-7

The Family Meeting Model

Objectives:

- To recognize that all families have differences and disagreements
- To teach the students the format for the Family Meeting
- To have the students practice using problem-solving skills

> NOTE: This format, as originally intended by Dr. Alfred Adler, the noted Austrian psychologist, can serve as a positive model for problem-solving and conflict-resolution within the family. It can also be used in other places where people work closely together; i.e. institutions, offices, schools, etc.

Activities:

1. Present the following information to the students, concerning setting up a Family Meeting:
   a. On an 8 1/2" × 11" piece of paper prepare an announcement.
      —Indicate the time, date, and place of meeting.
      —Post it in a prominent place at least two days before the scheduled date.
      —Leave a large area on the piece of paper blank for the "family" members to write in the topics they wish to discuss.
   b. Note that *all* family members are expected to attend. (If a member is not present, he/she will have to abide by the decisions made by the group until the next meeting.)
   c. Provide a pleasant atmosphere, such as comfortable seating and favorite refreshments.
   d. Prepare guidelines for the "family" group meeting. (These can be discussed and agreed upon during the first meeting.)
      Example:—the length of time allotted for the meeting
      —one person speaks at a time
      —each person speaks only for him/herself
      —no distractions are permitted; i.e., no telephone calls, no visitors or TV, etc.
   e. Rotate the chairperson who starts the meeting on time, keeps the group on task, and closes the meeting on time.
   f. Rotate the secretary who keeps minutes for the meeting, and writes and posts the solutions and the tasks each has agreed upon to carry out the solution.
   g. Decide on the problems to be resolved in order of importance to the group members.

2. To allow the students to *practice* their skills, have the class break up into groups of five or six to form "families."
   a. Have each group choose a chairperson and a secretary.
   b. Give each "family" member a copy of "Our Family Meeting," Activity 7-7A, to keep a record of the meeting's agenda.
   c. Ask each group to select a problem for discussion that they might be experiencing in the class right now.
   d. They will use the steps for problem-solving and decision-making.
   e. The secretary will keep notes during the meeting and read them to the group at the end of the session.
   f. When the activity has been completed, ask the students to share their impression (and group accomplishments) with the class.
3. The students may take home a blank copy of the Our Family Meeting to introduce the idea into their families. (Some of the topics to be explored might include: curfews, borrowing clothes, using the family car, meal-times, yelling, family vacations, hurt feelings, etc.)

Shedding a Little Light:
"Change and differences are constant, normal, and healthy factors present in every family. Expect it!" (*Peoplemaking*, Virginia Satir, Science & Behavior Books)

Name ______________________

Date ______________________

Our Family Meeting

1. MEETING DATE ______________________

   TIME ______________________

   PLACE ______________________

2. ISSUE OR PROBLEM FOR DISCUSSION

   ____

   ____

3. PROPOSED SOLUTIONS
   (Brainstorm at least 10 solutions. Encourage responses from all family members. Accept *all* answers at this time.)

   a. ______________________

   b. ______________________

   c. ______________________

   d. ______________________

   e. ______________________

   f. ______________________

   g. ______________________

   h. ______________________

   i. ______________________

   j. ______________________

4. Discuss each of the suggestions. After all members have had a chance to share their ideas and opinions, select the solution that everyone could agree to try.

Continued

5. THE SOLUTION SELECTED ______________________________

____

6. Decide how each person will work toward the solution. Be specific.

(a) Name ______________ Task ______________

(b) Name ______________ Task ______________

(c) Name ______________ Task ______________

(d) Name ______________ Task ______________

(e) Name ______________ Task ______________

(f) Name ______________ Task ______________

7. NEXT MEETING DATE ______________________________

NEXT MEETING TIME ______________________________

NEXT MEETING PLACE ______________________________

Review the results of the solutions proposed at this meeting.
Work out other solutions if necessary.
Prepare to solve new problems and conflicts.

III. DRUG INFORMATION ACTIVITIES

This section of the book provides information and activities focusing on drugs.

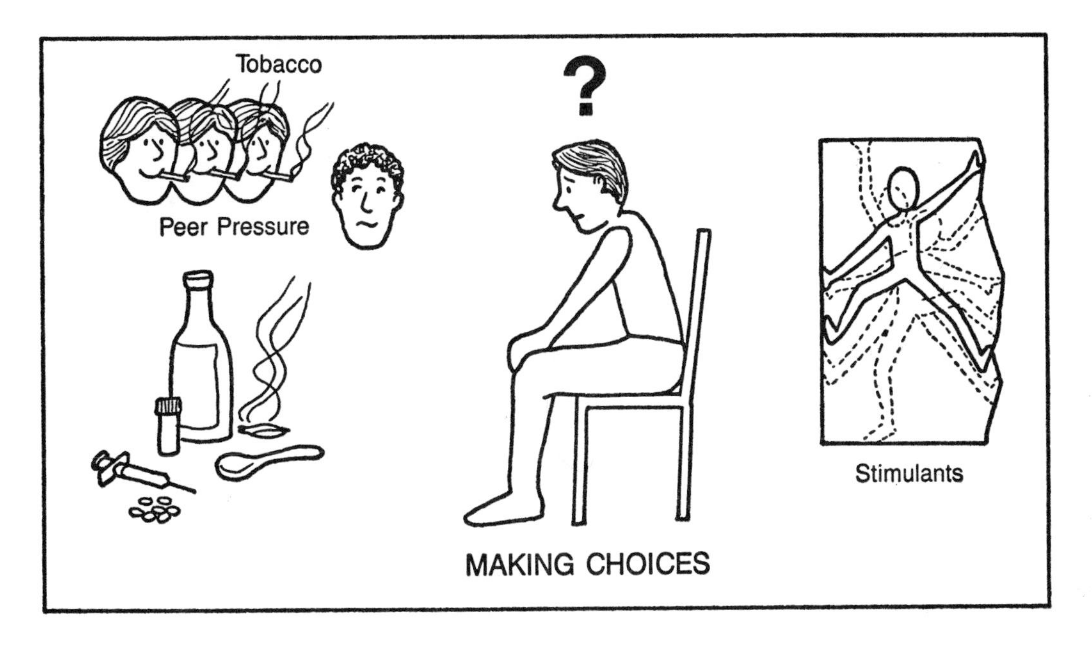

8 INTRODUCTION TO DRUGS

9 TOBACCO

Fact Sheet 10 .... Cigarette Smoking and Smokeless Tobacco
Fact Sheet 11 .... Effects of Cigarette Smoking on a Person
Fact Sheet 12 .... Effects of Smokeless Tobacco
Activity 9-1 The Health Dangers of Tobacco
Activity 9-2 Making a Decision About Using Tobacco

10 HEALTH AND PASSIVE SMOKE

Fact Sheet 13 .... Health and Passive Smoke
Activity 10-1 Polluting My Atmosphere

11 ALCOHOL

Fact Sheet 14 .... Alcohol
Activity 11-1 To Drink or Not to Drink
Activity 11-2 Alcohol and the Body
Activity 11-3 Drinking and Behavior

12 MARIJUANA

Fact Sheet 15 .... Marijuana
Fact Sheet 16 .... Marijuana and the Body
Activity 12-1 The Most-Used Illicit Drug

13 COCAINE

Fact Sheet 17 .... Cocaine
Activity 13-1 Cocaine Consequences

14 DRUGS AND DRIVING

Fact Sheet 18 .... Drugs and Driving
Fact Sheet 19 .... Drugs That Affect Driving
Fact Sheet 20 .... Marijuana and Driving
Activity 14-1 Behind the Wheel
Activity 14-2 Driving and the Law

15 DRUGS AND PREGNANCY

Fact Sheet 21 .... Drugs and Pregnancy
Activity 15-1 Passing on the Problem
Activity 15-2 Health Alert!

16 CHEMICAL DEPENDENCY

Fact Sheet 22 .... Chemical Dependency
Activity 16-1 What Is Chemical Dependency?
Activity 16-2 Help!

17 THE CHEMICALLY DEPENDENT FAMILY

Activity 17-1 Roles and Rules
Activity 17-2 The Need for Help
Activity 17-3 Breaking the Cycle—Getting Help

Introduction to Drugs

- A Drug is any chemical substance taken into the body—by mouth, inhaled, injected, or rubbed on the skin—that causes changes in the body and/or mind of the user.
- Drugs are *USED* properly when they are taken to prevent, treat, or cure illness. These are called *medicines.*
- Depending on how they are used, they can either improve or damage one's health. *Any* drug can be harmful if it is not used properly.
- Drugs are *MISUSED* when prescription or over-the-counter drugs are used improperly, deliberately, or unintentionally—for any of the following reasons:
  —by the wrong person
  —at the wrong time
  —in the wrong amount
  —for the wrong reason
- Drug *ABUSE* is the use of a drug for other than medical purposes, which results in the impaired physical, mental, emotional, and/or social well-being of the user.
- Drug effects depend on many variables including:
  —dose (amount taken)
  —time (how often it is taken)
  —other drugs present in one's body
  —weight
  —set (personality, mood, and expectations of the user)
  —setting (the environment)
- Studies indicate that drug abuse progresses from the use of at least one legal drug (*tobacco* or *alcohol**), and finally to other illicit drugs and/or prescription medications. (Kandel and Yamaguchi—1985).
- *CONTROLLED DRUGS* are those placed in special categories to prevent, curtail, or limit their manufacture and distribution. See Activity 8-1, "Controlled Drugs."
- *Alcohol* and *tobacco,* like prescription drugs, are *controlled.* They can be sold only to people of legal age.

**Alcohol* and *tobacco* are the most abused *legal,* mood-altering drugs.

Controlled Substances

Under the Controlled Substance Act of 1970, the Attorney General of the United States has the authority to place drugs into *five* categories based on their *relative potential for abuse*, the drugs' effect, and their pattern of use.

SCHEDULE I: (These drugs are *illegal*): a. have no medical use b. have a high potential for abuse c. have a high potential for dependency d. cannot be legally manufactured except under strict controls e. are not prescribable	Examples: LSD Mescaline Heroin **Marijuana*
SCHEDULE II: a. similar in their potential for abuse and dependency to Schedule I drugs b. do have a medical use c. mostly stimulants, narcotics, and depressants d. prescriptions *cannot* be renewed	Examples: Amphetamines Codeine Morphine **Cocaine*
SCHEDULE III: a. lower potential for abuse than drugs in Schedule I and II, but they can lead to dependency. b. have a medical use c. can be refilled up to five times in 6 months, if authorized	Examples: Paregoric Apririn with codeine
SCHEDULE IV: a. some potential for abuse but lower than Schedule I, II, and III drugs b. definite medical use c. can be refilled if authorized	Examples: Librium and Valium Many sedatives Some muscle Relaxants
SCHEDULE V: a. a low potential for abuse b. may either require a prescription—though in some states, it only requires the pharmacist to keep records of the sales and obtain an identification of the purchaser	Examples: Codeine based cough medicines Opium compounds for diarrhea

*Marijuana and Cocaine are the most abused *illicit*, mood-altering drugs.

OVER-THE-COUNTER DRUGS 8-2

Objectives:

- To recognize the current social attitude of looking for a chemical solution to relieve discomfort
- To look for alternative ways to deal with discomfort
- To recognize the influence of advertising on our decisions

> NOTE: • Americans spend $7 billion annually on non-prescription drugs, many of which have no effect on the condition for which they are taken. . . .
> • There are hundreds of different brand names of over-the-counter drugs. Most of them are made of different combinations of relatively few drugs. (Harry Avis, *Drugs & Life,* Wm. C. Brown Publishers—1990)

Activities:

1. Define Over-the-Counter Drugs.
   Over-the-counter drugs are medicines that do not require a doctor's order, or the assistance of a pharmacist. They can be found on open shelves in a drugstore or a supermarket. They are usually used to *relieve symptoms* of pain and discomfort, rather than to treat a disease. For example:
   a. Cold medicines do not cure colds, but they may relieve a stuffy nose.
   b. Aspirin can *relieve* a headache.
   c. Cough medicine can help you *cough less.*
2. To help the students recognize how often one has the opportunity to take some form of a drug during the course of an ordinary day, have them read Activity 8-2A, "Make My Day!" Discuss the responses and impressions with the class.
3. Have the students complete Activity 8-2B, "Back to Nature." They will have an opportunity to study *Warnings* on non-prescription medicines—to encourage that *safety practice.* They will explore non-chemical alternatives to relieve discomfort, to encourage that *health* practice.
   (For example: three ways to get rid of a headache without chemicals are (a) rest, (b) exercise, (c) play. Three ways to lose weight instead of using diet pills are (a) eat low-calorie food, (b) exercise, (c) no between-meal snacks, etc. Discuss the responses and impressions with the class.

4. a. Have the students bring in an ad for two different over-the-counter products used to treat *one* type of health problem. They will explore the following questions: (1) What is the "sales pitch"? (2) Who is the target audience? (3) What are the similar ingredients? (4) Were the advertisers' claims truthful? Discuss.
   b. You may bring in some old magazines, or ask the students to each bring in one old magazine, to cut out pictures and words.
   —Have the students form into groups of four.
   —Ask them to create an ad for a natural (non-chemical) remedy to cope with a particular health problem.
   —Then, have them "sell" their idea to their "audience."
   —Discuss how the media *pressures* people to buy their product. (Remind the students that advertising appeals to our *emotions.*)

Shedding a Little Light:
According to the Drug Abuse Warning Network (DAWN), aspirin was the eighth most common drug mentioned in Emergency Room cases of overdose and for at least 115 deaths in 1986.

All diet pills but one are manufactured by the same company.

Caffeine, *a central nervous system stimulant,* is found in coffee, tea, cocoa, and chocolate. It is added to many cola and non-cola soft drinks. It can be found in some OTC drugs for headache. cold, and stay-awake remedies

Some stay-awake remedies contain caffeine that is equivalent to 2 or 3 cups of coffee

Name ________________________________

Date ________________________________

Make My Day

Dear Diary,

Nothing much to write today. Today was just like yesterday and the day before. Mom is the one who hears the alarm at 6 A.M. I know, because I can smell the ________ coming from the kitchen. She calls me at 7 A.M. I wish she would do something about that cough and stop smoking those ________. On the way down for breakfast, I picked up some laundry to take with me to help Mom out. (I hate to carry my brother's shirts that are stained when he spits after chewing ________.)

I didn't have time to eat breakfast—so I just put a ________ bag in the cup of hot water to steep while I finished blow-drying my hair. Thank goodness my lunch was already packed. No change there either! I still take only one sandwich, one ____ cookie, and a diet ____. I guess taking that ________ has been working, because I've lost 8 pounds already.

The kids all dropped by after school and we almost ran out of diet ____. It was hot enough today for everyone to have two each. Later, while I was stretched out on the couch, Mom and Dad were having a before-dinner ________, and she was telling him about the terrific lunch she had with her friends at Chez Restaurant. The glass of white ____ she had was unusually delicate. Dad complained about his rough day. He was glad he could take ________ for his headache. Now, he was feeling much better. He told Mom that after eating supper and having his usual cold ____ with it, he was going to turn in early because there was a special conference called for 9 A.M. tomorrow. He wanted to be well-rested, so he would take ____. Mom said she probably would drop right off, because she was going to take ________ for her cough before she went to bed. My brother took a ________. He said he had to stay up most of the night to study for his final Spanish exam at college tomorrow.

Like I said, nothing special happened. So I'll say goodnight dear diary, before I have a cup of hot ________ and go to bed.

Oh, sorry—I wanted to tell you dear diary that even though it's boring sometimes—things are O.K. With all the problems drugs are causing in the world—we don't have to worry, because we don't take much of anything—and certainly none that would have any bad effects.

Good-night again.

Love,
Cassey

Shedding a Little Light:
Caffeine is banned by the International Olympics Committee.

Name ______________________

Date ______________________

Back to Nature

(1.) Complete the activity below. (2.) Name an over-the-counter (O-T-C) drug you can use. (3.) Study the *Warnings* on the medication bottle. Will it affect your performance during the day? (4.) Find a non-chemical alterative as a remedy.

PROBLEM	O-T-C DRUGS	WARNINGS	NATURAL SOLUTIONS
1. to fall asleep			
2. to wake up			
3. to lose weight			
4. to gain weight			
5. to relieve headache			
6. to relieve backache			
7. for an upset stomach			
8. for a cold			
9. for a toothache			
10. for muscle pain			

PRESCRIPTION DRUGS **8-3**

Objectives:

- To define prescription drugs
- To learn the safety rules for taking prescription drugs

Activities:

1. Define "prescription drugs." Prescription drugs are medicines that are *more potent* and have *more dangerous side effects* than do over-the-counter drugs.
   a. They can be obtained, legally, only on the *order of a doctor or a dentist* (a) for a *specific reason,* (b) for a *specific person,* and (c) prepared by a *pharmacist.*
   b. The order for the drug must be written on a *specific form* used by a physician for this purpose—which is then presented to the pharmacist.
2. You can bring in empty, clean bottles that once contained prescription medicines.
   a. Notice all the information that is required for each label. It states the name of one particular person, the name of the medicine, the amount and time to be given, the name of the doctor, the date, the prescription number and number of refills if needed. Here are two examples:

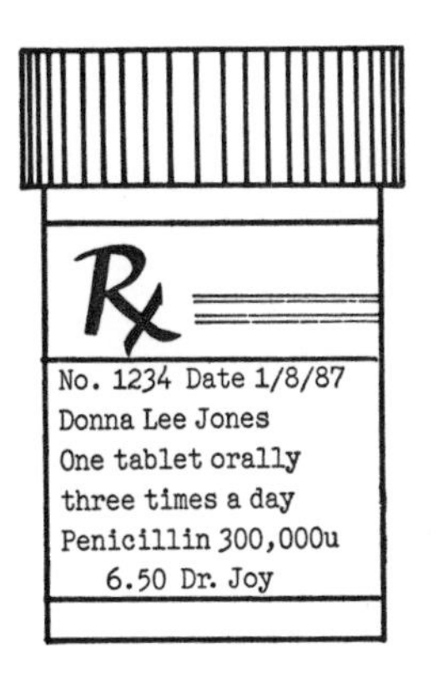

The medicine and dose are ordered on the basis of that particular person's:
—age
—weight
—general health
—type of illness

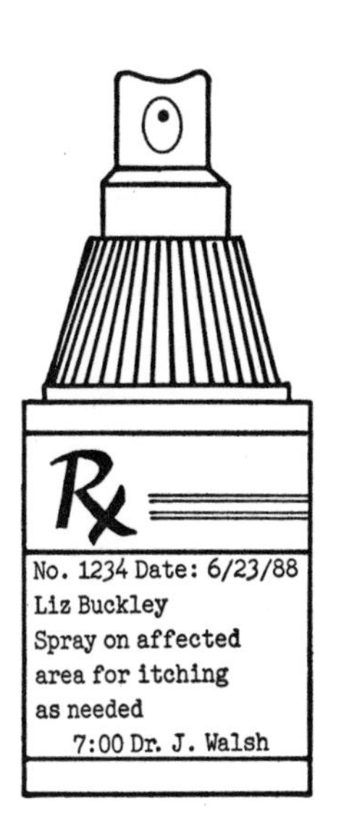

b. Review Fact Sheet 9, "Introduction to Drugs." (Note when drugs are *used* properly, *misused*, and *abused*.)

3. Copy and distribute "Safety Rules for Prescriptions Drugs," Activity 8-3A, to the students. Review the information. Discuss.

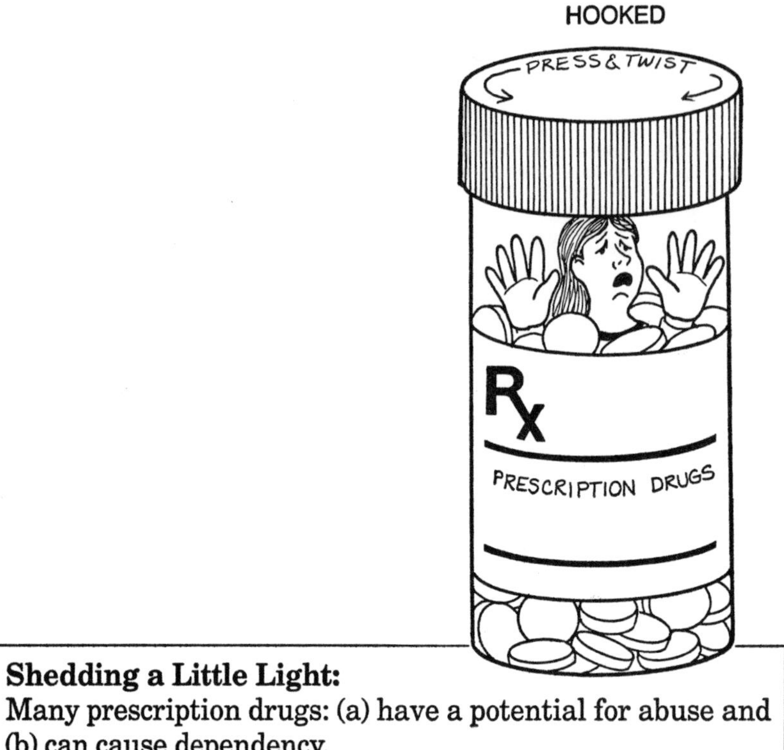

Shedding a Little Light:
Many prescription drugs: (a) have a potential for abuse and (b) can cause dependency.
See Controlled Substance—Schedule III, IV, V in Activity 8-1.

Name ______________________________

Date ______________________________

Safety Rules for Prescription Drugs

Dr. P. Smith

2357 PINEBROOK TPK
OLDHAM, N.J. 10251

555–7890
555–7897

For______________________________ Date ______________

Rx SAFETY RULES FOR TAKING MEDICINES

1. Take the medicine as directed.
2. Finish the entire prescription.
3. Discard any unused medicines.
4. Never share your medicines with anyone else.
5. Keep medicine in a safe place, out of the reach of children.
6. Keep medicines in their original container.
7. Do not take several medicines at the same time, unless the doctor is aware of *all* of them.
8. Mixing drugs (medicines) and alcohol can be fatal.
9. Never give medicines in the dark.
10. Never give medicine from an unlabeled container.
    WHEN IN DOUBT–THROW IT OUT.

Refill______ X ______________ M.D.

ATTITUDES ABOUT ALCOHOL AND OTHER DRUGS 8-4

Objective:

- To have the students explore personal attitudes about alcohol and other drugs in a variety of situations

> NOTE: There should be a non-judgmental attitude in the classroom. It is only important, at this time, that attitudes begin to surface.

Activities:

1. Define the word "attitude." (A manner of *thinking, feeling, and acting* that shows one's position or opinion.)
2. Lead the class in a discussion of the statement:
   "Attitudes are the Father of the Action." (My attitude about a subject determines how I *receive* the information—and then, how I will *use* the information. It influences my decisions and behaviors.)
3. Explore the following questions with the students. (The responses may indicate a greater acceptance of the abuse of alcohol than for the abuse of other drugs because of its legality and our social customs.)
   a. When you see an *adult intoxicated,* what do you think? How do you feel?
      When you see an *adult "high" on drugs,* what do you think? How do you feel?
   b. When you see one of the *students intoxicated,* what do you think? How do you feel?
      When you see one of the *students stoned on drugs,* what do you think? How do you feel?
   c. If you saw your *boyfriend/girlfriend intoxicated,* what would you think? How does it make you feel?
      If you saw your *boyfriend/girlfriend "high" on drugs,* what would you think? How would you feel?
   d. If a *member of your family* was *intoxicated,* what would you think? How would you feel?
      If a *member of your family* was *"high" on drugs,* what would you think? How would you feel?
      Many factors may influence one's reactions to these statements—including current alcohol or drug use, parental attitude toward use or non-use, past experiences, peer pressure etc. Becoming aware of our feelings, helps us to understand our behavior a little better.

4. Have the students complete Activity 8-4A, "My Attitudes." It is not necessary for the students to share this information.

5. Have the students complete "Parents' Problems" as shown in Activity 8-4B.
   a. Discuss the responses. After the discussion, vote on those Rules the class would like to use in creating a "Guide for Parents." (It will help them to clarify their values concerning drug use or non-use.)
   b. They can take the paper home to initiate a discussion with their parents.

6. Select students for a role-play:
   a. *An adult* who is *"moralizing"* about the use of alcohol or other drugs.
   b. The *young person* who is being *"preached to"* by the adult. (Give the actors a few minutes to prepare to play their part.)
   c. Have the actors interact on the theme for about 5 minutes.
   d. Get feedback after the performance.

      (1) What might the thoughts and feelings of the "young person" be about the "adult's" approach? (It is anticipated that he/she will get defensive as a result of the "righteous moralizing.")
      (2) What might be the thoughts and feelings of the "adult" in that role-play?
   e. Then, explore with the class, ideas about how the scene might be presented so that the "young person" would be less defensive and remain more "open" to the message.
   f. Ask for two other volunteers to assume the roles of "adult" and "young person," using the *new information* obtained from the discussion.

Name ______________________________

Date ______________________________

My Attitudes

1. List the first five words that come to your mind when you hear the word "drunk."

   a. ________________ b. ________________ c. ________________

   d. ________________ e. ________________

2. List the first five words that come to your mind when you hear the words "stoned" and "high."

   a. ________________ b. ________________ c. ________________

   d. ________________ e. ________________

   What attitude do your answers suggest? ______________________________
   (*Ex:* fearful, humorous, angry, confused, sad, embarrassed, etc).

2. What is the first word that comes to your mind when you hear the word "alcoholic"?

   ____

   What is the first word that comes to your mind when you hear someone say he/she is a "junkie" or an "addict"? ______________________________

3. How was alcohol used in your family? (Celebrations only; "beer blasts;" to "calm down" and relax; never used; at mealtime, etc.)

   ____

4. Fill in the blank:
   a. When I see someone drunk on the street, I ______________________________.
   b. If someone in my family had a drinking problem, I would

      ______________________________.

   c. I would feel __________ if my parents found me drinking a can of beer with my friends.
      I would feel __________ if my parents found me smoking a "joint."
   d. I've heard a lot of famous people talk about being an alcoholic or drug addict. They look O.K. to me. That makes me think ______________________________.
   e. So many famous people (actors, sports figures, politicians, or their spouses) have been in drug treatment facilities two or three times, it makes me think

      ______________________________.

   f. When I reach the legal drinking age and I am a host (hostess) at a party at which alcohol is served, I will tell my guests ______________________________

      ______________________________.

Name ______________________________

Date ______________________________

Parents' Problems

If you were a parent now, what rules would you impose on your own children regarding the use of alcohol? Explain why. Be specific.

Rule 1 ______________________________

Because ______________________________

____

____

Rule 2 ______________________________

Because ______________________________

____

____

Rule 3 ______________________________

Because ______________________________

____

____

Rule 4 ______________________________

Because ______________________________

____

____

Rule 5 ______________________________

Because ______________________________

____

____

Some Facts About Cigarette Smoking and Smokeless Tobacco

1. There are hundreds of chemical substances in cigarette smoke. Three of the most damaging are:
   a. *Tars*—damage delicate lung tissue and are considered the main cancer-causing agent in cigarette smoke.
   b. *NICOTINE*—is a deadly *poison* found only in tobacco leaves.
      —Nicotine is *smoked, inhaled,* or *chewed.*
      —It is absorbed through the lungs as well as the membranes of the mouth.
      —It is in cigarettes, cigars, pipe tobacco, and chewing tobacco. (It can be extracted as a colorless, oily transparent liquid and is used in a solution as an *insecticide.*)
      —One drop of *pure* nicotine can be fatal to humans.

   (1) It is a powerful stimulant to the brain and central nervous system that "hits" the brain within 4 seconds. Like the drug alcohol, after it initially stimulates, it has a *depressant* effect. (Although nicotine from smokeless tobacco enters the bloodstream more slowly than from cigarettes, studies show that average blood concentrations in regular users of smokeless tobacco are comparable to those found in smokers.)
   (2) Nicotine constricts (narrows) the blood vessels, cutting down the flow of blood and oxygen throughout one's body. Therefore, one's heart has to pump harder, increasing the chance of heart disease. It raises the blood pressure and narrows bronchioles (air passageways) in the lungs, also *depriving the body of oxygen,* and increasing the risk of stroke.
   (3) Nicotine is *addictive:* a *tolerance* develops. (One needs to use more and more for the desired effect. One NEEDS it to feel comfortable (*dependency*), and one suffers *withdrawal* symptoms (physical and psychological discomfort) when one tries to stop.)

   c. *Carbon Monoxide*—replaces needed oxygen in one's red blood cells. Even after one stops smoking, carbon monoxide stays in the bloodstream for hours, depriving the body of oxygen.

   Carbon monoxide is a waste product of *cigarette smoking, automobile exhaust, and unvented kerosene heaters.*

2. The effects of some medication taken by a person may be increased, decreased, or cancelled out by smoking.
3. Cigarette smoking by a pregnant woman may cause harm to the unborn child.
4. When a person quits smoking the body begins to repair itself (unless the damage was permanent).

NOTE:
- Cigarette smoking is the largest, preventable cause of illness and premature death in the country.
- Cigarette smoking is the major single cause of cancer deaths in the U.S. and is responsible for more deaths than all the other drugs combined.

Effects of Cigarette Smoking on a Person

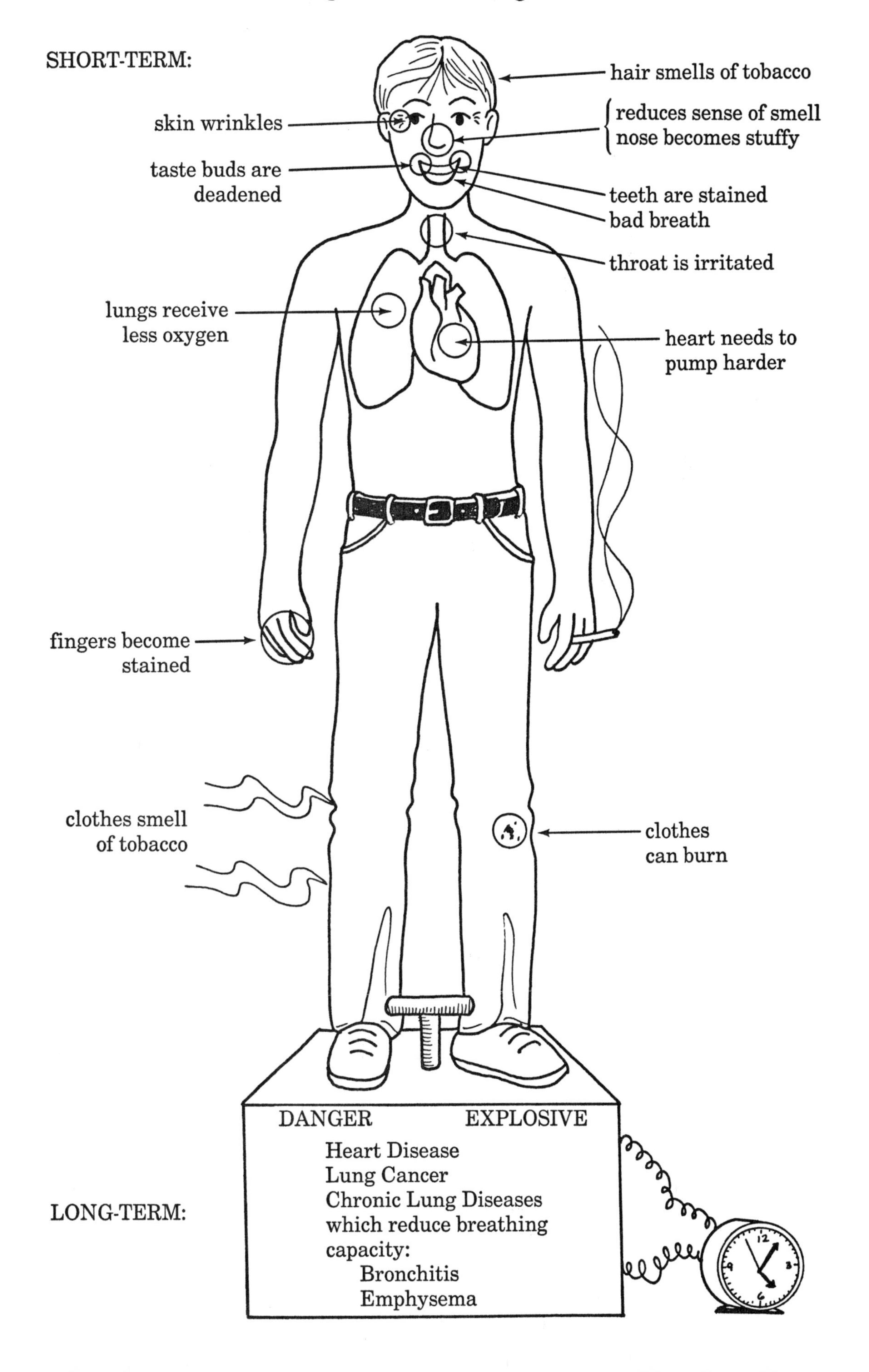

The Effects of Smokeless Tobacco

Entry:
Smokeless tobacco mixes with saliva. (a) Some of it is spit out.* (b) Some of the tobacco juice is absorbed through the lining of the *mouth* and directly affects the central nervous system. (c) The rest goes through the *stomach*, and then (d) through the lining of the *intestines* into the bloodstream.

Long-Term:
The chemicals in tobacco irritate the tissues of the mouth. White, leathery patches may form near where the tobacco is placed, between the cheek and the gum. It is called *leukoplakia.* This condition can lead to cancer of the mouth (in 5%) of the cases.

The risk increases with the longer duration of use.

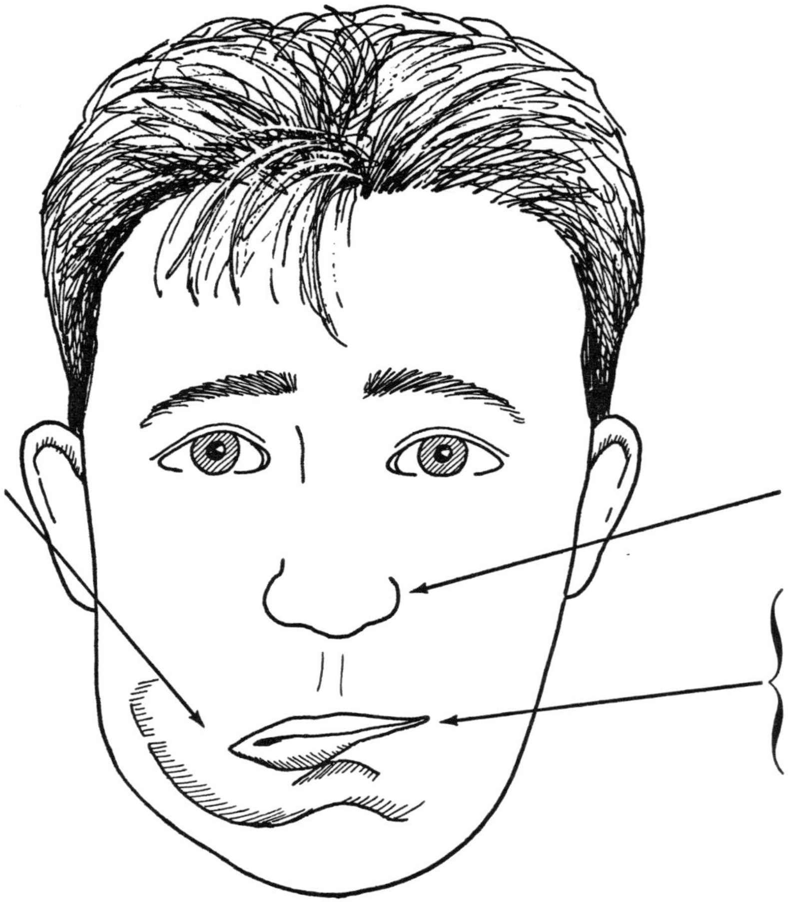

Smokeless tobacco includes both chewing tobacco and snuff.

Short-Term:
—Decreases the sense of smell

—Decreases a sense of taste
—Dental problems can develop
—Receding gums, especially where the tobacco is placed
—Bad breath
—Discolored teeth

*Frequent spitting is necessary to get rid of the tobacco juice.

Tins of smokeless tobacco now carry the statement:
"THIS PRODUCT IS NOT A SAFE ALTERNATIVE TO SMOKING CIGARETTES"

THE HEALTH DANGERS OF TOBACCO 9-1

Objective:

- To have the students research and study factual information about the dangers of cigarette smoking and smokeless tobacco

Activities:

1. Review and discuss Fact Sheets 10, 11, and 12.
2. To reinforce the idea that switching from smokeless tobacco to smoking cigarettes—or from cigarette smoking to smokeless tobacco—is not a safe alternative, have the class discuss the health risks that are *similar* in each method of using tobacco; i.e., heart disease, cancer, addiction.
3. The Surgeon General's Warnings must appear on all packets of cigarettes. It seems as though little attention is paid to them, however. To increase the impact of the health message, instruct the students to:
   a. study the ads in Activity 9-1A, "Truth or Consequences." Discuss the questions at the bottom of the page.
   b. study the four warnings. Then assign each student *one* of the "Warning Assignments" to be completed for homework. The students can share their information with the class to complete Activity 9-1B, "The Surgeon General's Warnings." (Answer to Warning #4: Carbon monoxide is a colorless, odorless gas found in tunnels, closed garages, near heavy traffic and by unvented kerosene lamps. It is *produced when carbon-containing fuels are incompletely burned.* It reduces the ability of blood to carry the oxygen.)
4. Have the students complete Activity 9-1C, "Getting It Right!" Have them review their answers with a partner. Answers to Activity 9-1C:

   1. True
   2. False
   3. True
   4. False
   5. True
   6. False
   7. False (males ages 10 to 17)
   8. True
   9. False (mucous membrane of mouth, small intestine)
   10. False
   11. True
   12. False (it is habit forming)
   13. True
   14. True

5. Have the students complete the crossword puzzle in Activity 9-1D, "Tobacco Trouble." Answers to Activity 9-1D:

ACROSS	DOWN
1. STIMULATES	1. NICOTINE
2. SMOKELESS	2. ADDICTIVE
3. SAFE	3. DISCOLOR

4. FETUS
5. CARBON MONOXIDE
6. RECEDE
7. LUNG
8. DEPENDENT

4. WITHDRAWAL
5. PREVENTABLE
6. CANCER
7. AUTO EXHAUST

6. Request the Optioscopic Lung from your local American Cancer Society office to view the healthy lung and the lung diseased by cigarette smoking.
7. Contact the local American Cancer Society, American Lung Association and/or the American Heart Association to have a speaker come in to give a talk or to request material for use in teaching about the dangers of smoking or chewing tobacco.
8. Arrange for a dentist or a dental hygienist to speak to the class about the effects of smokeless tobacco.
9. Invite a person from the Lost Chords (a person who has had his or her larynx removed due to cancer caused by smoking) to talk about his or her personal experiences dealing with the consequences of cigarette smoking.

Shedding a Little Light:

—Someone who smokes a pack a day takes in 200 doses of the addictive substance.

—When the Surgeon General mandated that cigarette packages must display Health Warnings, the leaders in the tobacco industry hired *ad men* to select the place on the packet where it would be *least noticeable.*

Name ______________________________

Date ______________________________

Truth or Consequences

Study the two ads. To what group are they appealing? How did you arrive at your answer?

Now, discuss the following questions with the class.

1. What is the purpose of advertising, and the motivation of the advertiser?
2. How effective do you think are the warnings?
3. Brainstorm ways to get the health messages across to the public more effectively.

Name ______________________________

Date ______________________________

The Surgeon General's Warnings

WARNING: The Surgeon General has determined that smoking is hazardous to one's health. As of October 1985, new warnings were issued by the Surgeon General. There are to be *four* warnings that are rotated every three months. Study the warnings and complete the assignment selected for you.

	WARNING	ASSIGNMENT
1	"Smoking causes lung cancer, heart disease, emphysema, and may complicate pregnancy."	Cut out three *different* ads for cigarettes that have this warning on it. On another piece of paper, describe the scene. Does the ad indicate the health hazards for smokers? Identify the audience that the ad wishes to target. How is the ad trying to appeal to people?
2	"Quitting smoking now greatly reduces serious risks to your health."	Locate two different smoking cessation programs and find out what methods are used. Write a report comparing the two methods. (The American Cancer Society is a good source.)
3	"Smoking by pregnant women may result in fetal injury, premature birth, and low birth weight."	List three complications that can develop for the unborn child if the mother smokes. Find this warning on an ad in a magazine. Cut it out and bring it to school. Now *create* an ad to tell mothers of the dangers.
4	"Cigarette smoke contains carbon monoxide."	List other places where carbon monoxide is found. How is the carbon monoxide harmful to us? What effect does it have on one's body?

Name ______________________________

Date ______________________________

Get It Right!

Read each statement and decide if it's true or false.

__________ 1. The tars in cigarettes are cancer-causing agents.

__________ 2. It is safe to smoke *filtered* cigarettes.

__________ 3. Nicotine is a poison found in tobacco.

__________ 4. Quitting smoking will not improve your health.

__________ 5. Leukoplakia is the medical term for the white patches that can appear in the mouth of a user of smokeless tobacco.

__________ 6. Smoke from cigarette harms only the smoker.

__________ 7. Males aged 25 to 40 are the greatest users of smokeless tobacco.

__________ 8. Cigarette smoking is the largest preventable cause of illness and premature death in the country.

__________ 9. Smokeless tobacco is absorbed only through the stomach when the saliva is swallowed.

__________ 10. Smokeless tobacco is a safer alternative to smoking cigarettes.

__________ 11. The nicotine in cigarettes and smokeless tobacco is addictive.

__________ 12. A regular user of tobacco should have no difficulty quitting any time he or she wants.

__________ 13. Violators of local, state, and federal smoking laws are subject to penalties.

__________ 14. I can choose not to smoke.

Select two of the statements you decided are false. On the lines below, rewrite each statement correctly and give one or two facts to support the revised statements. Use the back of this sheet if you need more space to write.

____

____

____

____

Name ____________________

Date ____________________

Tobacco Trouble

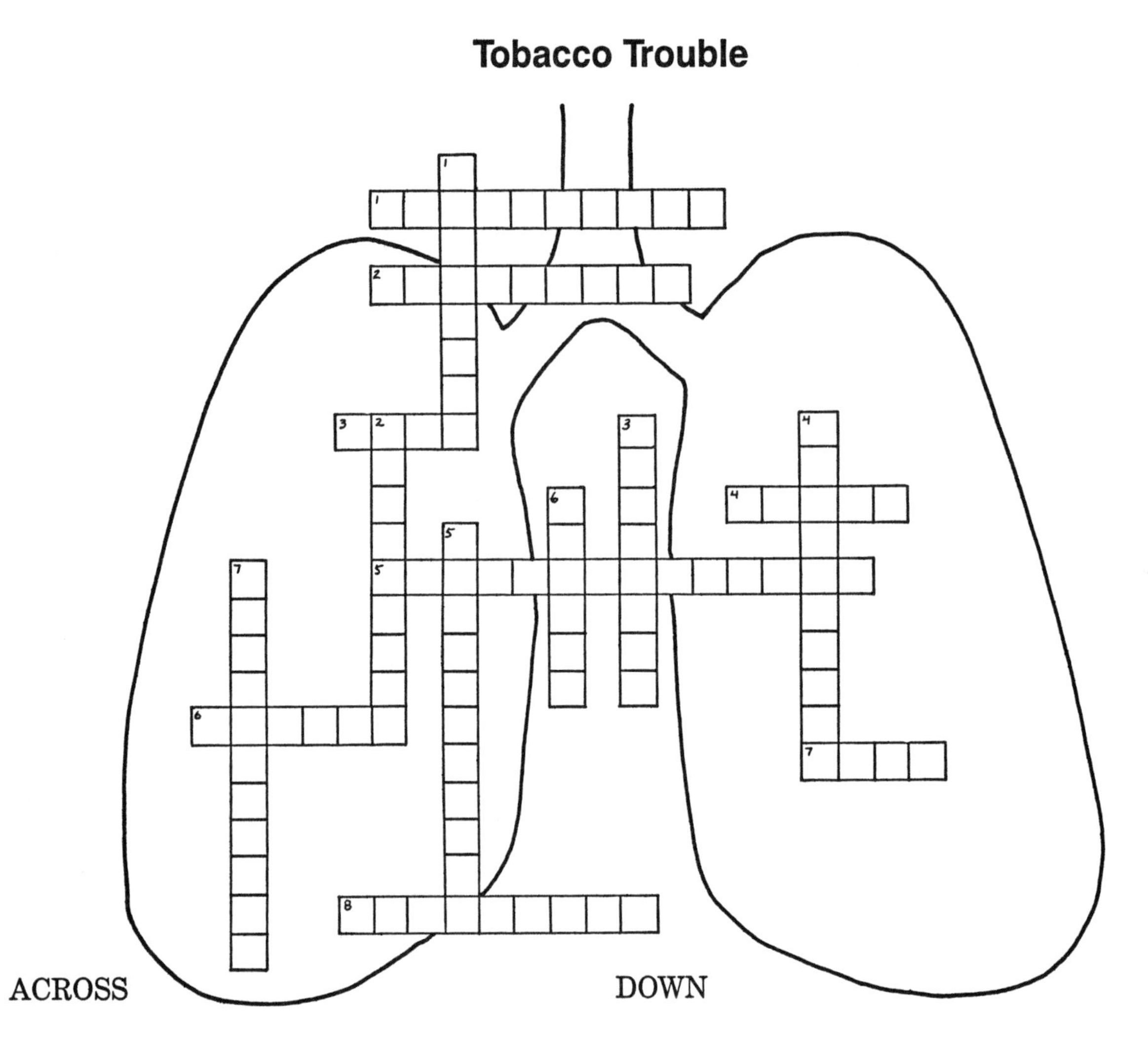

ACROSS

1. Nicotine only *initially* ____ the Central Nervous System
2. The largest single group using ____ tobacco are young males.
3. The Surgeon General says there are no ____ cigarettes.
4. Smoking by pregnant women can hurt the ____.
5. A waste product of cigarette smoking is ____ ____. (2 words)
6. Tobacco chewing and snuff dipping can cause gums to ____.
7. Cigarette smoking is the major single cause of ____ cancer.
8. Regular users of tobacco become ____ on it.

DOWN

1. The poison found in tobacco is called ____.
2. Nicotine is ____.
3. The use of tobacco causes the teeth to ____.
4. The discomfort a person feels when he or she stops using tobacco is called ____.
5. The largest single ____ cause of death is cigarette smoking.
6. The ____-causing substance in cigarettes is called tars.
7. Carbon monoxide is a waste product of ____ ____. (2 words)

MAKING A DECISION ABOUT USING TOBACCO 9-2

Objective:

- To help the students identify why some people use tobacco, and why some people do not use tobacco

Activities:

1. The class will brainstorm and discuss some reasons why young people might *begin* to smoke. Write the list on the chalkboard as they present the information (i.e., all my friends were smoking so....; to try it out; to be "cool"; it was something new.... etc.).

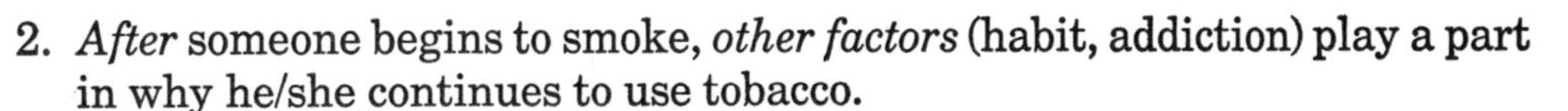

Peer Pressure

2. *After* someone begins to smoke, *other factors* (habit, addiction) play a part in why he/she continues to use tobacco.
   a. Have the students complete Activity 9-2A, "Why Do Some People Smoke?" After they have read the statements on the page, they will put the letter that appears in front of the sentence under one of the four headings that identifies the "pay-off" for the smoker.
   b. Then, ask them to think about some alternative behavior for each category to help someone to stop smoking. Examples: (1) Stimulation: exercise, take a risk and talk to someone new; (2) To reduce tension: relaxation breathing, jog, get absorbed in a new sport; (3) Rituals: keep your hands busy with other things; (4) Habits and/or addictions are hard to break—you may need outside help.
   c. The class will break up into small groups and, for the next 10 minutes, discuss their answers and suggestions.
   d. One person in each group will be selected to share the information with the class.

3. Direct the class to complete Activity 9-2B, "Why Some People DO NOT SMOKE!"
   a. They will read each statement, and circle one number for each statement that shows their beliefs about cigarette smoking.
   b. Next, the students will place the letter which appears in front of the sentence, plus the number that was circled, under one of the four headings below. Then, they will add up the score under each heading.

c. On a separate piece of paper, the students will write what they have learned about their personal beliefs concerning cigarette smoking. What was the most important factor in their decision to smoke or not to smoke?

d. Now, break up into small groups to share and discuss the information for approximately 10 minutes. (Some students may need more information about health dangers and social consequences of smoking.)

4. Distribute Activity #9-2C, "Smokeless Tobacco Questionnaire."

   a. When they have completed the questionnaire, review the hazards of using smokeless tobacco again. Encourage the students to share the information with other students.

   b. Discuss the ways people have successfully quit chewing tobacco or using snuff.

   c. Remind the students that *smokeless tobacco is not a safe* alternative to smoking cigarettes.

NOTE: See Chapter 7, "Making Decisions."

Name ______________________________

Date ______________________________

Why Do Some People Smoke?

Read the following statements carefully to understand some of the reasons why people smoke. Then, place the letter that appears in front of the sentence under one of the four headings below, which identifies the "pay-off" for the smoker.

A. I smoke cigarettes in order to keep myself from slowing down.
B. Handling a cigarette is part of the enjoyment of smoking it.
C. Smoking cigarettes is pleasant and relaxing.
D. I light up a cigarette when I feel angry about something.
E. When I run out of cigarettes, I find it almost unbearable until I can get more.
F. I smoke automatically without even being aware of it.
G. I smoke to stimulate myself, to perk myself up.
H. Part of the enjoyment of smoking a cigarette comes from the steps I take to light up.
I. I find cigarettes pleasurable.
J. When I feel uncomfortable or upset about something, I light up a cigarette.
K. When I am not smoking a cigarette, I am very much aware of the fact.
L. I light up a cigarette without realizing I still have one burning in the ashtray.
M. I smoke cigarettes to give me a lift.
N. When I smoke a cigarette, part of the enjoyment is watching the smoke as I exhale it.
O. I want a cigarette most when I am relaxed and comfortable.
P. When I feel blue or want to take my mind off cares and worries, I smoke.
Q. I get a real gnawing hunger for a cigarette when I haven't smoked for awhile.
R. I've found a cigarette in my mouth and didn't remember putting it there.

For Stimulation	To Reduce Tension	The Rituals	It's a Habit

List some HEALTHY ALTERNATIVE BEHAVIORS for each category to help someone stop smoking. Continue writing on the back of the page if necessary.

Name ______________________________

Date ______________________________

Why Some People Do Not Smoke!

Read each statement below, and circle one number for each statement that shows your belief about cigarette smoking. Then place the letter that appears in front of the sentence and the number you circled under one of the four headings below. Total your score under each heading.

Statements	Agree	Somewhat Agree	Somewhat Disagree	Disagree
A. Cigarette smoking might give me a serious illness.	4	3	2	1
B. My cigarette smoking sets a bad example for others.	4	3	2	1
C. I find cigarette smoking to be a messy habit.	4	3	2	1
D. Controlling my cigarette smoking is a challenge to me.	4	3	2	1
E. Smoking causes shortness of breath.	4	3	2	1
F. If I quit smoking cigarettes, it might influence others to stop.	4	3	2	1
G. Cigarettes cause damage to clothing and other personal property.	4	3	2	1
H. Quitting smoking would show that I have willpower.	4	3	2	1
I. My cigarette smoking will have a harmful effect on my health.	4	3	2	1
J. My cigarette smoking influences others close to me to take up or continue smoking.	4	3	2	1
K. If I quit smoking, my sense of taste would improve.	4	3	2	1
L. I do not like feeling dependent on smoking.	4	3	2	1

	Health	Example	Control	Personal Hygiene
Total				

Name ______________________________

Date ______________________________

Smokeless Tobacco Questionnaire

Interview five people who use/used smokeless tobacco and complete the questionnaire.

	A. PERSON USING . . . B. INTRODUCED TO IT BY . . .	AGE	LENGTH OF TIME USING?	TRIED TO QUIT? YES NO	HOW MANY TIMES?	DO YOU KNOW IT IS A HEALTH RISK? YES NO	IF YOU QUIT, WHAT DID YOU DO SUCCESSFULLY?
1	A. B.						
2	A. B.						
3	A. B.						
4	A. B.						
5	A. B.						

Do you know the health hazards of using smokeless tobacco? Tell someone else about the facts!

SMOKELESS TOBACCO IS NOT A SAFE ALTERNATIVE TO CIGARETTE SMOKING

Health and Passive Smoke

The dangers of second-hand cigarette smoke parallel those of direct smoke.
There is evidence that shows that the people nearby who inhale the toxic fumes generated by the smoker, particularly from the burning end of the cigarette, could get lung cancer and sustain heart damage.

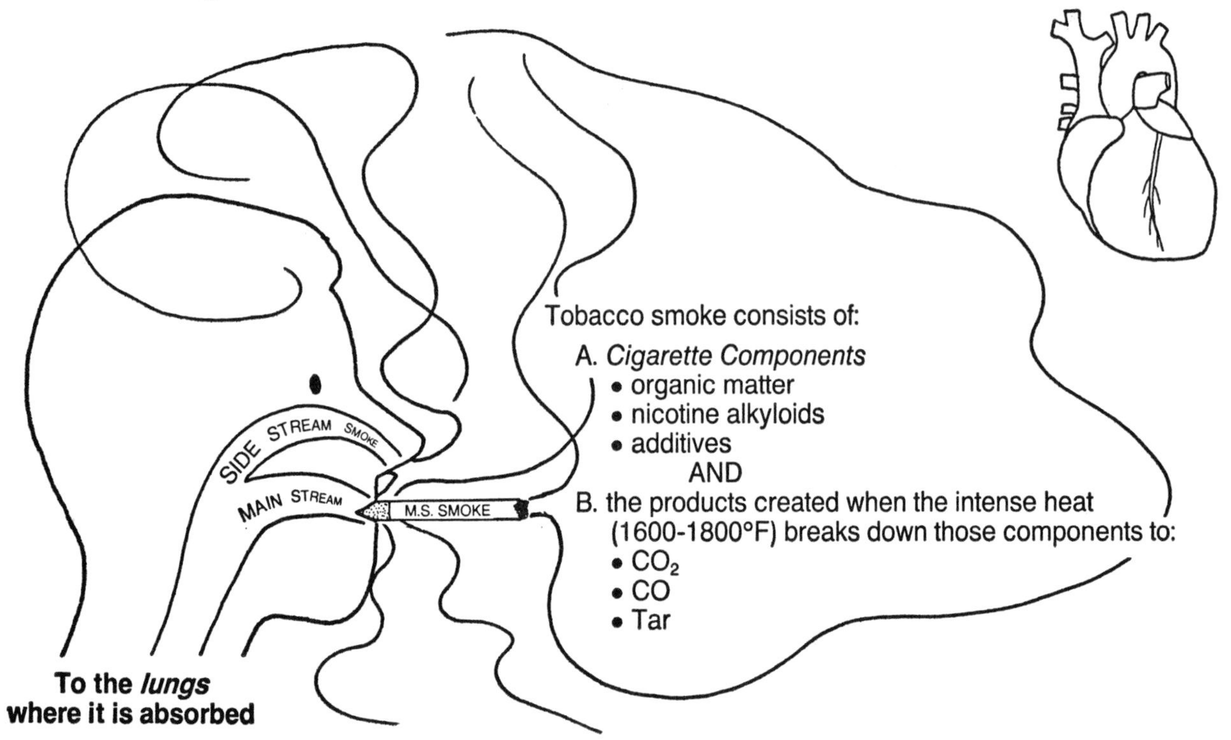

The ***amount, depth*** and ***duration*** of inhalation influences the degree of ***absorption.***

Major differences exist in the components of *mainstream* and *sidestream* smoke, largely determined by the degree of combustion:

—*Mainstream* smoke is inhaled into the lungs from smoking the cigarette, depositing large particles in the larger airways of the lungs.

—*Sidestream* smoke may come from someone else's tobacco or *one's own*, from the burning end of the cigarette *between* puffs, or while it is lying in an ashtray.

—*Sidestream* smoke is a mixture of irritating gases and carcinogenic tar particles that reach *deeper into the lungs* because they are small.

—*Sidestream* smoke is *dirtier* and chemically different from mainstream smoke.

Shedding a Little Light:
Passive smoking ranks behind direct smoking and alcohol as the *third leading preventable* cause of death.

Dr. Stanton A. Glantz, University of California at San Francisco — at a World Conference on lung health.

POLLUTING MY ATMOSPHERE 10-1

Objectives:

- To help the students identify some of the social and legal consequences of smoking cigarettes
- To help them understand the health dangers of passive smoke

Activities:

1. Have the students study Fact Sheet 13, "Health and Passive Smoke."
2. List some of the immediate effects of cigarette smoking on a non-smoker. (Odor on their clothes; reddened eyes; stuffy nose; coughing; may be accidentally burned by the lit end of the cigarette; could cause burns in their clothes or possessions, such as the upholstery of a car, etc.)
3. To challenge the students to view the subject of cigarette smoking from a "new" position, have them complete Activity 10-1A, "On the Far Side." Ask for volunteers to share any new perceptions they have arrived at as a result of doing this exercise.
4. Have the students break up into small groups. Give each student a copy of Activity 10-1B, "Second-Hand Smoke."
   a. Each group will discuss the situations presented in the activity. The students will write their opinion, and add notes in the space provided on the paper.
   b. Then, the class as a whole will brainstorm a "Bill of Rights for Non-Smokers." A "secretary" will record the information.
   c. The class will, by consensus, select the specific information to be included in the final draft of the "Bill of Rights." (A formal "document" can be created and placed in a prominent place in the classroom to encourage non-smokers to "stand up" for the right to health and safety.)
5. Have the students complete Activity 10-1C, "Who Wants to Kiss an Ashtray!" They will:
   a. read the article,
   b. take a position on the information on a scale of 1 to 5,
   c. then, on another piece of paper, write one page of facts and feelings to support their position,
   d. follow with a class discussion or small group discussion.

6. The students will complete Activity 10-1D; "No Smoking!" exploring legal implications for smokers to help them identify the regulations and penalties in their particular location.
7. Ask the students to check the policy of three insurance companies about the differences in the rates for smokers and non-smokers.
8. Have the students read the classified section of several newspapers to find ads for positions for *non-smokers only.*
   a. They can also look for ads for roommates who are non-smokers only. They can bring the ads to class.
   b. Ask: Would these consequences affect your decision to begin to smoke? What would your response be if you had all the qualifications for a job, but you were disqualified for the position because you smoked?

Name ________________________________

Date ________________________________

On the Far Side

1. Imagine that there was an "alien" visiting our planet and he sees people with white "sticks" between their fingers. They are sucking on them, and blowing smoke out of their mouths. He says he would like to try it. He asks if there is any information you would want him to know before he tries it.

____

____

____

____

____

____

____

____

____

____

____

____

____

____

____

____

____

2. Create an ad for a "new" product on the market that—
   a. is proven to be hazardous to your health,
   b. is responsible for at least 350,000 deaths a year in America,
   c. has not had to be approved by the Food & Drug Administration,
   d. is addictive,
   e. is used by children.

Name ______________________________

Date ______________________________

Second-Hand Smoke

Discuss the following statements in your group. Write your opinion and take notes in the space provided.

1. Smokers should always ask permission to smoke.

2. A smoker is in a room with four people, and only one person objects to him/her smoking.

3. You are attending a meeting about planning an important social event. Several people in the room are smoking. You are a non-smoker.

   What consequences might there be for your decision?

4. Someone is asked not to smoke, and he/she proceeds to light up.

5. Someone is already smoking when someone else joins the group and courteously asks that he/she not smoke.

Shedding a Little Light:
Cigarette smoke consists of more than 4,700 compounds, including 43 carcinogens.

Name ______________________________

Date ______________________________

"Who Wants to Kiss an Ashtray!"

On this page are excerpts from an article that appeared in the *Fayetteville Observer*. Read the material carefully.

FAYETTEVILLE OBSERVER: Monday, 19 January, 1987

Survey: Smokers Have Trouble Getting Dates

BOSTON (UPI)—While overweight people previously had the hardest time getting a date, smokers are now the least sought-after on a Saturday night, an informal survey of singles shows.

"It used to be that a person who was overweight was the hardest to match up," said Steve Penner, who recently completed a survey of 600 new members of the dating service he founded in 1982. "Smoking has definitely overcome that."

The survey, which sampled preferences of singles who have joined LunchDates within the past eight months, found that only 10 percent smoked and 78 percent strongly preferred dating non-smokers.

"I asked, 'What if we found a great match for you but the person smokes?'" Penner said. "And still 78 percent said they strongly preferred a non-smoker."

As a result of the survey Penner decided to make LunchDates, which currently has 1,500 active members who pay to be matched up for lunch, dinner or drinks, a non-smokers' dating service.

"When anybody calls for information about the service, the first thing we ask is if they smoke," Penner explained. "If so, we strongly discourage them from joining."

Penner said the new policy is honest, not discriminatory. "I don't want to take anyone's money under false pretenses," he said. "I can't match up a good-looking intelligent man or woman if they're a pack-a-day smoker."

He said some people have joined LunchDates twice—before and after quitting smoking—and enjoyed far better results as non-smokers.

Penner decided to do the survey after receiving complaints from smoking members. "People were calling up to complain they were not matched up well," he explained. "Inevitably it would be a smoker because hardly anyone will go out with them."

While admitting his survey is not scientific, Penner says his business has taught him a lot about the dating market. "In our position—interviewing and talking and matching up 5,000 single people since Lunchdates started—what we have is an up-to-date barometer of what single people are looking for," he said.

The quality most in demand these days is fitness, he said.

"Men say they want a fit woman, not a skinny one like they wanted three or four years ago," he said. Women base their decision "primarily on what the man does for a living," he said. "But he still can't be a heavy smoker or exceedingly overweight."

Penner feels his survey reflects the current health and fitness trend. "People are losing weight and getting in shape and smoking has become something they want to drop," he said.

Many non-smokers also describe the nicotine habit as a physical turn-off, Penner said. "I can't tell you how many times I've heard, 'When I kiss them it's like licking an ashtray,'" he said.

"The tobacco industry is always saying, 'If you smoke you get romance and love,'" Penner said. "It's just not true."

Select a position about what you have read by marking the scale below.

1	2	3	4	5
strongly agree	agree	undecided	disagree	strongly disagree

Now, on another sheet of paper, write one page of facts and your feelings to support your position.

Name ______________________________

Date ______________________________

No Smoking

Federal rules went into effect restricting smoking in Federal buildings nationwide. To get an idea about some state and local restrictions and penalties, read the information below. Then, research those restrictions and penalties placed on smoking in your local area. Be specific.

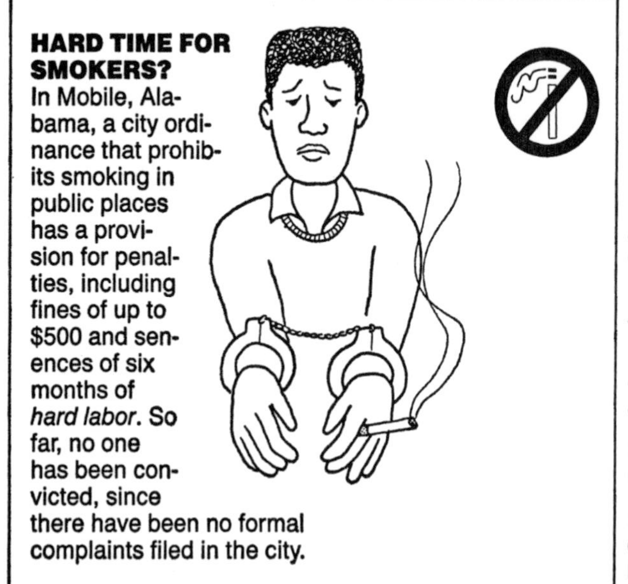

HARD TIME FOR SMOKERS?
In Mobile, Alabama, a city ordinance that prohibits smoking in public places has a provision for penalties, including fines of up to $500 and sentences of six months of *hard labor*. So far, no one has been convicted, since there have been no formal complaints filed in the city.

Smoking in New York State: Where to Light Up, Where Not

New regulations on smoking adopted yesterday by the New York State Public Health Council would go into effect May 7. Each violation could be punished by a $250 fine and 15 days in jail. Here are highlights:

At work No smoking allowed in any workplace, except in designated enclosed areas.

In public spaces No smoking in malls, meeting halls, theaters, arenas, museums, stores, banks, hospitals and health clubs. No smoking in schools, including colleges and vocational schools. Smoking allowed in hotel rooms and tobacco stores.

In common spaces No smoking in lobbies, waiting rooms, restrooms, taxis, limousines, elevators.

In restaurants and bars Restaurants of 50 seats or less could allow smoking. Those with 51 seats or more would be required to designate up to 70 percent of their seats for non smokers. Smoking would be allowed in bars.

LOCAL REGULATIONS FOR SMOKERS	PENALTIES FOR VIOLATION OF REGULATIONS

Alcohol

1. *Alcohol is a drug* that affects the way the body naturally functions. It is a *depressant* drug that *slows the body processes.* (When the body breaks down the ethyl alcohol molecule, it forms a water molecule and *ether. Ether* is used in medicine as an *anesthetic.*)
2. *It is the oldest and most abused drug in the world.*
3. A 12-ounce can of beer, a 5-ounce glass of wine, and 1 ounce of whiskey *all* contain the same amount of alcohol!
4. *Ethyl Alcohol* is the intoxicating ingredient present in many substances (including wine, beer, whiskey, vodka, gin, rum, most cough medicines, some mouthwashes, cooking extracts, and some over-the-counter sleeping medicines).
5. There are predictable, though varying, physical effects upon *everyone* who drinks alcohol. (This is why the law has set a specific blood alcohol level for defining drunkenness while driving.)
6. Alcohol affects many of the body organs and their functions, including the heart, stomach, liver, and brain. (See Activity 11-2, "Alcohol and the Body," and Appendix 2A-2 for further information.)

7. Some of the factors that may influence *how* alcohol affects the individual include:
   a. Amount of alcohol intake.
      Amount of *time* in which alcohol is taken.
   b. Body weight.
   c. Age (children and the elderly are the most sensitive).
   d. Previous drinking experience. (If one develops a *tolerance*, it takes *more* and more of the drug to get the desired effect.)
   e. The presence of other drugs in the system.
   f. The general health of the individual.
   g. The mood of the user; and the setting in which one is drinking.

8. The factors which influence the *speed* at which the alcohol is absorbed include:
   a. The presence of *food* in the stomach (*decreases* the speed of absorption).
   b. The use of *carbonated beverages* with alcohol (*increases* the speed of absorption).
   c. The *concentration* (proof) of the alcohol used.
      100% alcohol = 200 proof = strong poison
      50% alcohol = 100 proof
      43% alcohol = 86 proof
9. Alcohol is *addictive.*
10. Only *time* will cause a person to be sober. The liver detoxifies 1/2 oz. of pure alcohol per hour.

BEER

5 oz. 12 oz. 1 oz.

Each container has the same amount of alcohol.

TO DRINK OR NOT TO DRINK 11-1

Objective:

- To explore the reasons why some people drink alcohol, and why some people choose not to drink

21 years of age is the "legal drinking age" in almost every state in the United States.

Activities:

1. Have the students complete Activity 11-1A, "Down the Hatch."
   a. They are to select three of the "reasons" they think that some people drink alcohol.
   b. Each answer is then to be explained in the place provided. Encourage the students to be thoughtful about their answers.
   (Since previously unexplored attitudes may surface, answers may be kept confidential. *Volunteers* may discuss their answers.
   It is important for the teacher to maintain a non-judgmental attitude at this time, so the students will feel free to express themselves.)
2. Have the students complete Activity 11-1B, "No, Thanks!"
   a. They are to select three of the "reasons" listed on the page (or they may add their own answers) that indicate why some people may choose *not to* drink alcohol.
   b. Each answer is to be explained in a brief paragraph.
   c. Discussions in small groups or as a class may be initiated to explore the topic.

NOTE: Reinforce that *abstinence* is an acceptable choice!

Name ______________________________

Date ______________________________

Down the Hatch!

Read the following statements to review some of the reasons people say they drink alcohol. Select three of the reasons mentioned below that you wish to support or disprove.

I drink to have fun.	It helps me to forget stuff.
I don't want to feel left out.	It helps me to relax.
I want to try it.	It makes me stop "hurting inside."
I like to get "stoned."	It's a habit.
I do it to be sociable.	There is nothing else to do.
It calms me down.	Everyone else is doing it.
It quenches my thirst.	I like the taste.
It helps me to fit in.	There is nothing wrong with it.

1. ______________________________

2. ______________________________

3. ______________________________

Name ______________________________

Date ______________________________

No, Thanks!

Read the sentences below that tell why some people may *choose not* to drink alcohol. Select three reasons mentioned that you agree or disagree with. Explain your answer. (You may want to add and explain other reasons that do not appear on the list.)

My folks said I'd be grounded. I don't like the taste. I don't want to gain weight. I'm afraid I'll lose control. It's against my religion. I'll be kicked off the team.	I don't want to get into trouble. I'm too young to start. It feels "weird." I've seen what it does to some people. If I get caught I'll lose my license. Then my younger brother and sister will try it.	My parents would "freak out." I can use my money for other things. It makes me sick. I'm a recovering alcoholic. It's illegal. I signed the school pledge not to drink or use other drugs.

1. ______________________________

2. ______________________________

3. ______________________________

ALCOHOL AND THE BODY 11-2

Objective:

- To identify the effects of the drug alcohol on the body

Activities:

1. Have the students define the following words that are related to the effects of alcohol on the body:

intoxication	abstinence	sedation
tolerance	absorption	oxidation
depressant	addiction	abuse

2. Review Fact Sheet 14.
3. Reproduce and review Activity 11-2A, Alcohol in the Body fact sheet.

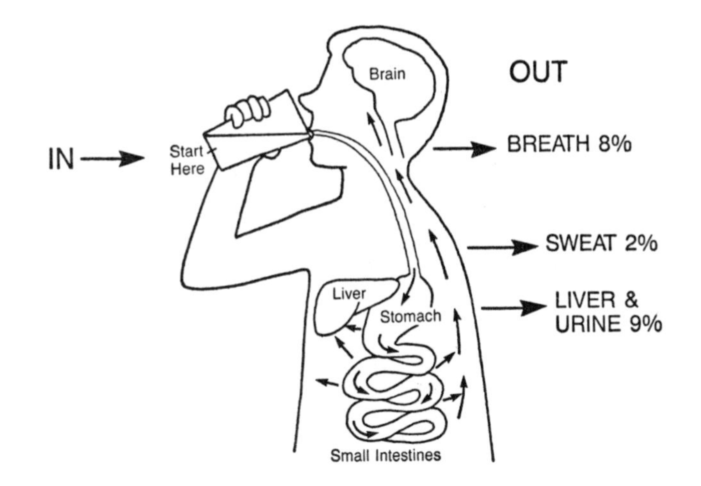

4. Later, direct the students to use Activity 11-2B to trace the pathway of alcohol through the body with a pen, label the organs of the body that are affected by alcohol, and list one fact about each organ.
   a. The students can exchange papers to check each other's answers.
   b. Encourage students to ask questions in class.
5. Complete the sentences in Activity 11-2C, "Body Parts," using the words in the box. (Additional information is available in Appendix 2A-2.) Answers to Activity 11-2C:
   (1) LIVER: detoxification, cleansing, poisons, 1/2 ounce, hour, oxidation, damage, cirrhosis.
   (2) STOMACH: esophagus, no, not digested, directly, capillaries, small intestines, rapidly, irritates.
   (3) BRAIN: bloodstream, minutes, sedative, depresses, impairs, coordination, behavior, judgment.

Alcohol in the Body

+ Study the Pathway of Alcohol through the Body.

* *Learn the effects of alcohol on the body.*

1

+ Alcohol is taken into the body through the MOUTH. This is called ingestion. The alcohol passes down the esophagus.

* *Its use increases the risk of cancer of the mouth and the esophagus.*

2

Alcohol has no food value.

+ No digestion takes place in the STOMACH. Some alcohol is absorbed into the bloodstream. The rest of the alcohol passes into the small intestines.

* *Alcohol irritates the stomach lining.* The acute effects of heavy drinking, such as gastritis or bleeding peptic ulcer, are more likely in the adolescent.

3

+ From the SMALL INTESTINES, most of the alcohol is absorbed rapidly directly into the bloodstream.

4

+ The BLOODSTREAM carries the alcohol to *all* parts of the body. (The brain is "bathed" in alcohol *almost immediately.*)

5

The LIVER is the "Chemical Factory" of the body.
It acts as a cleansing station to rid the body of poisons.

+ The LIVER removes alcohol from the blood. It breaks down the alcohol into carbon dioxide and water by a process called *oxidation*. OXIDATION OCCURS AT A CONSTANT UNCHANGEABLE RATE OF 1/2 OUNCE OF PURE ALCOHOL PER HOUR.

* *Excessive use of alcohol can damage the liver and lead to deadly liver disease (cirrhosis).*

6

The BRAIN is the "Control Center" of the body.

+ The Brain is "bathed" in alcohol almost immediately upon ingestion. Alcohol keeps passing through the brain until the liver has had enough *time* to remove all the alcohol from the bloodstream.

* *The brain is the organ most sensitive to alcohol.*
It affects judgment, learning, behavior, coordination, vision. Excessive amounts can cause the organs vital for life to stop functioning!

Name ______________________________

Date ______________________________

Follow the Pathway of Alcohol in the Body

1. Use pencil or pen to trace the pathway of alcohol through the body.
2. Label the organs of the body that are affected by alcohol.
3. List one fact about alcohol's effect on each organ of the body that is shown.

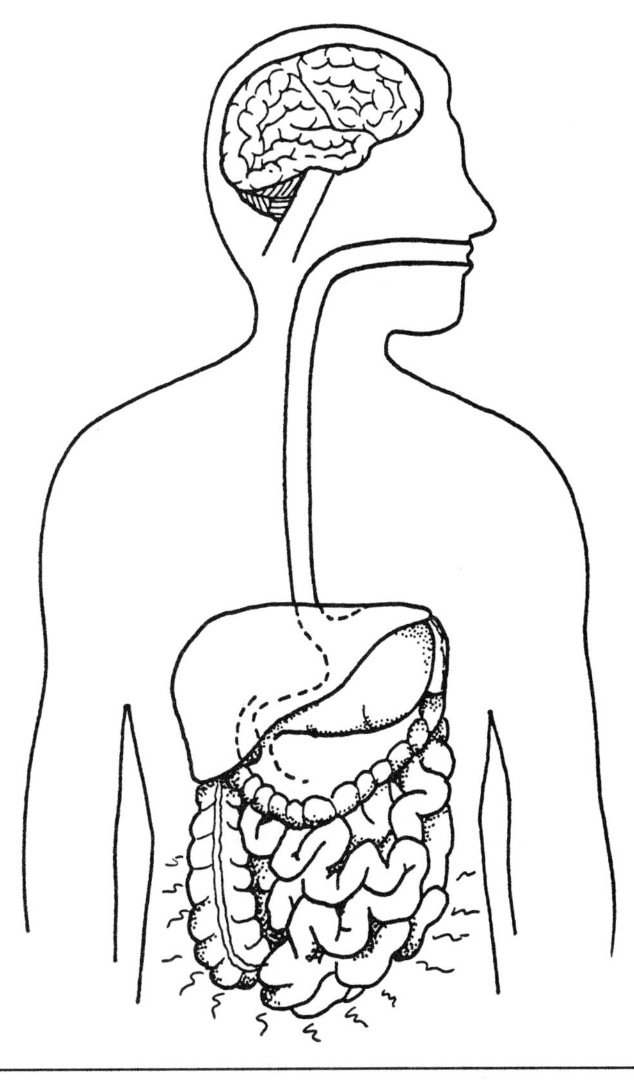

Shedding a Little Light:
Researchers have determined that women are more susceptible to the effects of alcohol than men because of an enzyme, alcohol dehydrogenase. Men make *far higher amounts* of the enzyme, which breaks down alcohol before it hits the bloodstream. (Dr. Marie Frezza, University School of Medicine, Trieste, Italy.)

Name ______________________

Date ______________________

Body Parts

Label each organ. Then complete the sentences below, using the words in the box. Not all of the words will be used.

1.

oxidation	digestion	hour
detoxification	cirrhosis	cleansing
1/2 ounce	damage	poisons

The liver aids in __________. It acts as a __________ station to rid the body of __________. The liver breaks down the alcohol in the body at a rate of __________ of pure alcohol per __________. This is called __________. NOTHING CAN CHANGE THE RATE OF THIS PROCESS. The excess use of alcohol can __________ the liver and lead to a serious liver disease called __________.

2.

completely	capillaries	directly
irritates	small intestines	not digested
esophagus	rapidly	no

Alcohol irritates the __________. It has ________ food value. Alcohol is ________ __________ in the stomach. A small amount of the alcohol is absorbed __________ into the bloodstream through the smallest blood vessels called __________. The rest of the alcohol passes into the __________ __________ where it is absorbed __________ into the bloodstream. Alcohol __________ the stomach lining. Acute abdominal distress, vomiting, and ulcers may occur.

3.

coordination	minutes	bloodstream
behavior	impairs	judgment
sedative	digests	depresses

The __________ carries alcohol to the brain within __________. Alcohol is a __________ drug that __________ the Central Nervous System. It __________ the functions of __________, __________, __________.

DRINKING AND BEHAVIOR 11-3

Objectives:

- To have the students identify the effects of alcohol upon the brain
- To have the students recognize what effect alcohol may have on their behavior

Activities:

1. Have the students study the information in the picture of the brain in Activity 11-3A.
2. The brain is the "Control Center" of the body. Drinking the drug alcohol cuts down on the ability of the brain (and the rest of the nervous system) to do its job.
   - When the brain is impaired, behavior is affected.
   - To help the students recognize what the effect on their behavior might be, they can use the Blood Alcohol Concentration (BAC) Wheel.

   a. *To make the BAC Wheel:*
      (1) Follow the directions given on the two BAC Wheel activity sheets 11-3B and 11-3C.

   b. *To use the BAC Wheel,* read the following directions:
      As an example: If you had four average-sized drinks of beer, wine or mixed drinks:
      (1) Line up the number 4 in the "number of drinks" row with the outer ring, which shows the weight of the person drinking the alcohol.
      (2) Read the figure that appears in the upper window. This is the BAC if that person has taken the 4 drinks within a quarter hour.
      (3) By looking at the bottom window, you can determine what the BAC would be with the passage of time. Experiment with different combinations.

> NOTE: Keep in mind the factors that influence the speed at which alcohol is absorbed, and the other factors that may influence how alcohol will affect the individual. (See Fact Sheet 14.)

   c. Study the probable behavior that would be visible at the degree of intoxication using Activity 11-3D, "Degree of Intoxication." (Note the numbered areas on the picture of the Brain [1 to 6] in Activity 11-3A.)

3. Almost 50 percent of people who died from falls had been drinking. Almost 70 percent of drowning victims had been drinking. Over 50 percent of fires that led to adult deaths involved alcohol.
   a. Instruct the class to collect articles from newspapers and magazines over a period of a week, chronicling problems resulting from alcohol-impaired behavior. (Examples: accidents—household, auto, train, airplane; violence—date rape, shootings, stabbings; suicides; drownings; etc.)
   b. With the information they have collected, have the class make a collage or poster to illustrate the negative effects of alcohol abuse.
   c. Place the collage in a prominent place in the classroom.
4. Have the students do Activity 11-3E, "What Happened?" They will break up into groups of four. Each group will choose one of the scenarios in the activity. The group will discuss their situation for about 10 minutes.
   a. They will take into account those factors that will influence alcohol's effect on the person,
   b. the behaviors that one can expect,
   c. what each one might have done in a similar situation, and
   d. make suggestions of how the situation could be prevented in the future, or what help is needed.

   When the "story is complete," the designated person in each group will share the information with the rest of the class.

NOTE:
- Stress the fact that 21 is the legal drinking age in most states.
- Recognize abstinence as an acceptable choice.

Shedding a Little Light:
Wine coolers typically look like soda or a fruit drink—but, some contain more alcohol than beer! (6% in wine coolers and 4% in beer.)

Name ____________________

Date ____________________

The Brain

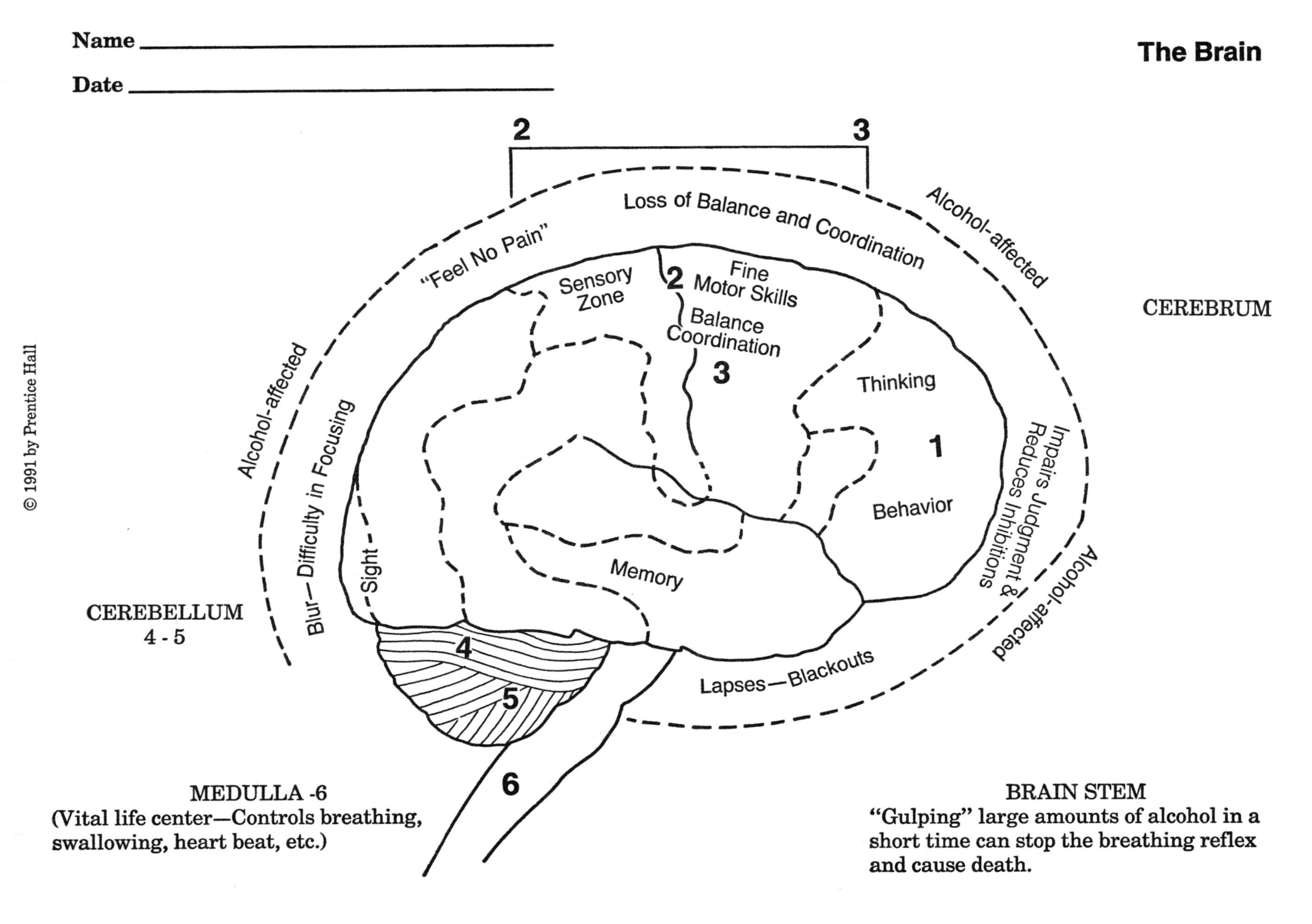

MEDULLA -6
(Vital life center—Controls breathing, swallowing, heart beat, etc.)

BRAIN STEM
"Gulping" large amounts of alcohol in a short time can stop the breathing reflex and cause death.

Name ______________________________

Date ______________________________

BAC Wheel

Part 1

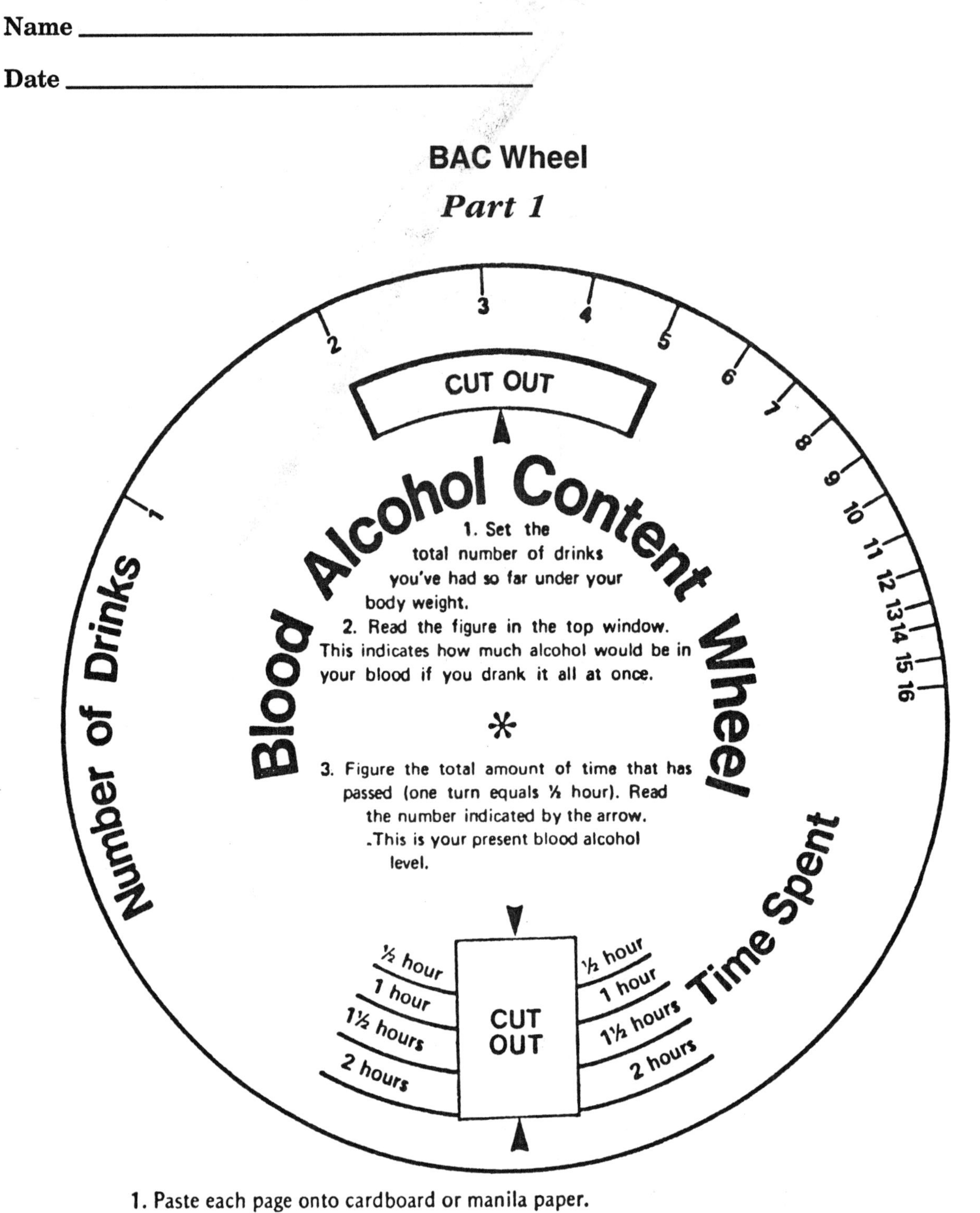

1. Paste each page onto cardboard or manila paper.
2. Trim around each circle.
3. Use a razor to cut the two sections marked "CUT OUT."
4. Put the smaller circle on top of the larger one, carefully fastening them together at the stars (centers) with a paper fastener.

Source: Reprinted from Peter Finn and Judith Platt, *Alcohol and Alcohol Safety,* Volume 2. Washington, D.C.: U.S. Government Printing Office, 1972.

Name ______________________________

Date ______________________________

BAC Wheel

Part 2

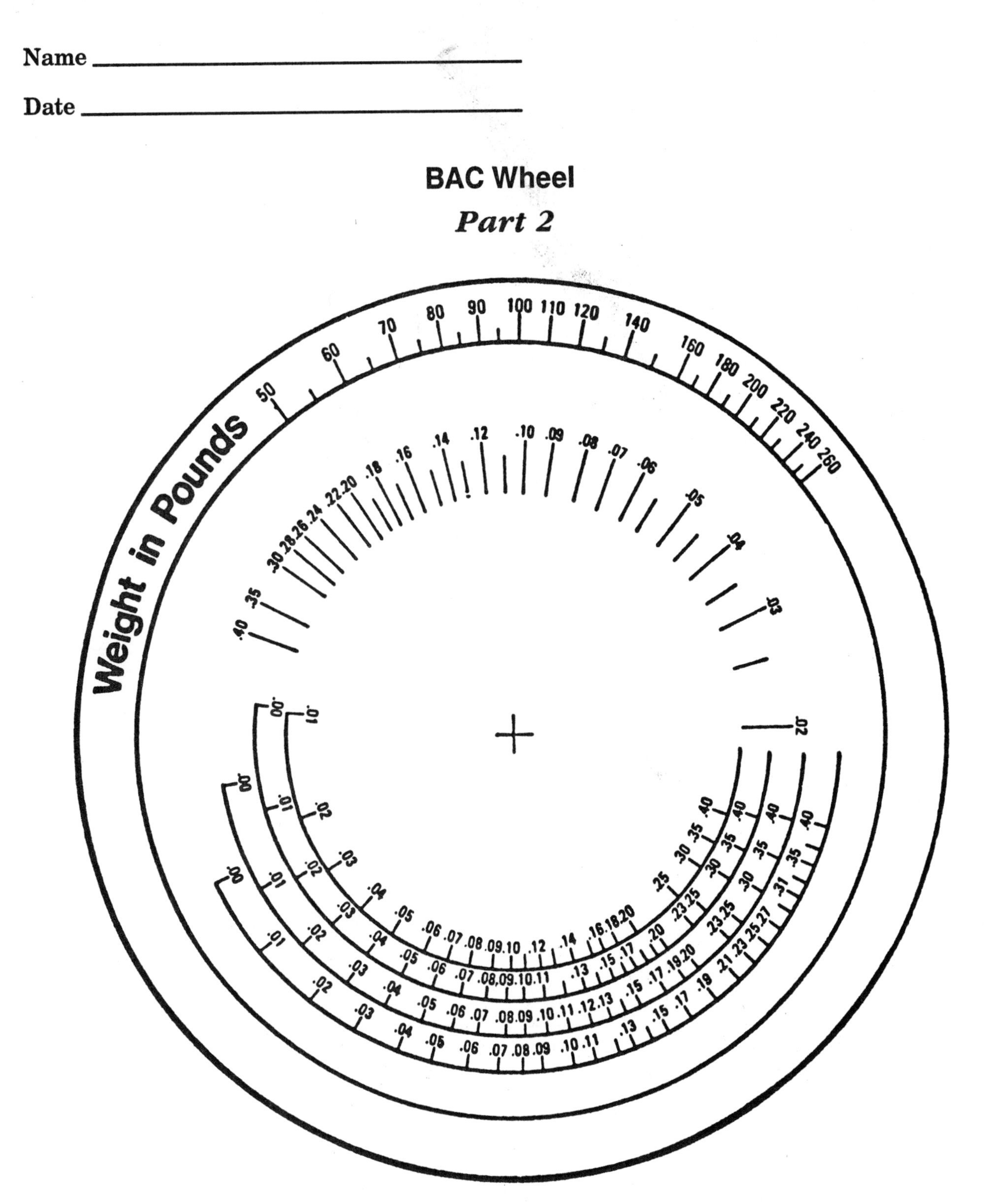

Source: Reprinted from Peter Finn and Judith Platt, *Alcohol and Alcohol Safety,* Volume 2. Washington, D.C.: U.S. Government Printing Office, 1972.

Name ______________________________

Date ______________________________

Degree of Intoxication

BAC READING	BRAIN AREA AFFECTED	FEELINGS AND BEHAVIOR	HOW IT LOOKS
.01-.04%	1	Usually no apparent changes in behavior are noted. Relaxation with minor impairment of *judgment* and *memory.*	
.05-.08%	2	*Walking, talking,* and *hand movements* become more clumsy. *Slows* the person's ability *to react.*	
.08-.10%	3	Speech, judgment, and balance are affected. Blurred vision. Slower reaction time. (Considered drunken driving in most states.)	
.10-.15%	4	Judgment, memory, and self-control are further affected. Irresponsible behavior is evident. There is a decrease in the sense of pain. Speech, hearing, and balance altered.	
.15-.20%	5	Behavior is greatly affected. Lack of motor control; mental confusion.	
.20-.30%	6	Unable to perform tasks. Confused or dazed state. Unconsciousness may occur. All physical and mental abilities are *severely* impaired.	
.30 plus	6	Unconsciousness, coma, or death possible.	
.40-.50%	6	The breathing process may stop functioning. Death.	JON SMITH 8-6-76 to 9-7-92

- If someone is unconscious, vomiting may cause the person to choke. Help is needed! Call for medical attention!
- A *person in a coma may also have unabsorbed alcohol in the stomach.* Even though no further alcohol is taken, the continuing absorption will increase the risk to his or her life.

Name ______________________________

Date ______________________________

What Happened?

Break up into groups of four.
Choose one of the following scenarios to discuss. Take into account:

a. the problem,
b. the factors that will influence alcohol's effect on a person,
c. the behaviors that could be expected,
d. make suggestions of how the situation could be prevented in the future, or what help is needed.

When the story is complete, designate a person in your group to share the information with the rest of the class.

1. Michael is a 32-year-old man. He is 5 feet 9 inches and weighs 165 pounds. Michael is an attorney. He is on his lunch hour, and has just had three glasses of beer with his sandwich. He wants to drop by the drugstore to pick up some gum to have his breath smell fresh because he is going into court in a few minutes.

2. Paul is a 50-year-old father of six. He is 6 feet tall and weighs 200 pounds. He has two jobs and often works late. It's 10 o'clock and he has just arrived home. He has had several scotches on the rocks to "unwind." He is dozing on and off on the couch, the television is on, and he is smoking his cigarette.

3. Sarah is a bartender. A young woman has been drinking at the bar for most of the evening. Sarah can't believe it! She doesn't notice any of the signs of drunkenness yet.

4. Chris has a date with Jean tonight. They have been seeing each other all through their senior year. They like each other a lot. Jean's folks aren't home tonight. Chris brought along a few bottles of wine cooler to celebrate their six-month "anniversary."

5. This is Tom's first semester at college. He seldom drinks. Tonight he is pledging for a fraternity. The two new pledges have to compete in a "chug-a-lug" contest. It's a private fraternity house, so they are not worried about getting caught. The other pledge "wins" because Tom "passes out." The fraternity members put Tom in his room to sleep it off.

6. Maggie has been drinking beer on the beach with her friends. The sun feels hotter now. She has a little trouble with her balance when she first gets up, but soon gets her balance. She starts toward the water to swim and cool off.

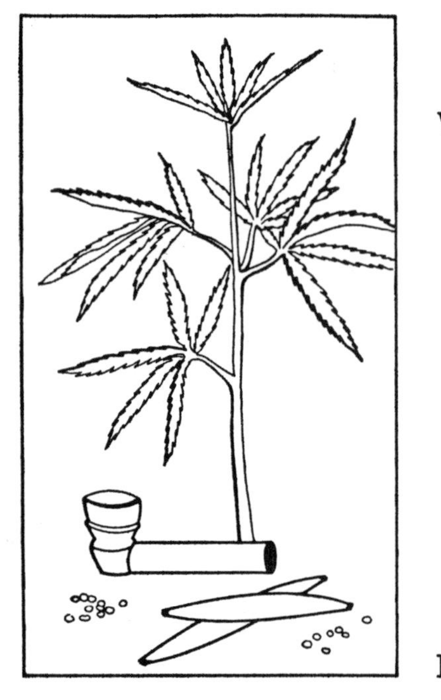

Marijuana

WHAT

- Marijuana is derived from the *Cannabis Sativa* plant which is grown in mild climates throughout the world.
- THC (delta-9-tetrahydrocannabinal), a chemical from the marijuana plant, is the principal mind-altering ingredient in marijuana.
- The strength of marijuana has *dramatically* increased. It now contains as much as 10 times the amount of THC as it did years ago.

HOW

- Marijuana can be either *smoked* or *ingested* (sprinkled in food).
- Smoking provides a more direct route to the brain, and the effects are felt in minutes.
- THC is fat-soluble. This means that it can be *stored in the body for long periods,* unlike alcohol, which is water-soluble and leaves the body more rapidly.
- It is stored in areas of high-fat content: (1) the lungs, (2) the brain, (3) the reproductive organs. (See Fact Sheet 16, "Marijuana and the Body.")
- Depending on the amount of marijuana use and the testing method, marijuana can be detected in the body up to *28 days after use.* (Hawkes, R. L., and C. N. Chian. "Urine Testing for Drugs of Abuse," National Institute of Drug Abuse Research Monograph, *73,* 1986.)
- There is no quality control for illegal drugs. Each dose is different.
- The drug's effect on the user's mood and senses varies according to:
  (1) the amount and strength of the marijuana,
  (2) the social setting,
  (3) the effects *anticipated* by the user,
  (4) the mood of the user.
- Marijuana is usually the first, and most frequently used, illicit drug.

NOTE: See "Drugs and Pregnancy," Chapter 15. See "Driving and Drugs," Chapter 14.

Marijuana and the Body

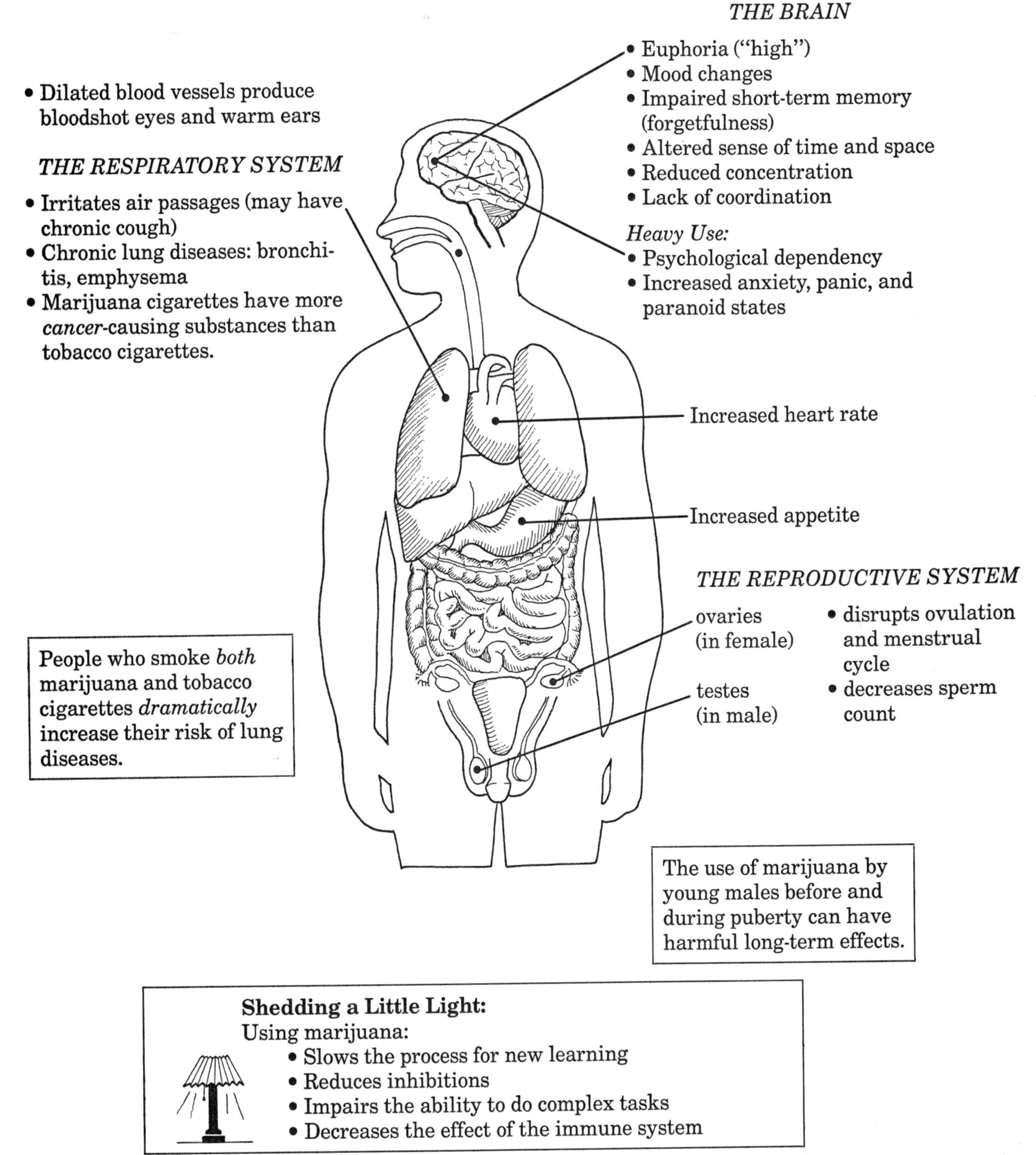

THE MOST-USED ILLICIT DRUG 12-1

Objective:

- To inform about the physical and psychological effects of the drug, marijuana

Activities:

1. Study Fact Sheet 15.
2. Distribute Fact Sheet 16 to the class. Review the information with the students.
3. Have the students complete Activity 12-1A, "A Review." They will fill in the words missing in the sentences, and answer the true/false statements. Answers to Activity 12-1A:
   PART ONE—1. THC; 2. stronger; 3. 28; 4. fat; 5. brain, lungs, reproductive system; 6. dependency.
   PART TWO—true, true, false, false, false, true.
4. Activity 12-1B, "Facing the Facts," is designed to have the students put their knowledge to work in a "real life" situation. This activity can be done as a class discussion, or the students may write their answers on a separate piece of paper and then discuss them.
   The answers should include:
   Fact
   a. Ann — Marijuana can be detected in the body up to 28 days.
   b. Bobby — Marijuana is illegal. (Explore the scenario that might take place with a detective, plus the legal penalties expected.)
   c. Frank — Combining drugs greatly increases the potency of their effect and, therefore, increases the risk of having an accident.
   d. Ashed — It is *not* smart to abuse *any* drug. Marijuana is *illegal* and can cause *dependency.*
   e. Sam — Since it is not fatigue, hunger, or worries, it is understood that the marijuana has affected his *short-term memory*—interfering with learning and processing the information for the future.
5. Have the students select a college anywhere in the country. Ask them to write to the college to obtain information about their college's drug policy. They can share the information with the class. (The students may be surprised that drugs on campus are unacceptable. The penalties might include immediate expulsion.)

Shedding a Little Light:

- Marijuana cigarettes contain more "tar" than tobacco cigarettes.
- They are inhaled more deeply,
- The smoke is held for a long time in the lungs,
- They are smoked to the very end where tar concentrations are highest.
- 90% of marijuana users also drink alcohol. (D.H. Gieringer, "Marijuana, Driving and Traffic Safety," *Journal of Psychoactive Drugs, 20,* 93-101, 1988.)

Name ______________________________

Date ______________________________

A Review

PART ONE
Fill in the blanks of the sentences below.

1. The mind-altering ingredient of marijuana is ____________________.
2. Marijuana in use today is __________ than it was years ago.
3. It is possible to detect the presence of marijuana in the body up to ____________ days.
4. The body stores THC for long periods because it is ____________ soluble.
5. It has the greatest effect on the __________, __________, and __________.
6. Regular use of marijuana can result in ____________________.

PART TWO
Read the sentences below. Then indicate whether each is TRUE or FALSE.

1. Marijuana cigarettes have more cancer-causing substances than tobacco cigarettes. __________
2. Marijuana affects the driver's ability to judge time and distance. __________
3. Marijuana is one of the small number of chemicals that cannot cross from the bloodstream of a pregnant woman into the bloodstream of her unborn child. __________
4. Marijuana use is responsible for most of the automobile accidents on the highway today. __________
5. The effect of each marijuana cigarette on the user's mood and senses is consistently the same. __________
6. Anyone who smokes both tobacco and marijuana cigarettes greatly increases the risk of lung disease. __________

Name ______________________________

Date ______________________________

Facing the Facts

Presume that all the people in the stories below are involved with the drug, marijuana. To determine what you know about this drug:

1. Read each story.
2. List the facts that indicate some of the difficulties the use of marijuana may create in each situation.
3. What information would you like to share with them in order to be helpful?

Ann
The Airline Stewardess

Ann is leaving to go to her new job today. She knows that it is company policy to do a drug test on all new employees.

She smokes marijuana two or three times a week. She is not worried about the test because she was very careful this week not to smoke at *all* for a full four days before the test.

Bobby
The "Buyer"

Bobby wants to know what all this hype is about marijuana. He drank a few beers, smoked cigarettes a lot lately—but he has not gotten around to smoking a "joint" yet.

Today he finally has a contact for a "buy." As he is giving him the money for the drug, an undercover detective who had been watching comes over to them and shows his badge.

Frank
The "Frat" Brother

Frank knows the dangers of drinking and driving while intoxicated. He's pretty careful about following the law.

Tonight he took only *one* beer about a half hour ago. He's just finishing smoking his second "joint" with his fraternity brothers.

Now he is going to be a good buddy and drive a new fraternity pledge to his home.

Ashed
The "Achiever"

Ashed will be attending high school this year. His girlfriend will be there, too. He's looking forward to marrying a girl like her some day, but right now he's concentrating on doing well in school. He wants to go to college when he graduates. He won't let anything stand in his way. No hard drug for him! He's decided that a "soft" drug like marijuana is smart because there are no long-term effects.

Sam
The Student

Sam seems to be having some trouble remembering the answers for the quiz tomorrow. He has been studying at the desk for awhile now.

He tries to understand the problem by reviewing the last few days:

a. He had 8 hours' sleep each day.
b. He didn't forget to eat lunch today.
c. He hasn't had time to exercise so he relaxed, as usual, with two "joints" almost every day to reduce the pressure.
d. He doesn't have any money worries.

Cocaine

WHAT

- Cocaine is a drug extracted from the leaves of the cocoa plant which grows in South America.
- It is sold (illegally) in three forms:
  cocoa paste   cocaine powder   "Crack"

WHY

- Cocaine is a powerful drug that *stimulates* the Central Nervous System. It increases alertness, activity, and excitement by speeding up the body's processes.
- It initially produces a sense of *euphoria.*
- The effects of cocaine last only a short time.
- Repeated use can lead to a rapid escalation to *dependency.*

HOW

- Cocaine is usually sniffed or *snorted* into the nose.
- It can be *injected* into the veins.
- *Smoking* this drug is called freebase. Freebase produces a shorter, more intense "high" because it provides a more direct route to the brain.
- *Crack is cocaine already in smokeable form.*
  It is smoked with a special pipe, or the pulverized chips can be sprinkled on a tobacco or marijuana cigarette.
  Since the effect is so pleasurable and so short lived, the craving for another dose can be overwhelming.
  It is highly addictive.

NEGATIVE PHYSICAL AND PSYCHOLOGICAL CONSEQUENCES with repeated use of cocaine include:

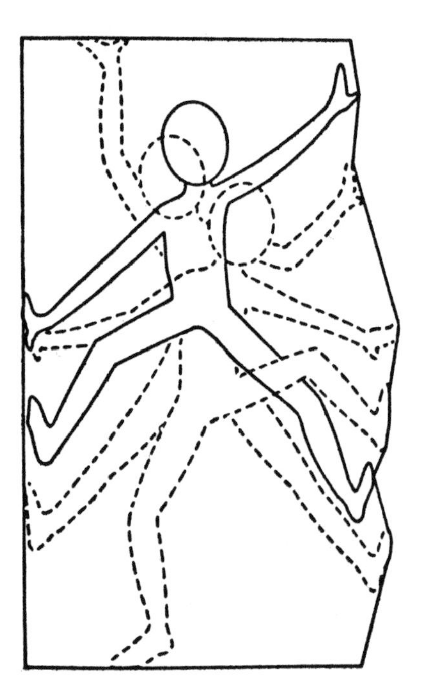

irritability
memory loss
hallucinations
fatigue
nasal sores
panic attacks
paranoia
malnutrition
sleep disturbances
lack of sex drive
irregular heartbeat
deep depression
violent behavior
chronic cough
convulsions
respiratory paralysis

Death due to a cocaine overdose is very quick. It can occur within minutes from the beginning of the symptoms: excitement, psychotic behavior, seizures, and respiratory paralysis are reported.
Because of the short time it takes to die from cocaine overdose, treatment is often not available soon enough.

COCAINE CONSEQUENCES

13-1

Objective:

- To provide information about the effects of repeated uses of cocaine, the students will (1) identify the physical and psychological effects of the drug and (2) explore the financial problems that can result from them

Activities:

1. Have the students define:
   euphoria hepatitis paranoia
2. The class can study and discuss Fact Sheet 17.
3. Using the body form showing the effects of cocaine in Activity 13-1A, have the class study some of the physical and psychological effects from the use of this drug. Note the effects on the eyes, nose, teeth, brain, lungs, heart, and circulatory system.
4. Later, have the students complete Activity 13-1B, "Hitting the Target," to identify at least five effects of cocaine on the body. The students will write a brief description of the effect on the "Target" site.
5. To explore the financial problems that result from the use of cocaine, have the students complete Activity 13-1C, "Sounding the Alarm." After the students have completed the activity, have the class discuss their answers.
6. Invite a speaker from Cocaine Anonymous to address the class. To prepare for the guest speakers:
   a. Have the students each list three questions for the visitor to answer. No names need be used.
   b. Collect the questions, place them in a box or other container, and present them to the guest speaker after the presentation.
7. Have the students read the scenarios and finish the stories in Activity 13-1D, "Wise Up." Then, have the class break up into groups of four and discuss their responses. After the discussion, have each group choose a spokesperson to report some of their conclusions to the class. (See the chapters on *Drugs and Pregnancy* and *Drugs and Driving* for additional information and activities.)

Shedding a Little Light:

- Using alcohol or another depressant drug to modify the effects of overstimulation from Cocaine risks an overdose and "double addiction."
- **Crack:** The name comes from the crackling sound it makes when it is smoked.

Name ____________________________________

Date ____________________________________

The Body Form

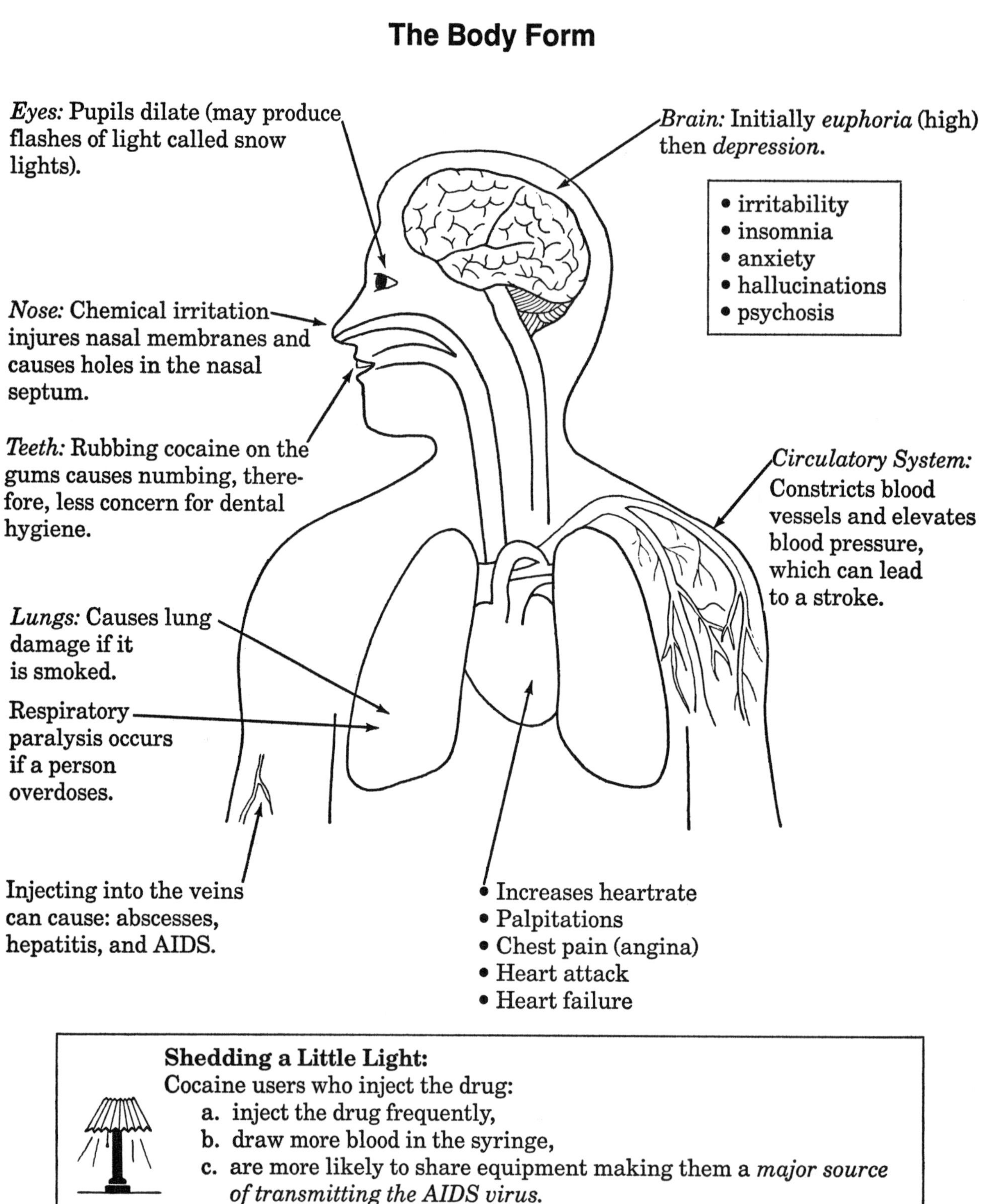

Shedding a Little Light:
Cocaine users who inject the drug:

a. inject the drug frequently,
b. draw more blood in the syringe,
c. are more likely to share equipment making them a *major source of transmitting the AIDS virus.*

(See "AIDS," Appendix 3A-1 to 3A-5.)

Name ________________________________

Date ________________________________

Hitting the Target

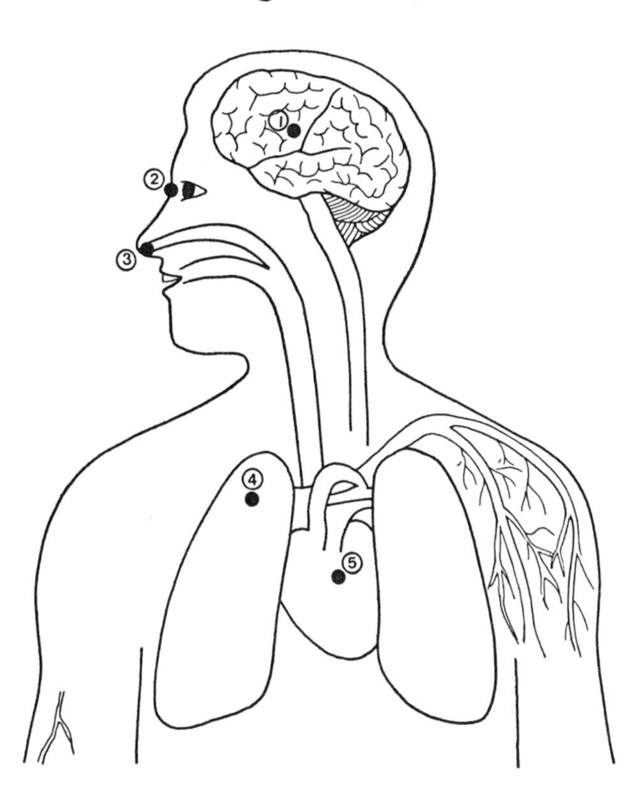

Identify each site of the body indicated with the black dot:

1. ______________________________

2. ______________________________

3. ______________________________

4. ______________________________

5. ______________________________

Write a brief description of the effect of cocaine on that target site:

____

____

____

____

____

____

____

____

____

____

Name ______________________________

Date ______________________________

Sounding the Alarm

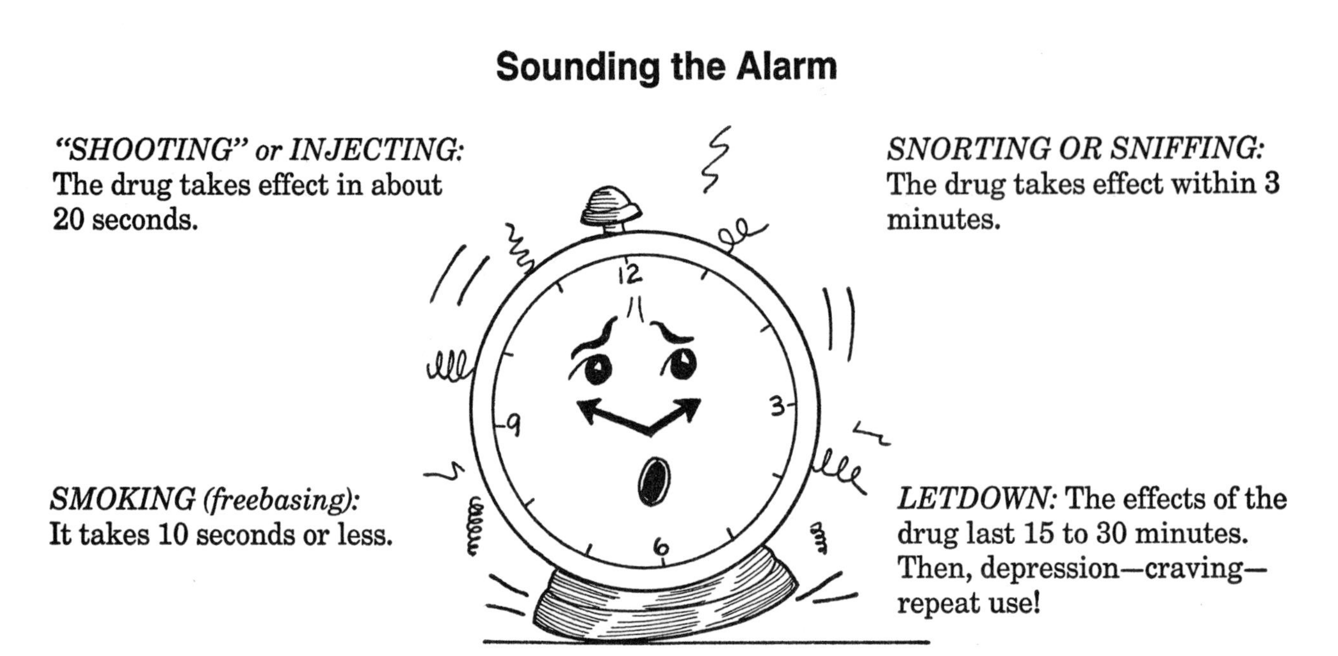

"SHOOTING" or INJECTING:
The drug takes effect in about 20 seconds.

SNORTING OR SNIFFING:
The drug takes effect within 3 minutes.

SMOKING (freebasing):
It takes 10 seconds or less.

LETDOWN: The effects of the drug last 15 to 30 minutes. Then, depression—craving—repeat use!

1. This activity would *NOT BE* of interest to anyone who is addicted to cocaine/crack. That person would not *care* about preparing for the future.

A vile of Crack costs $10. Due to the intense "high" and the short duration of the effect, the desire to "use" again can be overwhelming. Addiction is rapid. More and more money is needed to buy the drug to support the "habit."	
a. How much money would you spend:	b. Other ways you could spend it:
—once a day . . . . $________	________________________
—3 times a day . . . . $________	________________________
—7 days a week, 5 times a day . . . . $________	________________________
—every two hours around the clock . . . . . . $________	________________________

Shedding a Little Light:
The *need* for the drug can progress until it is preferred to family, friends, food, sex . . . .

Continued

2. This activity WOULD BE of interest to someone who was dependent on the drug.

You have only $6. A vile of crack is $10. You are feeling "ants crawling all over you." You are getting fearful and agitated. How will you get the money for your drug this time, and next time? List as many options as you can think of. Next to each, list any consequences that might result from getting the money.	
GETTING THE MONEY:	CONSEQUENCES:
______	______
______	______
______	______
______	______
______	______
______	______
______	______

How might that affect your future? ______

______

______

______

______

______

______

Name one person who cares about you and whose life would be affected also. ______

How? ______

______

______

______

______

______

Name ______________________________

Date ______________________________

Wise-Up

Read the following scenarios and finish the stories. Explain fully.

1. Your folks are out. You have a few friends come over for a few hours. One of your friends has some "coke" with him. You have tried it once or twice before. No big deal! You are about to "snort a line" when your 10-year-old brother walks in on you. He has always admired you, and tries to imitate some of the things you do.

____

____

____

____

2. Your friend has been using cocaine more often lately. You don't use drugs, and you're really getting worried about her. She's beginning to feel a little jumpy and has been using alcohol to bring herself "down."

____

____

____

____

3. Your parents are always talking to you about staying out of trouble. Don't they know you have to grow up and decide things for yourself? It's pretty exciting trying out new things. You've taken a few risks, and it has turned out O.K.: riding in a car that's going over the speed limit once; smoking a "joint" in someone's house; having a few beers at someone's party. You could always handle it, and so far your parents haven't found out. Now, someone offers you some "crack."

____

____

____

____

____

Drugs and Driving

- Auto accidents are the *leading* cause of death for people under the age of 25.
- Riding in an automobile, says the Federal Department of Transportation, is the *single greatest hazard* that young Americans face—greater than disease, suicide, or war.
- Good driving skills require:
  - (a) *a clear mind*—for good judgment and decision-making,
  - (b) *good reflexes* and *coordination*—to react appropriately,
  - (c) *good vision*—since almost 90% of the information we use for driving comes through the eyes.

DRIVING UNDER THE INFLUENCE OF ALCOHOL AFFECTS *ALL* OF THOSE SKILLS.

METHODS OF TESTING FOR BLOOD ALCOHOL CONTENT

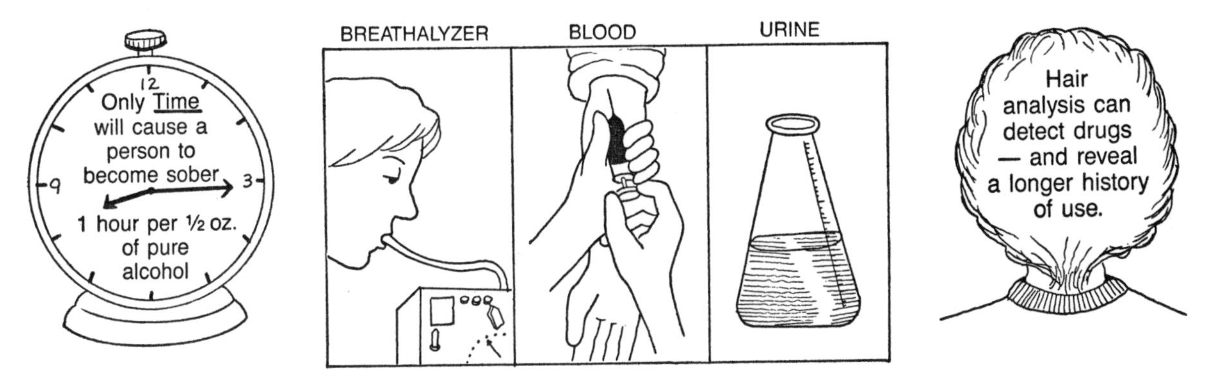

- The increased accident risk begins *before* drivers are impaired or intoxicated.
  - (a) At .04% BAC, chances of an accident *increase.*
  - (b) At .06% (impaired driving), chances of an accident *double.*
  - (c) At .10% BAC, chances of an accident are *6 times greater* than when sober.
  - (d) At .15% BAC, chances of an accident are *25 times greater* than when sober.
- Young people who break the law and drink before the legal age have auto accidents with a *lower percentage* of alcohol in their blood than adult drivers who drink and drive. Over *one-half* of young drivers involved in alcohol-related crashes have a BAC of *.02%.* This may be due to:
  - (a) lack of experience in driving,
  - (b) lack of experience in drinking,
  - (c) the *use of other drugs,* with a small amount of alcohol.
- Using two or more drugs at the same time *dramatically increases* the potency of the drug reaction upon the drug user—increasing the risk of injury (or death) to him/herself and others.

Drugs That Affect Driving

SEDATIVE-HYPNOTICS

Sedative-hypnotics (such as sleeping pills and barbiturates) slow brain activity. They *impair judgment, slow reflexes and coordination.*

ANTIHISTAMINES

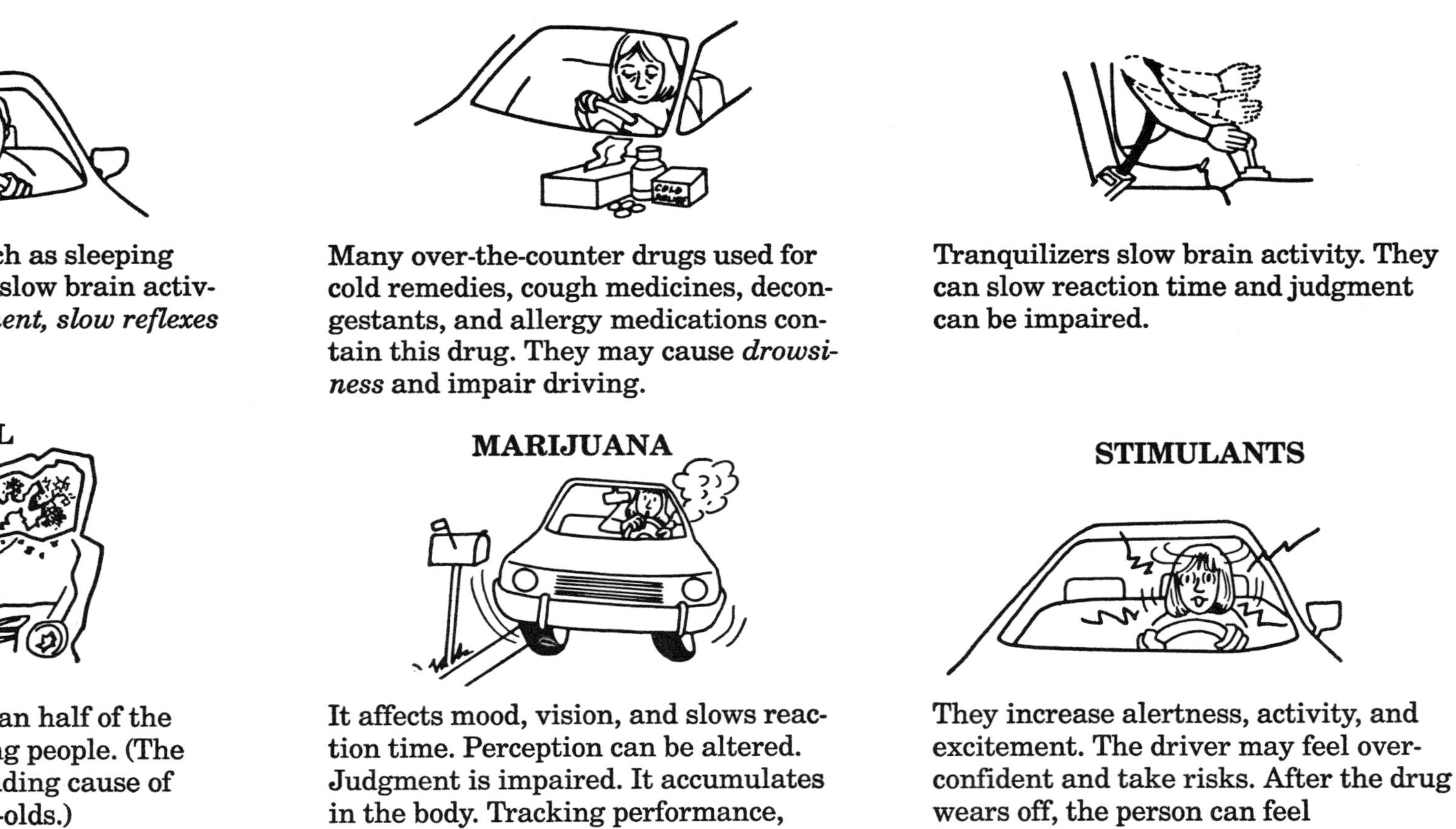

Many over-the-counter drugs used for cold remedies, cough medicines, decongestants, and allergy medications contain this drug. They may cause *drowsiness* and impair driving.

TRANQUILIZERS

Tranquilizers slow brain activity. They can slow reaction time and judgment can be impaired.

ALCOHOL

Alcohol is a sedative drug!

It accounts for more than half of the auto accidents for young people. (The auto accident is the leading cause of death for 15 to 19 year-olds.)

MARIJUANA

It affects mood, vision, and slows reaction time. Perception can be altered. Judgment is impaired. It accumulates in the body. Tracking performance, glare recovery, and motor coordination are affected.

STIMULANTS

They increase alertness, activity, and excitement. The driver may feel overconfident and take risks. After the drug wears off, the person can feel depressed.

Shedding a Little Light:

- Read the over-the-counter drug label warnings.
- Ask if prescription medicines will affect driving.
- DO NOT MIX ALCOHOL AND OTHER DRUGS. This combination accounts for many Emergency Room visits.

Marijuana and Driving

One marijuana cigarette can affect driving skills 6 or more hours after use, unlike one beer with an effect of about 1 hour.

Driving Skills That Marijuana Impairs	Driving Situations Requiring That Skill
Coordination:	All
Reaction time:	Changing traffic lights; sudden appearance of a child; abrupt slowing of a car ahead.
Ability to follow a moving object:	Lane change or movement of a car ahead.
Perception of flashing lights:	Flashing traffic lights; directional or braking signal by a car ahead.
Perception of objects near the edge of the field of vision:	Sudden appearance of another car from behind in an adjoining lane; sudden appearance of a pedestrian crossing the street.
Ability to recover quickly from the perceptual changes caused by bright light:	Sudden appearance of an oncoming car at the top of a hill or at the bend of a curve at night.

NOTE: Nearly all studies of traffic fatalities have shown that the majority of marijuana users also have high blood alcohol levels.

BEHIND THE WHEEL 14-1

Objective:

- To inform the students of the effects of alcohol and other drugs on driving performance

Activities:

1. Review Fact Sheet 18.
2. Have the students review Fact Sheet 19 and Fact Sheet 20.
3. There are many factors that influence how alcohol will affect an individual.
   a. To recognize that *body weight* affects the degree of intoxication, have the students make a "picture graph" by filling in the figures with the symbols designated in Activity 14-1A, "What's the Difference?" Observe the relationship of alcohol intake, body weight, and accident potential.
   b. Then, they are to list three other factors that influence the way alcohol affects a person. It can include:
      - the *amount* of alcohol taken,
      - the *amount of time* in which alcohol is taken,
      - age,
      - previous drinking experience,
      - the presence of other drugs in the system,
      - the general mood of the individual,
      - the setting in which it is used,
      - presence of food in the stomach.
4. Direct the students to complete Activity 14B, "Playing It Safe." The students can share their answers with the class, and discuss the responses.
5. Divide the class into groups of four to six students. Direct them to:
   a. design a "Drugs and Driving" poster or "Don't Drink and Drive" poster. Encourage creativity. The posters may be hung in the classroom for a period of time.
   b. "adopt" a class in a lower grade to present a lesson about drugs and driving, using the posters.
6. The students can evaluate their knowledge of the material covered by completing Activity 14C, "A Road Test." Answers: 1. c; 2. d; 3.a, b; 4. a; 5. d; 6. b; 7. a,c; 8. c,d; 9. e; 10. c.

Name ______________________________

Date ______________________________

What's the Difference?

There are many factors that influence how alcohol will affect an individual. To recognize that *body weight* affects the degree of intoxication, fill in each figure below as indicated:

	BAC %	*CONDITION*	*CHANCE OF ACCIDENTS*
Color all areas blue	.00-.04	You are *affected.*	Accidents increase.
Color all areas green	.05-.09	You are *impaired.*	Accidents double.
Color all areas black	.10-.14	You are *drunk.*	6× greater increase.
Color all areas red	.15 and up	You are *dead drunk.*	25× greater increase.

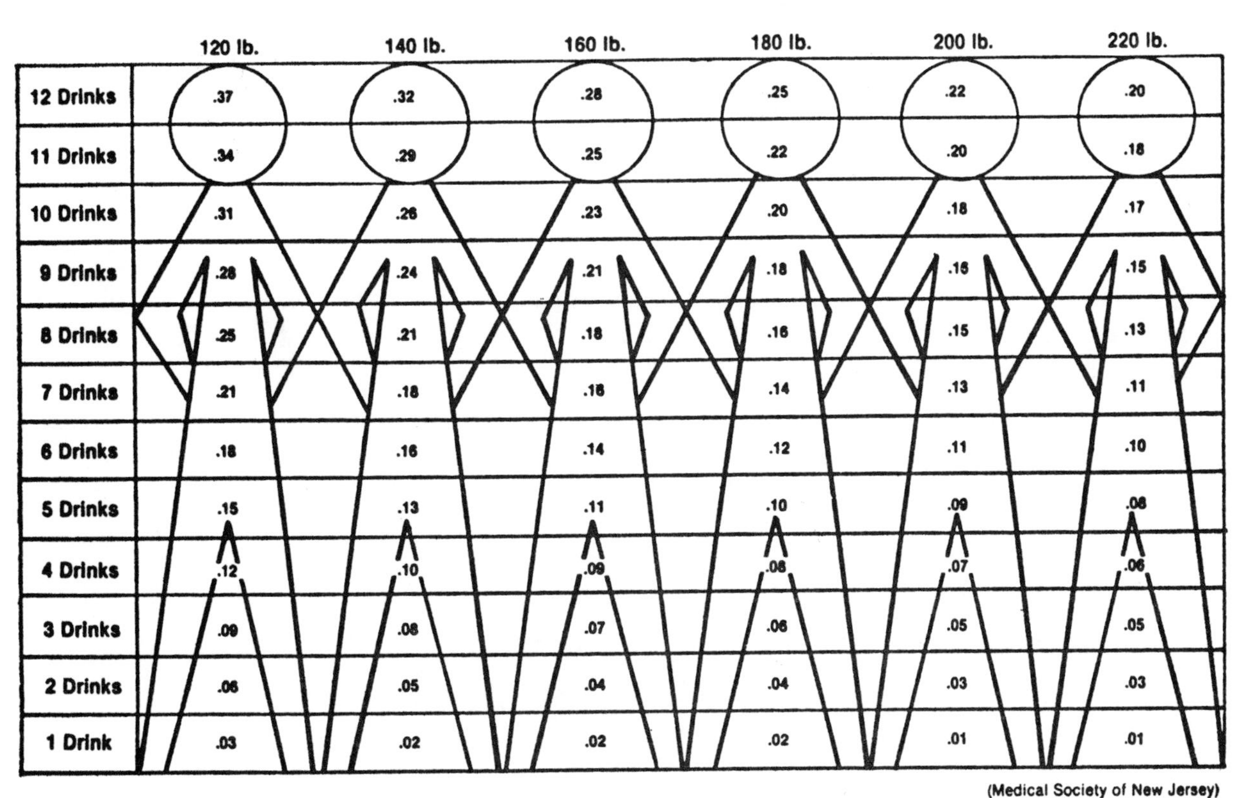

	120 lb.	140 lb.	160 lb.	180 lb.	200 lb.	220 lb.
12 Drinks	.37	.32	.28	.25	.22	.20
11 Drinks	.34	.29	.25	.22	.20	.18
10 Drinks	.31	.26	.23	.20	.18	.17
9 Drinks	.28	.24	.21	.18	.16	.15
8 Drinks	.25	.21	.18	.16	.15	.13
7 Drinks	.21	.18	.16	.14	.13	.11
6 Drinks	.18	.16	.14	.12	.11	.10
5 Drinks	.15	.13	.11	.10	.09	.08
4 Drinks	.12	.10	.09	.08	.07	.06
3 Drinks	.09	.08	.07	.06	.05	.05
2 Drinks	.06	.05	.04	.04	.03	.03
1 Drink	.03	.02	.02	.02	.01	.01

(Medical Society of New Jersey)

(Medical Society of New Jersey — one hour period)

List three other factors that influence how alcohol affects a person:

1. ______________________________

2. ______________________________

3. ______________________________

Name ________________________________

Date ________________________________

Playing it Safe

Complete the following stories on a separate sheet of paper.

1. Your friend has just gotten his driver's license. He wants to take you for a drive around the neighborhood. You jump at the chance! He stops off at a friend's house. Your driver decides to drink a few beers with his friend. After they finish a six-pack, he wants you to get back into the car so he can take you home. You don't drive. No one is at your house. You ---------
2. Mrs. Potter is a single parent who has to work. She sends her 3-year-old son Chris to a day care center. You work as a teacher's aide after school. You notice that the neighbor who picks up Chris on her way home has the smell of liquor on her breath today, and she seems unsteady on her feet. You ---------
3. Mary has had too much to drink. Her friend wants to help her to "sober up" before she drives home, so she gives her a cup of coffee. Mary gets her coat to leave for her car. You ---------
4. Your older brother shouts out to your mother, who is working in the kitchen, "I'm taking the keys to the car. I need to pick up something at the store. I'll be right back." You notice he looks "high." You ---------
5. You are being picked up for a date by someone you really like and want to impress. When he comes, he seems a little slow to respond to your questions and the whites of his eyes appear red. He is driving a new red convertible. He hands you a long-stem red rose. You ---------

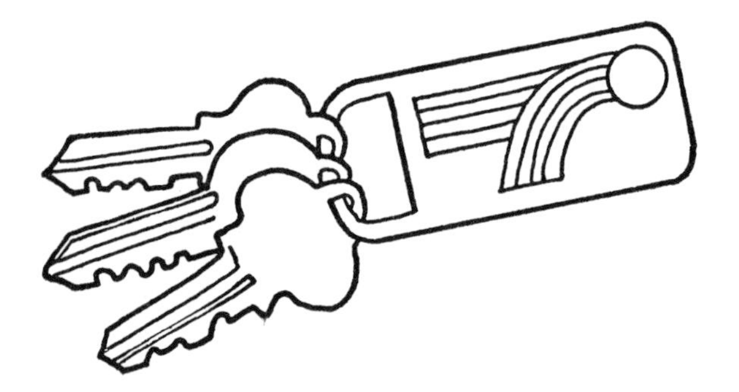

Name ______________________________

Date ______________________________

A Road Test

1. The single greatest hazard that young Americans face is:
   (a) disease, (b) suicide, (c) automobile accidents, (d) war.

2. Alcohol use accounts for a large number of:
   (a) household accidents, (b) automobile accidents, (c) boating accidents, (d) all of the above.

3. Alcohol is a (select two of the answers):
   (a) depressant, (b) stimulant, (c) aphrodisiac, (d) drug.

4. An instrument *most often* used to show if a driver has been drinking alcohol is:
   (a) a breathalizer, (b) a barometer, (c) litmus paper, (d) a vision chart.

5. Studies show that driving performance may be impaired with blood alcohol concentration levels as low as:
   (a) 0.04%, (b) 0.10% (c) 0.08%, (d) 0.02%.

6. The effect of using two or more drugs (including alcohol) at the same time may *greatly increase* the drug's effect on the person. This dangerous phenomenon is called the:
   (a) Total Effect, (b) Synergistic Effect, (c) Pasteur Phenomenon, (d) Saturation Level.

7. A driver who has taken "uppers" (stimulants) may (select 2 of the answers):
   (a) overestimate his abilities, (b) drink more coffee, (c) take more risks, (d) drive alone.

8. Using marijuana will (select 2 of the answers):
   (a) enhance driving skills, (b) have no effect on driving, (c) will show up on drug tests days later because it accumulates in the fatty cells of the body, (d) will alter vision and perception of the driver.

9. The drug alcohol is present in which of the following:
   (a) beer, (b) champale, (c) wine cooler, (d) most over-the-counter cough medicines, (e) all of the above.

10. ____________ can detect drug use, and also reveal a longer pattern of use than urine and blood tests:
    (a) X-ray exams, (b) skin scratch test, (c) hair analysis, (d) CAT scan.

DRIVING AND THE LAW 14-2

Objective:

- To have the students learn about the laws and penalties of their state related to drugs and driving

Activities:

1. Invite a speaker from the Intoxicated Driver Resource Center in your area to speak to the students about their program of education and referral. (Be sure that they include the *fee* to the driver for miscellaneous costs.)
2. Invite a law enforcement officer to talk to the class about his/her work dealing with drivers under the influence of alcohol and other drugs (including assessment, arrest, arraignment, etc.).
3. Persons who are found guilty of driving while under the influence of alcohol and other drugs are subject to substantial legal penalties. To learn more about this, have the students research and collect information on:
   a. State DWI laws and penalties for the *first offense*, the *second offense*, and the *third offense*; open container-in-the-vehicle, etc. (These may include suspension of the driver's license, revocation of the driver's license, fines, community service, and jail terms.)
   b. The *insurance penalties* for driving under the influence of alcohol or other drugs.
   c. Elect a secretary to organize and type the information. (It would be effective to create a poster presenting the information in large, clear printing.)
      —Post the material in a prominent place for easy referral by the students.
      —You may also have the students copy the information on the form provided in Activity 14-2A, "Penalty Box," to keep for their own use.
4. Inform the students that in an effort to further motivate young people to stop using drugs, several states (Oregon, New Jersey, and Missouri are among them), have passed laws that encourage teenagers to stay away from drugs to *protect their privilege to drive.* Provisions in these laws have stipulated that students of driving age found in *violation of any drug or alcohol laws would lose their driving privilege* for 6 months to a year (depending on the state).

   Students found in possession of alcohol or other drugs *before* receiving a driver's license would have to *wait* 6 months to a year (depending on the state) past the normal date of eligibility before applying for a driver's license. (This penalty would be imposed *whether or not a motor vehicle was involved.)* Does a similar law exist in your state?

a. To explore the economic and social impact of having a driver's license suspended or revoked for violating drug and driving laws, have the students brainstorm the following questions:
   (1) After determining the amount of the fine for either a first, second, *or* third offense, determine how you would pay the fee.
   (2) How *else* would you have used the money? (concerts, clothes, gifts, saving for a car, saving for college, etc.)
   (3) How would you get to a job?
   (4) How would you pick up a date?

5. It is necessary to complete Activity 11-3, "Drinking and Behavior," before doing the next activity. Then instruct the students to complete Activity 14-2B, "Predicting Possible Performance," to recognize (a) how *time* and *weight* influence the degree of intoxication; (b) how your *B*lood *A*lcohol *C*ontent (BAC) might predict your possible performance in daily life activities, including driving; (c) what consequences might result from your behavior. (Be specific about the consequences and penalties for each driver.)

Shedding a Little Light:
In October 1990, a pilot, co-pilot, and flight engineer were given jail sentences from 12 to 18 months for being intoxicated *behind the wheel of an airplane.*

Name ____________________

Date ____________________

Penalty Box

FIRST OFFENSE:	*INSURANCE COSTS:*
SECOND OFFENSE:	*PHASES AND FEES OF THE LOCAL ALCOHOL COUNTERMEASURE PROGRAM:*
THIRD OFFENSE:	*ADDITIONAL INFORMATION:*

Name ______________________________

Date ______________________________

Predicting Possible Performance

1. A young man who is 5 feet, 9 inches, weighing 169 lbs., consumes four 8-oz. cans of beer in an hour. Use the BAC wheel to find his probably BAC level after 1/2 hour.
   a. Complete the following activity to determine the effect of the alcohol on the man and his activities over a period of time. Be specific about any penalties given for driving.

Time	*BAC level*	*Visible Effects*
1/2 hour	____________	____________________
		____________________
		____________________
		____________________
1-1/2 hours	____________	____________________
		____________________
		____________________
		____________________
3 hours	____________	____________________
		____________________
		____________________
		____________________

   b. In the first 1/2 hour, how might it affect his performance:

      walking ______________________________

      lathering his face and shaving ______________________________

      figuring out his income tax ______________________________

   c. What consequences, if any, would there be for the young man if he was stopped by a police officer while driving his car within the first hour after he had been drinking?

   ____

   ____

Continued

2. A young woman who is 5 feet, 2 inches tall, weighing 110 lbs., consumes four 5-ounce glasses of wine within 1 hour.
   a. Complete the following activity to determine the effect of the alcohol on the woman and her activities over a period of time. Be specific about any penalties given for driving.

Time	*BAC level*	*Visible Effects*
1/2 hour	____________	____________________
		____________________
		____________________
		____________________
1-1/2 hours	____________	____________________
		____________________
		____________________
		____________________
3 hours	____________	____________________
		____________________
		____________________
		____________________

   b. Within the first hour, how would it affect her performance:

applying eye makeup ____________________

preparing a meal ____________________

filling out a job application ____________________

   c. What consequences, if any, would there be for the young woman if she drove her car within the first hour, should she be stopped by a police officer? ____________________

____

____

____

____

Drugs and Pregnancy

THE MOTHER

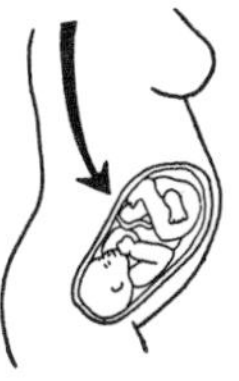

1. Almost *every* drug used by the mother has an effect on the developing baby.
2. The substances pass through the placenta from the mother's bloodstream into the baby's bloodstream.
3. The mother may not be aware of her pregnancy in the early stages. Although a woman may discontinue taking drugs once she learns of her pregnancy, there may *already* be consequences for the fetus.

THE CHILD

1. Drugs have such profound effects on the developing baby because the *liver*, which breaks down a drug to rid the body of the poison, does not completely develop until *after birth.*
2. A *baby* born to a woman who is addicted to alcohol and/or other drugs may show signs of being *addicted at birth.*
   - The baby, then, must be treated for the physical problems associated with *withdrawing* from a drug.

THE DRUG

1. The child born with birth defects due to the mother's use of *alcohol* during pregnancy is said to have FAS. (See Activity 15-1 about FAS, [Fetal Alcohol Syndrome].)
2. *Smoking* during pregnancy causes: (a) dramatic reduction in the oxygen supply to the fetus, (b) decreased birth weight *in direct proportion to the number of cigarettes smoked,* (c) increased risk of miscarriages.
3. *Marijuana* use during pregnancy may cause the baby to be born with birth defects similar to FAS.
   - A decreased birth weight is *in direct proportion to the number of marijuana cigarettes* used.
4. *Cocaine/Crack* used by pregnant women causes: (a) impaired oxygen delivery to the fetus, (b) an abrupt rise in blood pressure, (c) early increase of uterine contractions, (d) high incidents of hemorrhage and anemia for the mother after she gives birth.
   - There appears to be a greater increase of SIDS (Sudden Infant Death Syndrome—unexplained natural early death of the young baby.)

Shedding a Little Light:
- *AIDS can be transmitted from the mother to her child.*
- *NO SAFE* level of alcohol has been established.
- Developmental disabilities due to the use of alcohol and/or other drugs are preventable.

PASSING ON THE PROBLEM 15-1

Objectives:

- To identify the dangers of taking drugs during pregnancy
- To become aware of the effects of alcohol and other drugs on the unborn baby, the family, and the community

Activities:

1. Review and discuss Fact Sheet 21.
2. To learn more about the Fetal Alcohol Syndrome (FAS):
   a. Have the students define the following words:
      cleft palate hyperactivity syndrome
      detoxified fetus placenta
   b. Now, review FAS in Activity 15-1A.
   c. Assign each of the students to read a chapter in the book *The Broken Cord* by Michael Dorris, published by Harper and Row. (It describes the problems of children born with FAS, as well as its devastating effects on the family and on society.)
   d. The students can report to the class on the chapter that they were assigned. Discuss the information.
3. Invite a speaker from the March of Dimes to talk to the class about birth defects resulting from taking drugs during pregnancy.
4. Alcohol remains the *most abused* drug. The use of crack/cocaine is increasing.
   a. Use the chalkboard to write some of the more severe effects that will be experienced by the children of women who abuse these drugs during pregnancy.
      First list each effect, and then ask the students to suggest a behavior that might result from it.
      (E—will indicate the EFFECT of the drug use.
      R—will indicate the RESULT of that limitation.)
   b. Then, brainstorm with the class how some of the limitations of the children will impact on: (a) the family, (b) the schools, and (c) their future work.

Example:

Alcohol FAS	Crack/Cocaine
1. E = exhibits no self control R = (impulsive behavior) 2. E = no abstract thinking R = (no problem-solving skills) 3. E = unable to follow directions R = (on a box of gelatin) 4. E = does not distinguish right from wrong R = (may take things that do not belong to him/her) 5. E = needs frequent reminders to do ordinary things R = (personal hygiene, eat, etc).	1. E = convulsion, cerebral palsy R = (limited physically) 2. E = hyperactivity R = (short attention span) 3. E = has trouble interpreting nonverbal signals R = (difficulty in social interaction) 4. E = easily frustrated R = (acts out anger) 5. E = overwhelmed by too much activity or noises R = (irritability)

5. Have the students study "Drugs and AIDS, The High Risk Group" in Activity 15-1B to understand how the "problem is passed on."
6. The students can complete Activity 15-1C, "Make a Change," to test their knowledge. Answers:

ACROSS

1. RETARDATION
2. NO SAFE
3. MEDICINE
4. BREASTFEEDING
5. WITHDRAWAL
6. BIRTH WEIGHT, NUMBER

DOWN

1. DRUNK
2. FAS
3. ANY
4. BIRTH
5. SEIZURES
6. LIVER
7. AIDS
8. OXYGEN
9. FAE
10. ADDICTED

Shedding a Little Light:
Predisposition to problem drinking can be inherited. Studies show several psychological, neurophysiological, and biochemical differences in Children of Alcoholics. The change is seen before, during, and after alcohol abuse.

FAS
(Fetal Alcohol Syndrome)

Since biblical times it has been noted that babies born to drinking mothers showed signs of physical and mental problems. Modern studies first published in 1973 confirmed these observations. These characteristics of babies born with alcohol-related birth defect are called the *Fetal Alcohol Syndrome* or *FAS.*

FAS IS A PATTERN OF PHYSICAL, MENTAL, AND BEHAVIORAL DEFECTS THAT MAY DEVELOP IN AN UNBORN BABY OF A PREGNANT WOMAN WHO CONSUMES ALCOHOL.
LESS SEVERE BIRTH DEFECTS ASSOCIATED WITH ALCOHOL USE ARE CALLED FAE—*Fetal Alcohol Effect.*

A.
PHYSICAL

- shorter height
- lighter weight
- skeletal defects
- poor coordination
- genital defects
- cleft palate
- heart valve defects

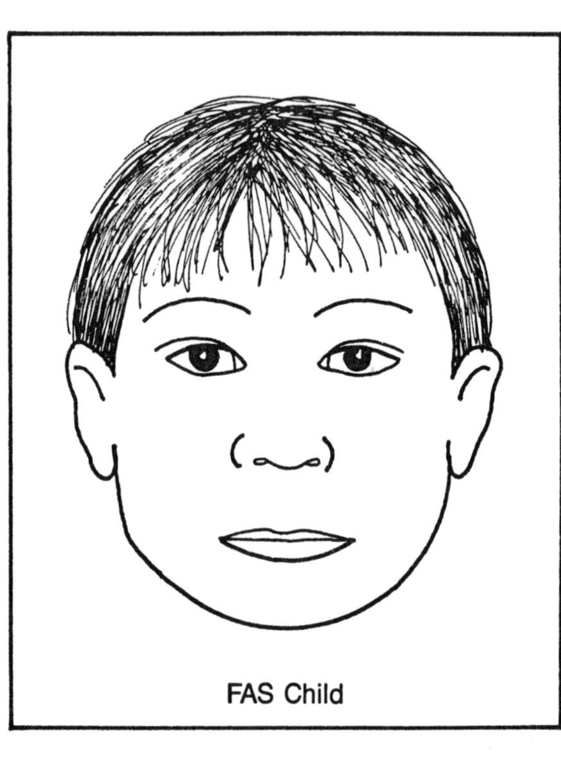

FAS Child

B.
MENTAL

- mental retardation
- learning disabilities (short attention span, behavioral difficulties)
- central nervous system involvement causing irritability and hyperactivity

C. *FACIAL DEFORMITIES with distinctive features;*
Smaller head, widely spaced eyes, flatter nose, sunken nasal bridge, short receding chin

Shedding a Little Light:
1. It is the third leading cause of birth-defect-mental retardation.
2. Most of the child's problems will last a lifetime.
3. It is preventable!

Drugs and AIDS
The High Risk Group

AIDS is a disease caused by the HIV virus. It attacks a person's immune system, making it ineffective in fighting off infections and diseases. There is no cure for AIDS at this time. It is deadly.

> Transmission of the AIDS virus from person to person requires that the virus leave the infected person through the blood or semen and enter the other person's bloodstream. One exposure to the AIDS virus is enough to become infected.

ROUTES OF TRANSMISSION

A. PAST OR PRESENT ABUSERS OF INTRAVENOUS DRUGS

Infection can come from *sharing needles.* Some blood always remains in the *syringe.*

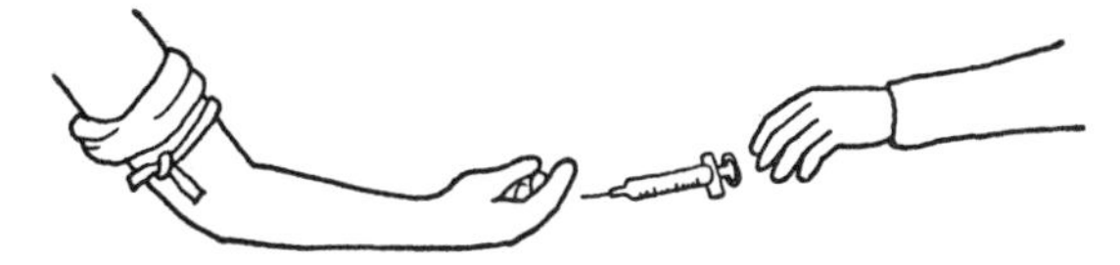

The IV drug user has become the "gateway" of the virus to the heterosexual community.

C. INFANTS BORN TO INFECTED MOTHERS

Often, the mother has a drug history, or a sexual partner with an IV drug history.

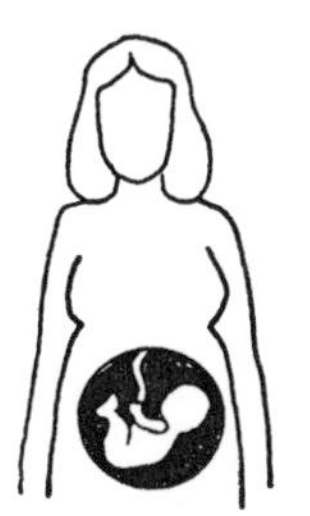

AIDS can be transmitted from:
- mother to fetus during pregnancy through the placenta
- from mother to infant during the birth process
- from mother's milk to infant during breastfeeding

B. SEXUAL CONTACT WITH SOMEONE INFECTED WITH THE VIRUS

Sexual intercourse, vaginal intercourse, anal intercourse, and oral-genital sex with a partner who was a past or present IV drug user may transmit the virus.

Women of childbearing age must know their child could be infected if the mother has been infected.

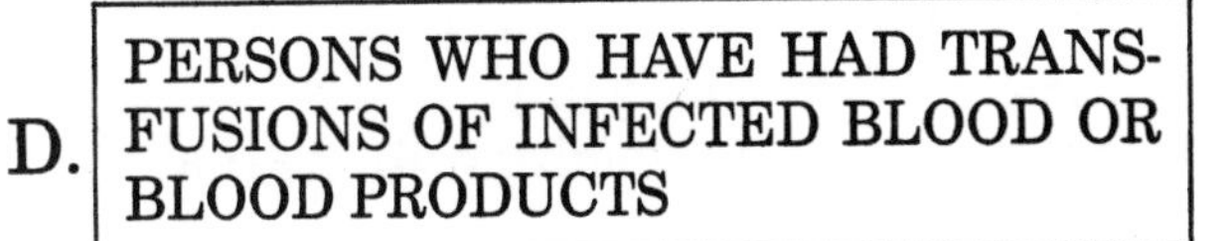

D. PERSONS WHO HAVE HAD TRANSFUSIONS OF INFECTED BLOOD OR BLOOD PRODUCTS

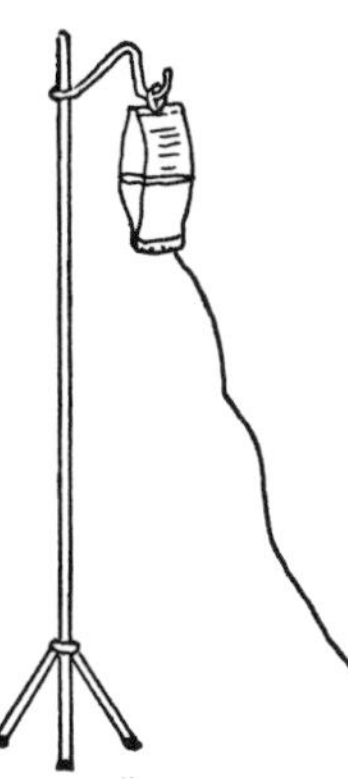

The risk of contracting this disease from blood products has been greatly reduced.

There is no danger in *donating* blood.

(See AIDS Appendix 3A-1 to 3A-5)

Name ______________________________

Date ______________________________

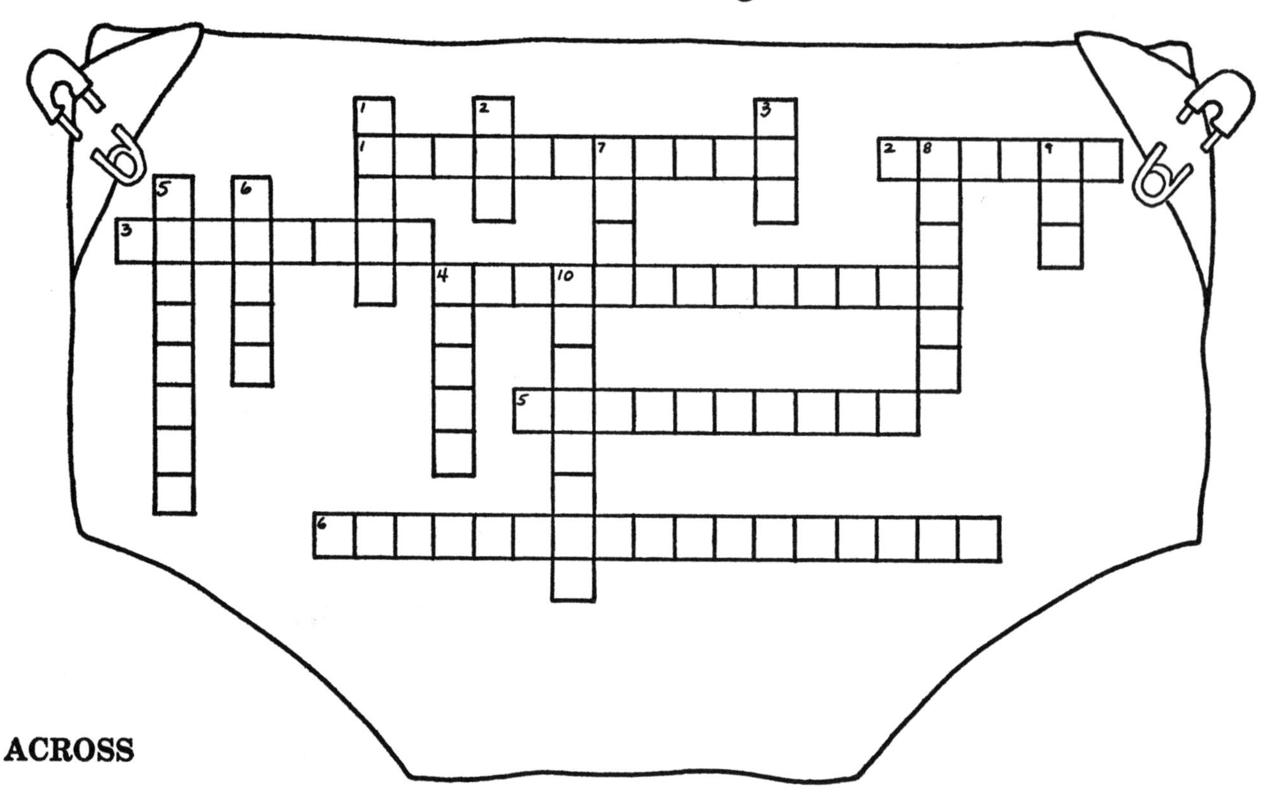

ACROSS

1. FAS is one of the leading causes of ____.
2. ____ ____ level of drinking has been established. (2 words)
3. Pregnant women should check with a doctor before taking any ____.
4. AIDS can be transmitted to the baby through ____.
5. Babies who are addicted at birth will have ____ symptoms.
6. Smoking cigarettes decreases the child's ____ ____ in direct proportion to the ____ of cigarettes smoked. (3 words)

DOWN

1. A drunk pregnant woman has a ____ fetus.
2. Marijuana use during pregnancy may produce defects similar to ____.
3. ____ amount of alcohol can affect the unborn baby.
4. A baby's liver does not completely develop until after ____.
5. Cocaine-affected babies can have ____.
6. The organ of the body that detoxifies drugs is the ____.
7. An infected mother can transmit ____ to her child.
8. Smoking slows down the delivery of ____ to the fetus.
9. The less severe birth defects that may develop for the baby if the pregnant woman consumes alcohol is called ____.
10. Babies born to a woman who is addicted to alcohol or other drugs can be born ____.

HEALTH ALERT! 15-2

Objective:

- To inform the students of the government warnings on alcoholic beverages and the penalties for non-compliance

Activities:

1. Inform the students that a bill was signed into law by Ronald Reagan on November 18, 1988, requiring alcoholic beverages produced to have a warning label:

> **WARNING**
>
> 1. According to the Surgeon General, women should not drink alcoholic beverages during pregnancy because of the risk of birth defects.
> 2. Consumption of alcoholic beverages impairs your ability to drive a car or operate machinery, and may cause health problems.

—Companies may be penalized up to $10,000 a day for not complying.
—Advocates of this label say the current wording may not go far enough and are urging the bureau to strengthen it.

2. Have the students break up into small groups. Using the facts they have learned in this section on *drugs and pregnancy*, ask each group: (a) to design another warning to improve on the message or (b) to create an ad or a "1-minute" TV spot to inform pregnant women about the dangers of alcohol and pregnancy. They will present their "creations" to the class.

Chemical Dependency

GETTING SICK

1. Abuse of alcohol and other mood-altering drugs can lead to the disease of *chemical dependency* (addiction).
2. Chemical dependency is a chronic, progressive, and potentially fatal disease.
3. It is characterized by three criteria: A *tolerance* develops. It now requires more and more of the drug to give the desired effect. *Dependency* occurs when the body and/or the mind become accustomed to the presence of the drug and its effects. The unpleasant physical and emotional symptoms resulting when *the drug is stopped* are called *withdrawal symptoms.*
4. The drug becomes the *most* important thing in the person's life, taking more and more time and energy. Essential daily functions begin to be neglected.
5. The inability to function effectively (due to the use of alcohol and other drugs) causes many problems for the chemically dependent person in all areas of his or her life: family, job, school, money, health, and legal. *Nevertheless, the person continues to use drugs despite the problems it is causing.*
6. Chemical dependency is a potentially fatal disease if it is not treated.

The biggest deterrent to getting help is
the DENIAL that a problem with drugs exists!

Continued

GETTING WELL

1. Chemical dependency is a *treatable* disease.
2. While there is *no cure*, it can be arrested. A person with this disease can return to a happy, useful, *drug-free* life.
3. There are many people who are specially trained to help those who are addicted to alcohol and other drugs when they want to begin the process of getting well. There are *treatment centers* and *self-help groups*.
4. Alcoholics Anonymous, Narcotics Anonymous, Cocaine Anonymous, and Pills Anonymous are each a fellowship of men and women who come together to offer each other hope, experience, and support to live a productive life, free of alcohol and other drugs.
5. Al-Anon, Nar-Anon, and Families Anonymous are fellowships of wives, husbands, children, relatives, and friends whose lives are affected by the alcohol/drug-abuser. Through the group experience, they share their strength and hope with each other in order to understand and overcome the problems resulting from this family disease. The chemically dependent person *need not* be willing to get help in order for family members to seek treatment.

RELAPSE

1. After the chemically dependent person has successfully stopped using the drug of choice—he or she may *NEVER* again use *ANY* mood-altering drugs *without activating his/her disease..*
2. The use of any drug that causes the disease to re-activate is called *Relapse.* All the former destructive symptoms will return, probably even *more intense* than before.
3. It is important for the person to reach out for help immediately and abstain from any further drug taking.

WHAT IS CHEMICAL DEPENDENCY? 16-1

Objective:

- To inform the students of facts about the disease of chemical dependency

Activities:

1. Review "Getting Sick" on Fact Sheet 22.
2. No one sets out to be chemically dependent. It is a subtle, insidious, "downhill" process. It can be explained as a *change in RELATIONSHIP* (1) to oneself, (2) to others, and (3) to drugs. (Keep in mind the amount of time and energy a *relationship* requires.)
   a. Review with the students the stages and pattern of progression of dependency by studying the information and diagrams in: Activity 16-1A, "Social/Experimental/Recreational Use"; Activity 16-1B, "More Regular Use"; Activity 16-1C, "Daily Preoccupation"; and Activity 16-1D, "Dependency/Addiction."

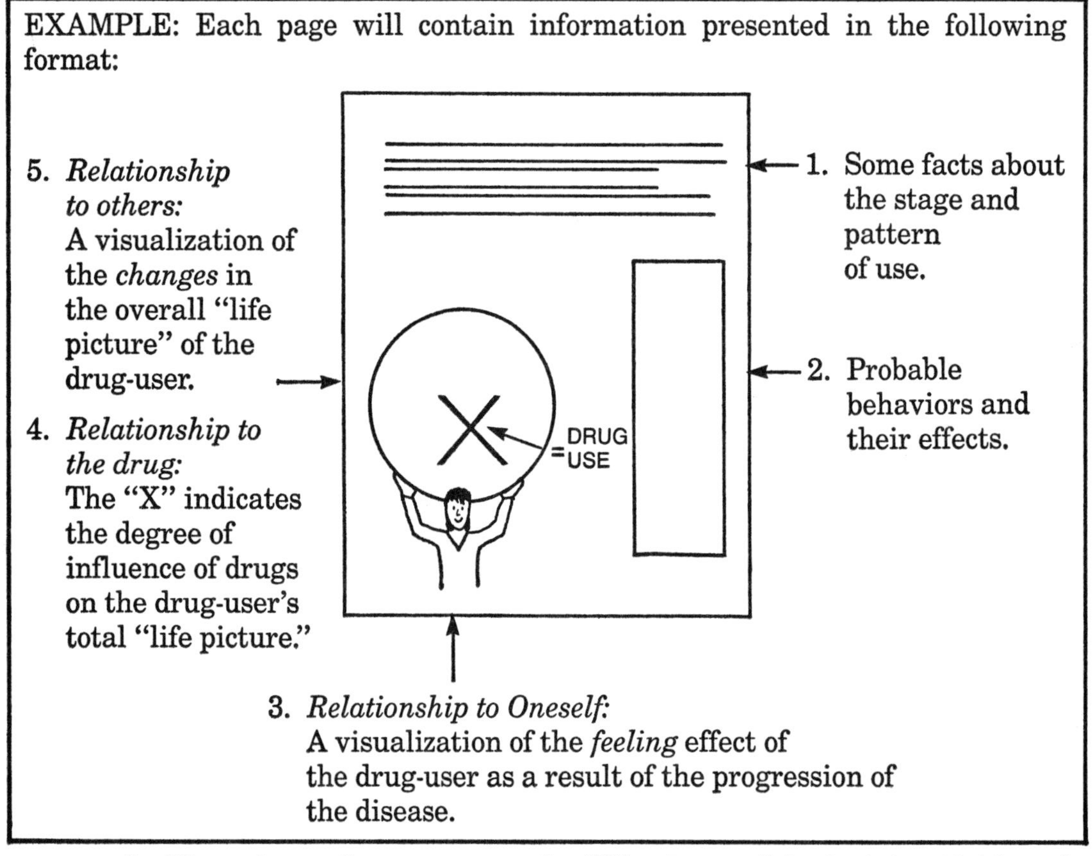

   b. Have the students compare the "life pictures" in Activity 16-1A and 16-1B. Note the beginning of losses.

c. Have the students critique the *thoughts* and *feelings* that the drug-abuser may be experiencing in Activity 16-1C, considering his "life picture" and the fact that his attempts to *stop* have been unsuccessful.
d. In Activity 16-1D, note the all-consuming power of the drug. Reinforce that it is a treatable disease.

3. Distribute Activity 16-1E, "The Course of Chemical Dependency," to the students for an overall view of progression and recovery.
4. Have the students complete Activity 16-1F, "Can You Tell?"
5. The students can complete the crossword puzzle, "Hooked," in Activity 16-1G. Answers:

   ACROSS—1. ALCOHOL, 2. BRAIN, 3. WITHDRAWAL, 4. RELAPSE, 5. CURED, 6. FATAL, 7. DISEASE; DOWN—1. ADOLESCENT, 2. DENIAL, 3. TOLERANCE, 4. ACTIVATE, 5. NAR-ANON.

6. Instruct the students to complete the alcohol questionnaire in Activity 16-1H. *The students will not share their answers.* (Be prepared with appropriate referral information if any student approaches you for help.)
7. Have the students complete Activity 16-1I, "Understanding the Problem, An Alcoholism Quiz." Then review the answers to that activity using "Understanding the Problem, Alcoholism Answer Sheet" in Activity 16-1J.

I. Social/Experimentation/Recreational Use

1.

The drug is being used "recreationally" in a social group with friends. The person using alcohol or another mind/mood-altering drug likes the good *feeling* it gives him/her.

RELATIONSHIP TO OTHERS:

THE LIFE PICTURE

5.

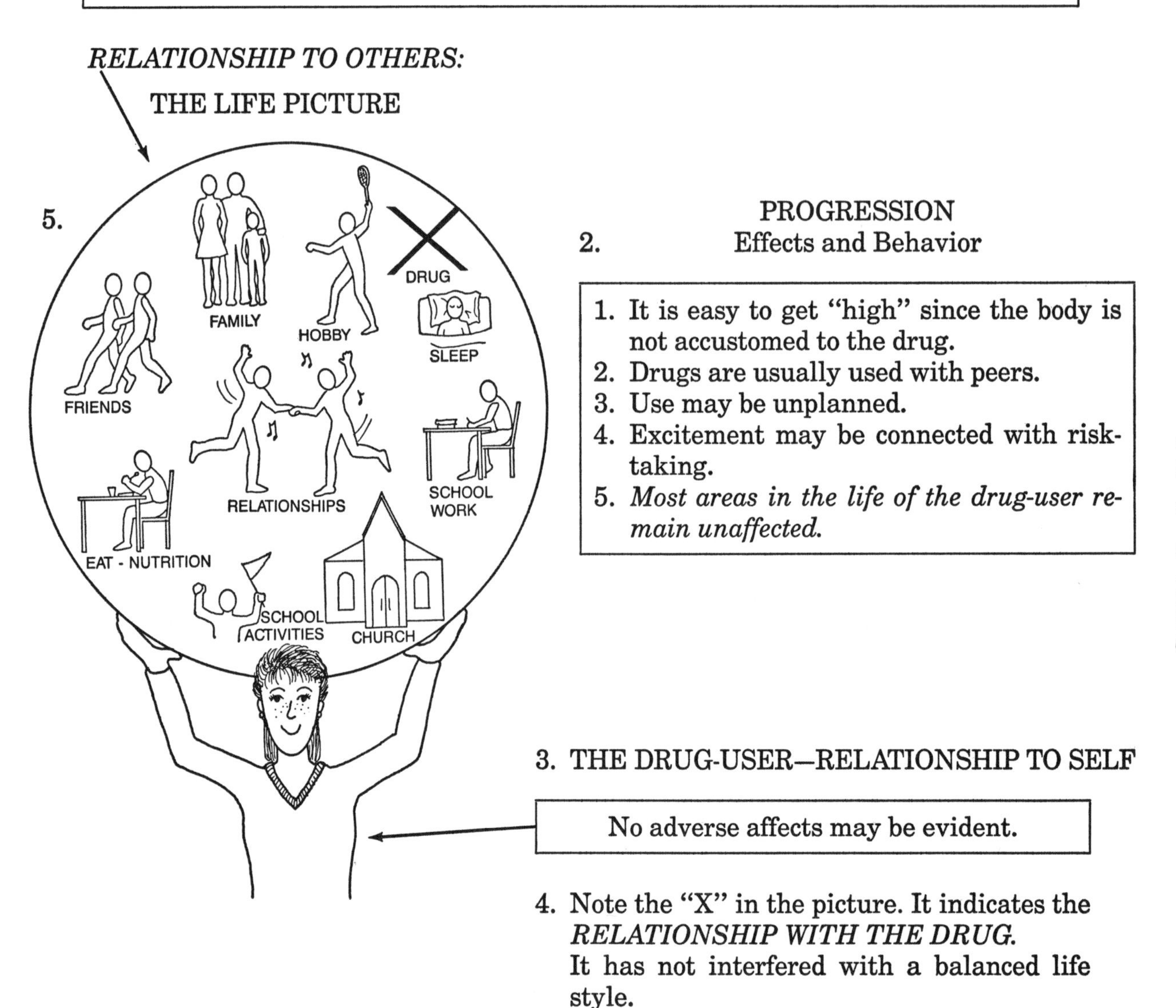

2. PROGRESSION
Effects and Behavior

1. It is easy to get "high" since the body is not accustomed to the drug.
2. Drugs are usually used with peers.
3. Use may be unplanned.
4. Excitement may be connected with risk-taking.
5. *Most areas in the life of the drug-user remain unaffected.*

3. THE DRUG-USER—RELATIONSHIP TO SELF

No adverse affects may be evident.

4. Note the "X" in the picture. It indicates the *RELATIONSHIP WITH THE DRUG.*
It has not interfered with a balanced life style.

II. More Regular Drug Use

1.

The person begins *looking* for the "good" feeling, and returns to using drugs again. The pattern of more regular use, along with some *negative behavioral changes*, can show a move towards a possible dependency. Why is it being used? What behavioral changes occur as a result of the drug use? Finding the answers to these questions can help determine the stage of use.

RELATIONSHIP TO OTHERS:

THE LIFE PICTURE

5.

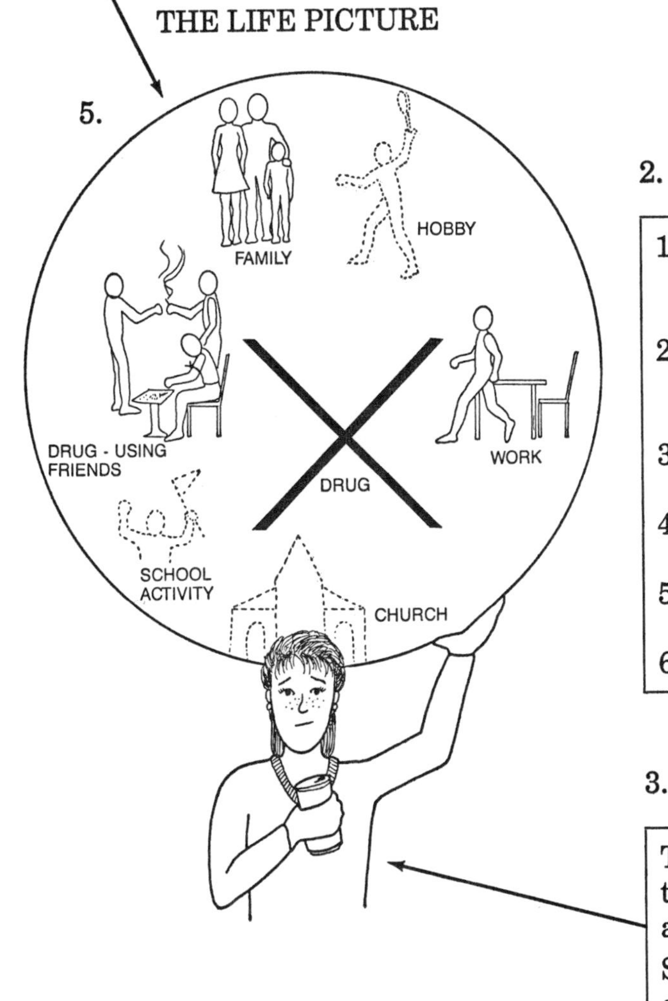

2. PROGRESSION
Effects and Behavior

1. Drug use increases in frequency. More activities include the use of alcohol and other drugs.
2. *Tolerance* for the drug increases. It now takes more of the drug for the desired effect.
3. Lying begins, to explain changes in behavior.
4. Stealing may become a means to pay for drugs.
5. Drinking alcohol or using another drug may be done alone.
6. *Plans* are made to get "high."

3. THE DRUG-USER—RELATIONSHIP TO SELF

The drug use now requires more time and attention—taking away from normal healthy activities.

Some negative emotions are experienced: guilt, loss of self-respect, anxiety, fear.

4. Note The RELATIONSHIP TO THE DRUG enlarging, indicated by the "X" in the picture.

III. Daily Preoccupation

1.

Preoccupation with drugs is one of the major indications of a chemical problem. Increasing amounts of time, energy, and money are spent on thinking about being "high" and insuring that a *steady supply of drugs* is available. The user accepts this as normal.

RELATIONSHIP TO OTHERS:

THE LIFE PICTURE

5.

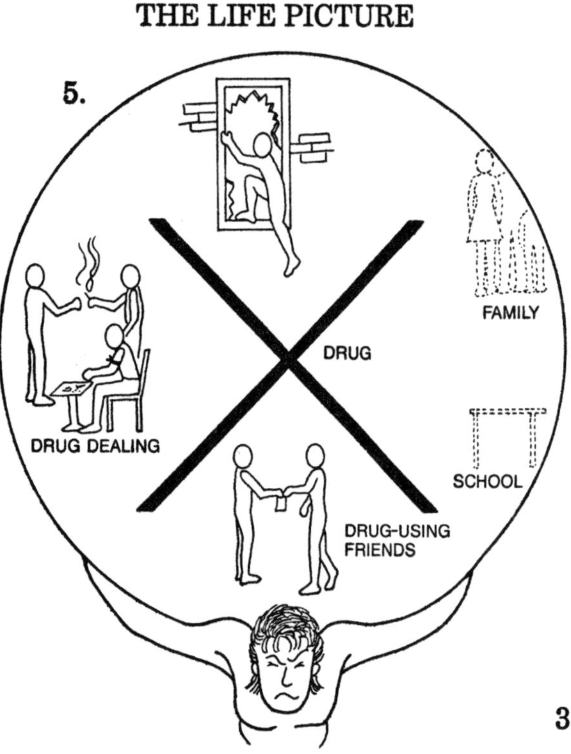

2. PROGRESSION
Effects and Behavior

1. The use of drugs increases.
2. Being "high" becomes "normal."
3. *Unsuccessful* attempts are made to stop using alcohol or other mood-altering drugs.
4. Solitary use increases.
5. Behaviors for obtaining money for drugs may conflict with personal values (i.e., stealing, selling sex).
6. The drug abuser denies that drugs are the problem.

3. THE DRUG-USER—RELATIONSHIP TO SELF

Family, health, financial, and legal problems multiply. The physical and emotional pain increases. The user feels "hooked."

4. The RELATIONSHIP TO THE DRUG ("X") continues to *squeeze out* other relationships and activities in the drug-abuser's life.

IV. Dependency/Addiction

1.

> *There is a complete loss of control.* The chemically dependent person can no longer predict what will happen when he/she begins to use any mood-altering drug. Now, daily, almost constant use is *necessary.* Denial increases....
>
> *Strong defenses* create the delusion that there is *no* problem, even in the face of *overwhelming evidence* that the use of chemicals has led to severe physical, mental, and emotional problems.

RELATIONSHIP TO OTHERS:

THE LIFE PICTURE

5.

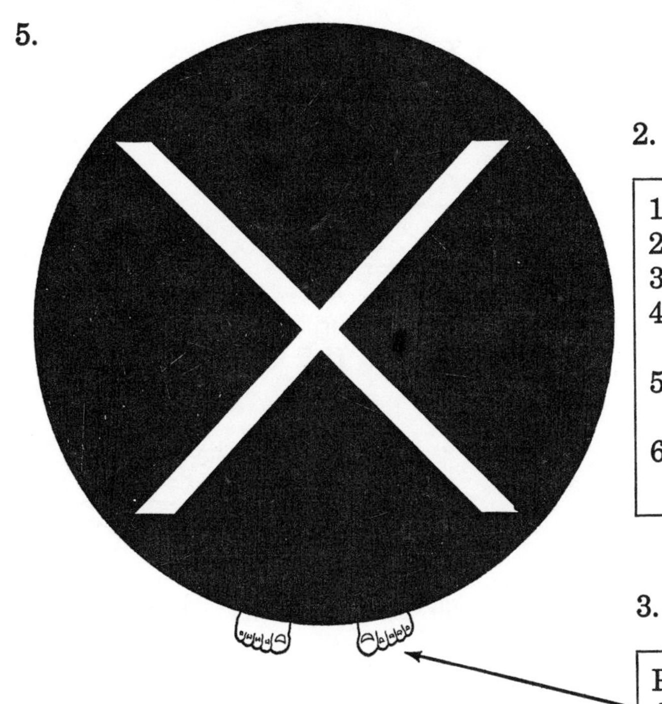

2. PROGRESSION
Effects and Behavior

1. Guilt, shame, and self-hatred increase.
2. Physical deterioration continues.
3. Legal problems increase.
4. Family and old friends may not be there for support.
5. The person now *needs* the drug physically and psychologically just to function.
6. The person fears stopping because of the physical and mental pain that will cause.

3. THE DRUG-USER—RELATIONSHIP TO SELF

> Professional help is needed to stop taking drugs and to "get out from under" the problems of his lifestyle.

4. THE RELATIONSHIP TO THE DRUG ("X") IS NOW ALL-CONSUMING. It is now the center of life.

The Course of Chemical Dependency

GETTING SICK | **GETTING WELL**

PROGRESSION | *RECOVERY*

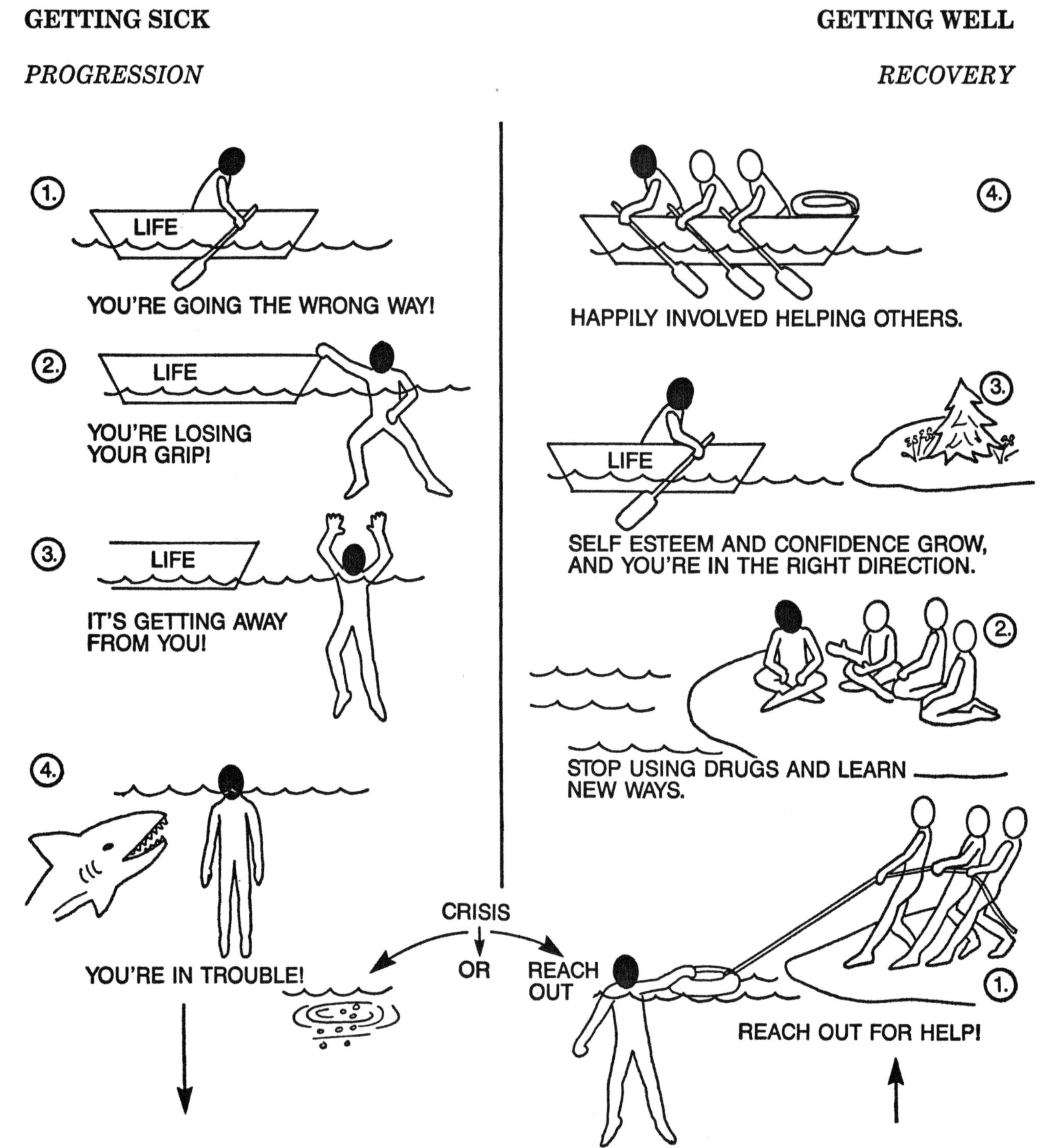

Can You Tell?

1. Read each story.
2. List the *facts* that indicate there may be a problem with alcohol or another drug for each story.
3. Select two stories from the page. On another sheet of paper, write a paragraph explaining what you would like to say to each of them in order to be helpful.

Homemaker

It seems that the doctor gave her some pills to calm her nerves when she felt upset.
Fortunately, she has been able to have them renewed repeatedly.
The doctor knows she's a respected member of the community and will not take them needlessly.
She is beginning to take a pill when she approaches a distressful situation to help her feel comfortable.
She never leaves home without the pills.

Businessman

He has at least two or three cocktails with his business lunch. The pressures of the job are getting to him.
He usually doesn't talk to anyone about how he feels. He takes longer lunch hours lately. His boss is beginning to notice. He drinks several beers when he comes home from work to unwind, and falls asleep. His wife spends a lot of time alone.

Teen

She liked the feeling she got when she "used" some marijuana with her pals.
Now, she "uses" alone.
She is beginning to lie to her family about where she goes. Almost everyone of her friends drinks or smokes marijuana.
School work seems to be getting harder.

Street Person

What else is there for him? He has lost everything. He does not care anymore!
He feels there is no hope.
He is running into physical problems now. The doctor at the clinic told him his liver is "bad."

Doctor

She has easy access to drugs. The hours are long and people expect a lot of her.
She needs to "wind down."
"If you can't take time out—at least you can take something to make it easier to *keep going*," she says.
She isn't worried about getting "hooked" because she is a doctor and knows all about drugs.

Name ____________________

Date ____________________

Hooked!

ACROSS

1. The most abused drug in our society by far is ____.
2. The body organ most sensitive to alcohol is the ____.
3. The unpleasant physical and emotional symptoms that result when the drug is stopped is called ____.
4. When a chemically dependent person returns to using a drug after a period of recovery, it is called a ____.
5. Chemical dependency cannot be ____, but it can be arrested.
6. Chemical dependency is a potentially ____ disease if it is not treated.
7. The ____ of chemical dependency is insidious.

DOWN

1. Families in which one or more member abuses a drug increases the risk of ____ chemical abuse.
2. ____ is the greatest roadblock to accepting help.
3. When the body needs more and more of the drug to get the desired effect, it is called ____.
4. A cocaine user who is in recovery cannot drink beer or it will ____ his/her disease.
5. ____ is a self-help group for families of drug addicts.

Teenager Alcohol Questionnaire

1.	Do you lose time from school due to drinking?	Yes	No
2.	Do you drink because you are shy with other people?	Yes	No
3.	Do you drink to build up your self-confidence?	Yes	No
4.	Do you drink alone?	Yes	No
5.	Is drinking affecting your reputation—and do you care?	Yes	No
6.	Do you drink to escape from study or home worries?	Yes	No
7.	Do you feel guilty after drinking?	Yes	No
8.	Does it bother you if someone says you drink too much?	Yes	No
9.	Do you have to take a drink when you go out on a date?	Yes	No
10.	Do you make out generally better when you have a drink?	Yes	No
11.	Do you get into financial troubles over buying liquor?	Yes	No
12.	Do you feel a sense of power when you drink?	Yes	No
13.	Have you lost friends since you started drinking?	Yes	No
14.	Have you started hanging out with a crowd where the stuff is easy to get?	Yes	No
15.	Do your friends drink less than you do?	Yes	No
16.	Do you drink until the bottle is done?	Yes	No
17.	Have you ever been to a hospital or been "busted" (arrested) for drunk driving?	Yes	No
18.	Have you ever had a complete loss of memory from drinking?	Yes	No
19.	Do you "turn off" to any studies or lectures about drinking?	Yes	No
20.	Do you think you have a problem with liquor?	Yes	No

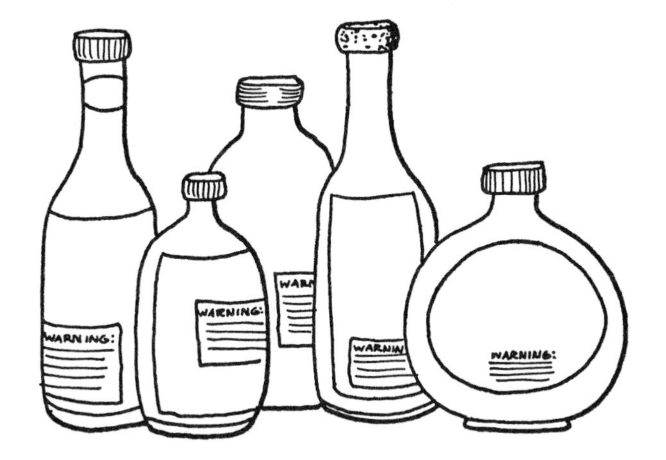

A "yes" to two or more of the above questions ought to be a warning that the respondent is on shaky ground. Alcoholism? Possibly. These are some of the early warning signs.

Name ______________________________

Date ______________________________

Understanding the Problem, an Alcoholism Quiz

	True	False
1. Alcoholism is a potentially fatal disease.	________	________
2. Most alcoholics live on the "streets."	________	________
3. If you only drink beer, you cannot become an alcoholic.	________	________
4. If an alcoholic uses his or her "will power," he or she can stop drinking without any difficulty.	________	________
5. As a child in a home with an alcoholic parent, I know that if I "behaved better" my parent would stop drinking.	________	________
6. If an alcoholic parent loved his or her family enough, he or she would stop drinking.	________	________
7. No treatment is available for the alcoholic.	________	________
8. Alcoholism is a disease.	________	________
9. Alcoholism is a moral weakness.	________	________
10. There is no cure for alcoholism.	________	________
11. If everything ran more smoothly at school or work, the person would not drink anymore.	________	________
12. Alcoholism affects the person's body, mind, and spirit.	________	________
13. A person who is an alcoholic hurts only him or herself.	________	________
14. After treatment, the alcoholic can lead a happy, satisfying life.	________	________

An Alcoholism Quiz—ANSWER SHEET

1. True —Alcoholism is a potentially fatal disease *if not treated.*
2. False—it affects people from all walks of life.
3. False—It is the *ethyl alcohol* in *any* substance that can lead to a problem.
4. False—It is *not* a problem of will power.
5. False—*No one* can cause someone else to drink.
6. False—The parent probably *does* love his or her family, but has lost control and needs help to stop.
7. False—There are treatment centers and self-help groups available for the alcoholic.
8. True —It is a disease. It has predictable symptoms, runs a course, and has specific treatment.
9. False—It is not a moral weakness. It is a disease. The person needs help to get well.
10. True —There is no cure, but it can be *arrested* through abstinence and continuing support.
11. False—You cannot make someone else stop drinking. The one who is drinking is responsible for that.
12. True —It affects every aspect of a person's life.
13. False—Everyone around the person is affected by his or her behaviors (at home, at school, at work, friends, and society as a whole). A large percentage of accidents, suicides, date rapes, and other violence are alcohol-related.
14. True —If the alcoholic remains *drug-free* (abstinent) and continues attending AA, he OR or she can lead a happy, fulfilling life.

    False—If the alcoholic begins to recover and *then returns to using alcohol or other drugs,* the disease will reactivate with all its devastating problems.

HELP! 16-2
(for the Chemically Dependent Person)

Objective:

- To have the students explore sources of help for problems with alcohol and other drugs

Activities:

1. Invite a member of Alcoholics Anonymous, Narcotics Anonymous, Pills Anonymous, or Cocaine Anonymous to speak to the class. (Keep in mind that alcohol is the most abused drug.)
2. Inform the students that the class will prepare a directory of resources in the school and community that provides help for people who have a problem with alcohol or other drugs.
   a. Include telephone numbers for mental health agencies, local hospitals, Alcoholics Anonymous, Narcotics Anonymous, etc.; the name and location of the "contact person" at your school; a hotline number; two drug treatment centers in your area; etc.
   b. A student may be designated to call a number on the list to inquire about their services and to request written information be sent. Another student can be assigned to call one other number, and so forth.
   c. After all the information has been collected, the information can be shared with the class.
   d. Select a committee to compile the information into a resource directory.
   e. Leave the directory in a convenient location for referral.
3. Invite a person from a Drug Treatment Center in your area to speak to the class. (Request that the speaker explain the types of treatment available, including detoxification, in-patient, out-patient, aftercare.)

ROLES AND RULES 17-1

Objectives:

- To explore the effects of chemical dependency on the family
- To identify the roles and rules in a chemically dependent family

NOTE: Although the directions are lengthy, this activity and Activity 17-2, "THE NEED FOR HELP," can be completed in one class session.

Activities:

1. Review Activity 5-8, "My Family System," to reinforce the idea that:
   a. a family is a system in which each member is important,
   b. the family is important for our very survival,
   c. each member affects all other members.
2. Use a mobile to illustrate how *each member* helps to keep the *system* in *balance.*
   a. Remove *one* of the forms suspended from the mobile.
   b. Ask: What happened to the mobile? (Some of the answers may include: "It goes out of balance," "It *tips*," "It gets messed up," etc.)
3. To visualize a family "out of balance" due to the use of alcohol and other drugs, you will create a *living portrait* of a drug-affected family. (In this particular instance, the drug-abuser will be "the father." You may choose to repeat this activity in the future, designating another family member as the drug-abuser, and note how it will affect the family system.)
   a. You will use the Teacher Information Sheet 17-1A, "Freeze," as a model to follow.
   b. To set the stage, reproduce and study the rules (or mottos) for this family found in the Teacher Information Sheets 17-1B, 17-1C, and 17-1D.
      —Tape or tack them up on the walls in the room for background scenery (as though they were "family pictures").
      —They will remind the family members that *NOTHING* must interfere with the drug-abuser's lifestyle!
   c. Now, select six volunteers and follow the directions in the Teacher Information Sheet 17-1E, "The Cast of Characters."

Freeze: The "Tip" Family Portrait Model
Teacher Information Sheet

All roles in the family are taken to relieve the pain, restore the "balance," and help keep the family together.

The roles will also take attention and responsibility away from the alcohol- or other-drug-abuser, *unintentionally* allowing him to avoid facing his real problem. He can continue his drug-centered lifestyle.

Shedding a Little Light:
Children of alcoholics are at a *higher risk* of becoming chemically dependent themselves.

DON'T "TELL" FRIENDS

NO VISITORS ALLOWED

KEEP SECRETS

DON'T "TELL" GRANDMA

DON'T "TELL" YOUR SISTER

DRUG ABUSER
self-hatred
anger
fear
guilt
shame
remorse
ENABLER
anger
low self-worth
guilt
self-doubt
inadequacy
HERO
hurt
guilt
fear
low self-worth
inadequacy
DON'T FEEL
Hidden
"FROZEN" FEELINGS
SCAPEGOAT
hurt
anger
inadequacy
rejected
low self-worth
CLOWN
fear
loneliness
anger
insecurity
low self-worth
inadequacy
FORGOTTEN CHILD
loneliness
isolation
fear
low self-worth
anger

INCONSISTENT MESSAGES
DON'T MAKE WAVES
DAD WILL FREAK OUT
PROMISES ARE NOT KEPT
DON'T TRUST
THINGS WILL GET WORSE
NO ONE WILL UNDERSTAND

A Cast of Characters

Volunteer #1—*The User* is *THE STAR* of the portrait.

(1) Place him in the *center* of the "picture."

(2) Have prepared a 8" × 10" piece of paper on which the word "DRUG" is printed in large letters.

(3) The "father" will hold the paper close to his face so he can see *nothing else.* He *cannot* let go of the paper *nor* can he remove it from the center of his attention! HE IS FOCUSED ONLY ON THE "DRUG."

(4) *Tip* his head to the left (and instruct him to keep it in that position for the rest of the activity) to indicate that he is "off balance" and his lifestyle is drug-centered.

Ask the class:

(1) What does a father usually do for a family? (Answers may include: support his wife, go to work, care for his children, belong to clubs, have hobbies, etc.)

(2) Can he do those things now? Why?

(3) How will the family survive? (To restore "balance" and help the family survive, other family members "*adjust*" to the unhealthy situation. They take positions or *roles* to "fix" the problem.)

As the father can no longer fill his role, the "mother" may assume *his* responsibilities to *restore balance.* But, in doing that she *enables* him to *continue his lifestyle.*

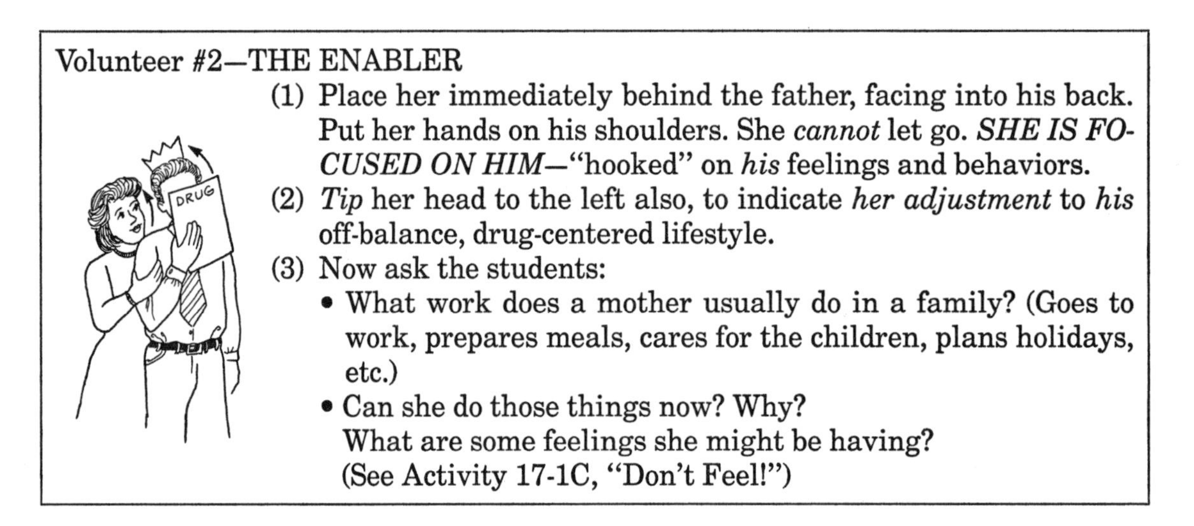

Volunteer #2—THE ENABLER

(1) Place her immediately behind the father, facing into his back. Put her hands on his shoulders. She *cannot* let go. *SHE IS FOCUSED ON HIM*—"hooked" on *his* feelings and behaviors.

(2) *Tip* her head to the left also, to indicate *her adjustment* to *his* off-balance, drug-centered lifestyle.

(3) Now ask the students:

- What work does a mother usually do in a family? (Goes to work, prepares meals, cares for the children, plans holidays, etc.)
- Can she do those things now? Why?
  What are some feelings she might be having?
  (See Activity 17-1C, "Don't Feel!")

Continued

As the mother may be overinvolved, or overwhelmed, an older child may take over some of the parental responsibilities:

Volunteer #3—THE OVERACHIEVER (HERO)
(1) Place him/her near the parents, facing his brothers and sister.
(2) *Tip* his/her head to the left to indicate "fitting in."
(3) Ask the students:
- What does a child usually do? (homework, play, join teams, rely on their parents for direction and support)
- Can he/she do that now? Why?
- What things can he/she do to help the family? (mind the younger children, prepare supper, excel in school and sports)
- What are some feelings he might be having? (See Activity 17-1C.)

This child causes no problems and makes no "waves." What a relief!

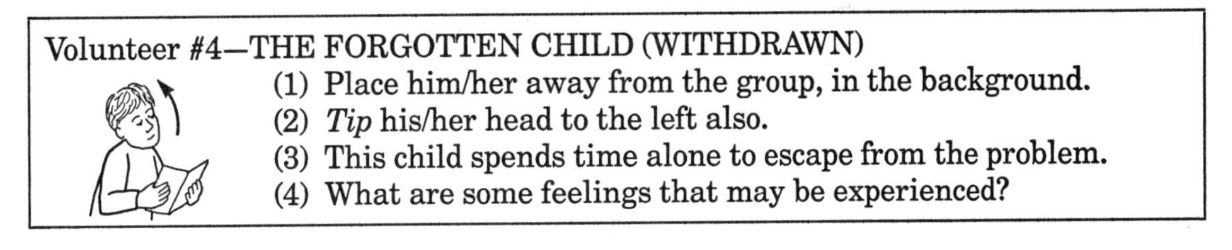

Volunteer #4—THE FORGOTTEN CHILD (WITHDRAWN)
(1) Place him/her away from the group, in the background.
(2) *Tip* his/her head to the left also.
(3) This child spends time alone to escape from the problem.
(4) What are some feelings that may be experienced?

This child will bring some comic relief to help the family.

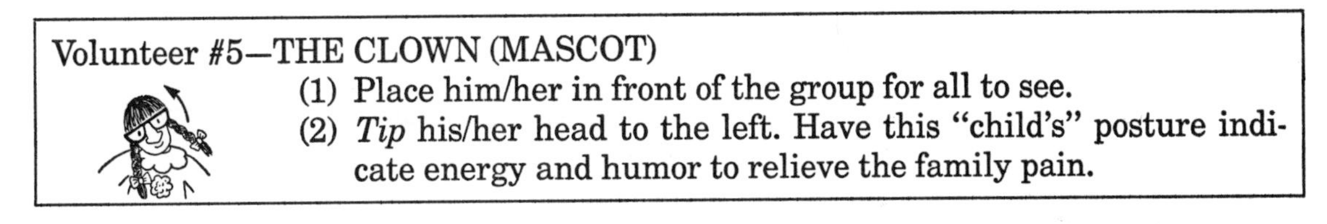

Volunteer #5—THE CLOWN (MASCOT)
(1) Place him/her in front of the group for all to see.
(2) *Tip* his/her head to the left. Have this "child's" posture indicate energy and humor to relieve the family pain.

And, this child may rebel and get into trouble. (Now that ought to keep everyone's attention away from other problems!)

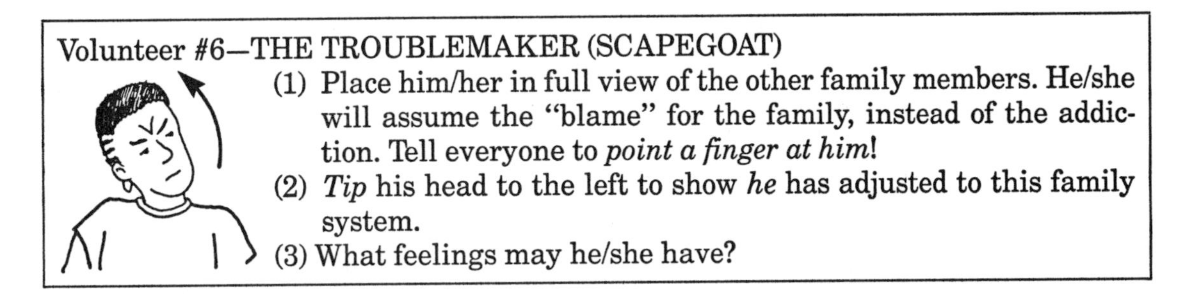

Volunteer #6—THE TROUBLEMAKER (SCAPEGOAT)
(1) Place him/her in full view of the other family members. He/she will assume the "blame" for the family, instead of the addiction. Tell everyone to *point a finger at him*!
(2) *Tip* his head to the left to show *he* has adjusted to this family system.
(3) What feelings may he/she have?

Now, do Activity 17-2, "The Need for Help."

THE NEED FOR HELP 17-2

Objective:

- To help the students identify the *need* for *each* member of a family to receive help to be free of the effects of chemical dependency

Activities:

1. For this activity, continue to use the "living" Family Portrait of the "Tip" Family, which was created in Activity *17-1A, "Roles and Rules."*
   a. Instruct the students who volunteered to "pose" for the "picture" to *retain their poses and "roles" until directed to do otherwise by the teacher.*
   b. Now, indicate that the "father" has received treatment for his disease of chemical dependency by:
      (1) removing him from the center of the picture,
      (2) throwing away the "DRUG" paper he once held in front of his face,
      (3) directing him to hold his head straight-up (instead of tipping it toward the left, which had indicated his adjustment to his drug-centered lifestyle).
   c. Instruct the students to observe the other family members who remain in the "portrait." Ask: What has happened to the other family members? (There should be *no* change in *their* position, despite the changes the father has made.)
   d. Next, select *one of the children* from the "Tip" family. Indicate that he/she has "left home" by placing the volunteer in another part of the room, "far removed from the family." (Whisper to the student to remind him/her to *remain* in the *original* role and position as before.)
   e. Ask the students to comment on what they observe. (Note that nothing has changed but the *geographical* location of the "child.")
   f. Thank the volunteers for their assistance. The class may applaud them to further distance them from their performances. Check to see that each volunteer is comfortable.
   g. Inform the class:

(1) *Each* family member is affected by chemical dependency. (2) *Each* family member is "stuck" in his/her role. (3) *Each* family member will carry the roles and rules into their adulthood. (4) *Each family member must receive help* to return to full functioning.

BREAKING THE CYCLE—Getting Help 17-3

Objectives:

- To inform the students that members of a family affected by alcohol and other drugs can learn to cope and be happy
- To identify sources of help

Activity:

1. Inform the students that no one is responsible for *someone else's* drinking or drug use. Introduce them to the "3 Cs":

   YOU DIDN'T CAUSE IT!
   YOU CAN'T CONTROL IT!
   YOU CAN'T CURE IT!

2. The *good news* is that there is help available for family members affected by chemical dependency. Ask the students to read the questions on the Alateen literature provided in Activity 17-3A, "Alateen—Is It for You?"
3. Invite a member of Al-anon, Alateen, or Nar-anon to speak to the class.
4. Have the students identify the site and time of an Alateen meeting in your area. They can find the number to call in their telephone directory.
5. Invite a person from a drug treatment center in your area that has a *program for family members* also to speak to the class.
6. Post the name and location of a "contact person" at your school.

NOTE: For *your* information, see the *New Attitudes and Behaviors* for the children from Chemically Dependent Families, Activity 17-3B.

ALATEEN
IS IT FOR YOU?

Alateen is for young people whose lives have been affected by someone else's drinking. The following twenty questions are to help you decide whether or not Alateen is for you.

1. Do you have a parent, close friend or relative whose drinking upsets you?
2. Do you cover up your real feelings by pretending you don't care?
3. Does it seem like every holiday is spoiled because of drinking?
4. Do you tell lies to cover up for someone else's drinking or what's happening in your home?
5. Do you stay out of the house as much as possible because you hate it there?
6. Are you afraid to upset someone for fear it will set off a drinking bout?
7. Do you feel nobody really loves or cares what happens to you?
8. Are you afraid or embarrassed to bring your friends home?
9. Do you think the drinker's behavior is caused by you, other members of your family, friends, or rotten breaks in life?
10. Do you make threats such as, "If you don't stop drinking, fighting, etc., I'll run away"?
11. Do you make promises about behavior such as, "I'll get better school marks, go to church or keep my room clean" in exchange for a promise that the drinking and fighting stop?
12. Do you feel that if your Mom or Dad loved you, she or he would stop drinking?
13. Do you ever threaten or actually hurt yourself to scare your parents into saying, "I'm sorry," or "I love you"?
14. Do you believe no one could possibly understand how you feel?
15. Do you have money problems because of someone else's drinking?
16. Are meal times frequently delayed because of the drinker?
17. Have you considered calling the police because of drinking behavior?
18. Have you refused dates out of fear or anxiety?
19. Do you think that if the drinker stopped drinking, your other problems would be solved?
20. Do you ever treat people (teachers, schoolmates, team mates, etc.) unjustly because you are angry at someone else for drinking too much?

If you have answered yes to some of these questions, Alateen may help you. You can contact Al-Anon or Alateen by looking in your local telephone directory or by writing to:

AL-ANON FAMILY GROUP HEADQUARTERS, INC.
P.O. BOX 862, MIDTOWN STATION
NEW YORK, N.Y. 10018-0862

Al-Anon Family Group Headquarters, Inc. 1981

1-275M-81-100/1.00 S-20 PRINTED IN U.S.A.

BREAKING THE CYCLE
New Attitude and Behaviors

Teacher Information

Following are *new attitudes and behaviors* that can be encouraged and practiced to help adolescents from chemically dependent families break the cycle of self-defeating behaviors and fixed responses:

HERO/CARETAKER: Overachiever	SCAPEGOAT/PROBLEM CHILD: Rebel
Needs to learn: (1) to relax (2) to have fun (3) to be spontaneous (4) how to follow (5) how to ask for help (6) how to compromise (7) to accept mistakes and failure	Needs to learn: (1) to express anger constructively (2) to express hurt feelings (3) to be involved in activities that bring them positive attention (4) to forgive him/herself (5) to learn to negotiate
FORGOTTEN CHILD: Withdrawn	**MASCOT/CLOWN: Comic relief**
Needs to learn: (1) to recognize his/her importance (2) to recognize his/her feelings; deal with loneliness (3) to recognize his/her needs and wants (4) to initiate activities (5) to make choices for oneself	Needs to learn: (1) how to recognize and accept his/her anger and fear (2) to accept support from others (3) to accept responsibility (4) to take oneself seriously, and accept his/her importance

APPENDICES

Appendix 1-A

FACTORS THAT INCREASE THE RISK OF SUBSTANCE ABUSE

1. Poor self-esteem
2. Families in which one or more member (generally parents or older siblings) smoke, drink alcohol, or abuse other drugs.
3. Family disruption by:
   (a) divorce,
   (b) death in the family,
   (c) poor parent/child relationship,
   (d) family rules and discipline that are *undefined, permissive,* or *harsh.*
4. Socializing mostly with friends who are substance-abusers, making it even more difficult to resist the "peer pressure."
5. Exposure to the media presentation of substance abuse as an important part of popularity, fun, and sex appeal.
6. Poor social skills
7. Poor academic performance

(These factors appear to increase the *probability* of drug use—they should not be considered factors *indicating* drug use.)

Appendix 1-B

The Path of Chemical Dependency in Adolescence

Most professionals in the chemical dependency field have seen various forms of progression charts for adult addiction to alcohol and other drugs. The above is the first we have found for adolescents, and we believe it is thorough and should be useful to anyone working with adolescents.

Out thanks to Bay Haven Chemical Dependency and Mental Health Programs at Samaritan Health Center, Bay City, Michigan, for granting us permission to share this chart with our readers. Further information about Bay Haven's program is available by writing to: 713 Ninth Street, Bay City, MI 48708. Telephone (517)894-3799.

Appendix 1-C

INDICATIONS THAT A CHILD MAY BE LIVING WITH FAMILY ALCOHOLISM

*GENERAL BEHAVIORS IN THE SCHOOL SETTING**

- morning tardiness (especially on Mondays)
- consistent concern with getting home promptly at the end of a day or activity period
- poor hygiene evident; body odor
- improper clothing for the weather
- regression; thumbsucking, enuresis, infantile behavior
- scrupulous avoidance of arguments and conflict
- friendlessness and isolation
- poor attendance
- frequent illness and need to visit nurse, especially for stomach complaints
- fatigue and listlessness
- hyperactivity and inability to concentrate
- sudden temper and other emotional outbursts
- exaggerated concern with achievement and with satisfying authority by children who are already at the head of the class
- extreme fear about situations involving contact with parents

*INDICATIONS DURING ALCOHOL EDUCATION ACTIVITIES**

- extreme negativism about alcohol and all drinking
- equation of drinking with getting drunk
- greater familiarity with different kinds of drinks than peers
- inordinate attention to alcohol in situations in which its evidence is marginal; e.g., in a play or movie not about drinking
- normally active child becomes passive during discussion
- normally passive or distracted child becoming active or focused during alcohol discussions
- changes in attendance patterns during alcohol education activities
- frequent requests to leave the room
- lingering after activity to ask innocent questions or simply to gather belongings
- mention of parent's drinking to excess on occasion
- mention of drinking problem of friend's parent or other relative
- strong negative feelings about alcoholics
- evident concern with whether alcoholism can be inherited

*Deutsch, Charles, ***Broken Bottles, Broken Dreams.*** 1982, Teachers College Press, New York.

Appendix 2A-1

SEDATIVES

This group of drugs *depresses the central nervous system* and *slows the body processes.* There are two main groups of sedative medications: *barbiturates* and *tranquilizers.* MIXING THESE DRUGS WITH ALCOHOL CAN PROVE FATAL!

Drugs

Barbiturates—Nembutal, Seconal, Amytal, Phenobarbital Tuinal
Methaqualone—Quaalude, Mequin, Parest
Tranquilizers—Valium, Librium
**Alcohol*

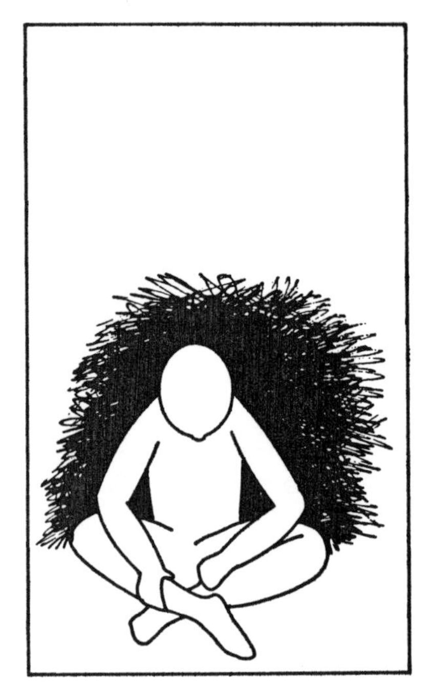

Street Names

Yellow jackets, reds, red devils, red birds, blues, blue heaven, purple hearts, tooeys, rainbow, ludes, barbs, downs

Medical Use

Anti-convulsant, relief of tension and anxiety, induce sleep, reduce symptoms of alcohol withdrawal. These drugs, even when given by prescription, can be abused, and *lead* to addiction.

Route of Administration

Ingestion, injection

Effects of Barbiturates

- Relaxation of body's muscles
- Intoxication appears similar to that of alcohol (without the odor of alcohol present)
- Staggering and stumbling movements; slurred speech
- Drowsiness

Effect of Tranquilizers

- Calms the person's emotions without interfering with the ability to remain alert and think clearly

> *NOTE: Abusers of stimulants and hallucinogens may take sedatives to calm down. Sedatives are* physically *and* psychologically *addictive. Withdrawal from these drugs should be done under medical supervision.*

Appendix 2A-2

ALCOHOL'S EFFECT ON THE LIVER AND THE HEART

The *liver* is the body's chemical factory:

1. It helps us digest our food.
2. It also acts as a cleansing station, deactivating the poisonous effects of alcohol, medicines, and other drugs, so they lose their harmful effects on the body.
3. All the alcohol absorbed from the stomach and the small intestines is carried directly to the liver through the bloodstream.
4. *Oxidation* is the process by which approximately 95 percent of the alcohol is changed to carbon dioxide and water for elimination from the body. A small amount of alcohol is released, unchanged, through sweat, breath, and urine.
5. Only the liver can start the process of breaking down alcohol in the body. It does this only at a *constant, unchangeable* rate of *one-half ounce* of pure alcohol per hour (12 ounces of beer, 4 ounces of wine, 1 1/2 ounce of 86 proof whiskey all contain the same amount of alcohol).
6. There is *no drug, food* or *exercise* that will increase the speed at which the liver breaks down the alcohol.
7. The "overload" of alcohol that the liver cannot deal with immediately, *continues to circulate* throughout the body within the bloodstream, affecting the brain and other organs.
8. With the intake of excessive amounts of alcohol, the liver "concentrates" on removing the alcohol from the blood, and "neglects" its other jobs or functions.
9. The liver becomes too busy metabolizing (breaking down) the alcohol to manufacture and release glucose (sugar) into the bloodstream. Glucose is the primary source of energy that the brain cells use.
10. Excessive use of alcohol can lead to liver damage.

Diseases of the Liver

1. *Fatty liver* is the mildest form of liver disease which results when there is a high intake of alcohol, and the liver neglects the breakdown of fat. At this point, if alcohol intake is stopped, the liver is able to return to normal.
2. *Hepatitis* is the next stage of damage if drinking continues. This indicates the inflammation of liver cells.
3. *Cirrhosis* is the most severe, often fatal, form of liver disease. All functions of the liver begin to fail. The excess alcohol kills the cells and they are replaced by scar tissue.
4. *Liver failure* as a result of cirrhosis, causes the following:
   a. An accumulation throughout the body of toxic (poisonous) products that were usually broken down in the liver.
   b. The sugar level in the blood falls because glucose is no longer produced, thus depriving the brain of nutrients.
   c. Blood-clotting substances usually produced by the liver decrease, and the danger of massive bleeding becomes likely.
   d. Kidneys begin to fail.
   Complete liver failure is fatal.
      - Alcohol causes the *heart* to lose its natural rhythm.
      - It weakens the strength of the heart muscles' contractions.
      - It may also cause the heart to enlarge.
      - It can cause heart failure in the advanced stages of alcoholism.

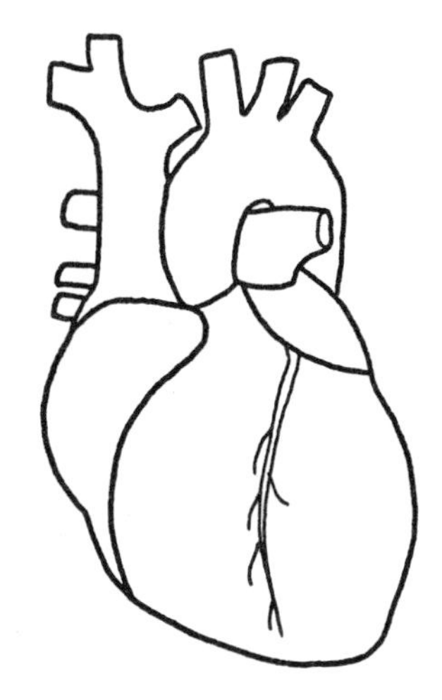

Appendix 2-B

STIMULANTS

A stimulant is a drug that *increases alertness, activity, and excitement by speeding up the body's processes.*

Drugs

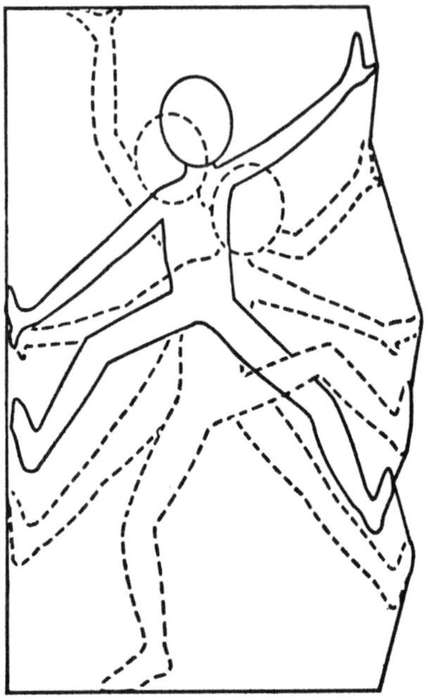

Amphetamines, *cocaine*, ritalin, caffeine

Street Names

Ups, bennies, whites, Christmas trees, uppers, dex, hearts, speed, black beauties

Medical Use

To treat overweight; to treat depression; cocaine can be used as a local anesthetic in eye, ear, nose, and throat surgery; for the treatment of narcolepsy (uncontrollable falling asleep during daily activities)

Route of Administration

Injection, inhalation, ingestion

Effects

- Speed up the body's processes
- Decrease in appetite
- Dryness of the mouth
- Pupils become dilated
- Rise of body temperature and blood pressure
- Increase of activity, irritability, and nervousness
- Large doses may lead to a "speed run" (increased agitation, fearfulness, hallucinations, and possible psychosis)

Note: The use of these drugs can cause a strong psychological dependence. Withdrawing from these drugs can cause the user to experience extreme fatigue and become very depressed (crash). (Cocaine is still classified as a narcotic, acting as a stimulant. The addiction to cocaine can be so consuming that all *survival functions—the need for food, water, sex, and protection—become secondary to the drive for cocaine.)*

Appendix 2-C

MARIJUANA/HASHISH/THC
(Cannabis Sativa)

Street Names

Pot, grass, joint, jays, sticks, Mary Jane, reefer, roach (*hashish*—hash, Panama red, Acapulco gold—contains a stronger concentration of THC)

Medical Use

None approved

Route of Administration

Swallowed (sprinkled on food), smoked (using rolling paper or pipes)

Effects

- Sense of euphoria and a relaxation of inhibitions
- In the early stages of intoxication, there may be loud talking and inappropriate laughter
- Distortion of the senses and of perception
- Increase in appetite
- In the later stages, the user may be sleepy or stuporous
- Whites of the eyes are reddened
- An odor similar to burnt rope may cling to the clothes and breath
- See FACT SHEET 15 for more information.

Note: It can take about 30 days for a single dose to be completely eliminated from the body. The drug available today is more potent than that which was available several years ago. Marijuana cigarette smoke has more cancer-causing substances than tobacco cigarette smoke. Long-term use can cause damage to the lungs, brain, and reproductive organs. Marijuana is often kept in small plastic bags. Stems and seeds may also be visible. Butts of the cigarettes (roaches) are saved for later use.

Appendix 2-D

NARCOTICS/OPIATES

Drugs

Dilaudid, Talwin, Percodan, Darvon, morphine, methadone, codeine

Medical Use

a. Relief from pain
b. Codeine—cough suppressant; relief from pain
c. Paregoric—stop diarrhea; relief from tooth pain

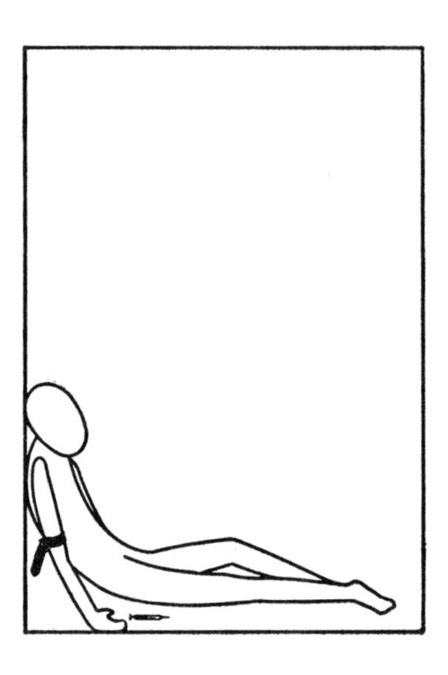

Route of Administration

Ingestion, inhalation, injection

Effects

- Euphoria → drowsiness → becoming stuporous
- Pupils become constricted
- Nodding

Illegal Drug
Heroin
Street Names of Heroin
Smack, stuff, scag, horse, dope
Medical Use
None

*Note: Narcotics are highly addictive. There is danger of infection from using unsterilized equipment. The disease AIDS may be contracted by the use of contaminated needles and syringes. *IV drug use is a high-risk activity for contracting AIDS; among minority populations (especially black and Hispanic) it is the greatest risk. (AIDS-Appendix 3-1). Needle marks or scars may be seen, usually on the arms. Syringes, bent spoons, bottle caps, cotton, eye droppers, or needles may be found.*

Appendix 2-E

INHALANTS

Substances

Glue (especially airplane glue), nail polish remover, aerosol sprays, spot remover, lacquer, cleaning fluid, liquid correction fluid for typewriters

Street Names

Popper, bolt, locker room, rush, ames

Medical Use

None

Route of Administration

Inhalation

Effects

- May appear uncoordinated, dizzy, and confused
- May appear drunk or in a dreamlike state
- An odor of the substance can be detected on the breath and clothing
- Frequent nausea and vomiting
- Impaired judgment
- May have blue lips due to lack of oxygen
- Long-term use can cause damage to the brain, kidney, and liver

> Note: *Plastic bags may be used to intensify the results. If the user becomes unconscious, death can result due to suffocation. Paper bags or rags may be found in the area. Death can result from displacing oxygen in the lungs or by depressing the central nervous system causing respiratory arrest.*
> *The use of poppers and other inhalants have been linked to Kaposi's Sarcoma; one of the opportunistic infections associated with AIDS.

INHALANTS ARE LEGAL SUBSTANCES THAT ARE READILY AVAILABLE AND INEXPENSIVE. THEREFORE, THEY ARE FREQUENTLY ABUSED BY CHILDREN!

Appendix 2-F

HALLUCINOGENS

Hallucinogens are drugs that precipitate imaginary visions, also known as hallucinations.

Drugs

LSD, PCP, mescaline, peyote

Street Names

Acid, angel dust, supergrass, killer weed, scramblers, blotter, buttons, cubes, mesc

Medical Use

None

Route of Administration

Ingestion. PCP may be inhaled or sprinkled on parsley or marijuana and smoked

Effects

- Senses of sight, hearing, as well as body image and time are distorted
- Perception, mood, and behavior are affected in a manner depending upon the emotional condition of the user and the environmental conditions
- Users may sit quietly in a dreamlike state
- There may be a feeling of depersonalization of body image and feelings of severe anxiety

Note: LSD is a colorless, odorless, and tasteless drug. "Flashbacks" (reexperiencing the hallucinations) can occur without using the drug, over a long period of time. Experiences can vary each time the drug is taken. PCP has produced dangerous symptoms. Its use may precipitate violent, bizarre, and unpredictable behavior.

Appendix 3A-1

AIDS
FACT SHEET

1. AIDS is a disease caused by the human immuno-deficiency virus (HIV).
2. This virus destroys the *helper* T cells which are responsible for activating the immune system's defenses, making it ineffective in fighting off infections and disease.
3. The rare diseases and infections that invade, overwhelm, and destroy the body are called "opportunistic" diseases.
   - These illnesses would not pose a threat to healthy individuals, but are fatal to a person with a damaged, vulnerable immune system.

Note: Efforts to develop a vaccine are hampered by the fact that the virus constantly changes. Scientists are shooting at a moving target.

4. The AIDS virus has been found in blood, semen, urine, vaginal secretions, spinal fluid, tears, saliva, and breast milk. Of these, only *semen, vaginal secretions,* and *blood* are implicated in transmission.
   - There are also some cases in which babies have contracted AIDS through infected breast milk.

**See Routes of Transmission* in Appendix *3A-2*

"When you sleep with someone, you are, in effect, sleeping with all the people that person ever slept with... Similarly, intravenous drug users who borrow 'a set of works' inject themselves with the blood of every person who ever shared the implement." (Dr. Molly Coyle, former Commissioner of Health for the State of New Jersey)

Appendix 3A-2

DRUGS AND AIDS
THE HIGH-RISK GROUP

AIDS is a disease caused by the HIV virus. It attacks a person's immune system, making it ineffective in fighting off infections and diseases. There is no cure for AIDS at this time. It is deadly.

Transmission of the AIDS virus from person to person requires that the virus leave the infected person through the blood or semen and enter the other person's bloodstream. One exposure to the AIDS virus is enough to become infected.

ROUTES OF TRANSMISSION

A. PAST OR PRESENT ABUSERS OF INTRAVENOUS DRUGS

Infection can come from *sharing needles.* Some blood always remains in the *syringe.*

The IV drug user has become the "gateway" of the virus to the heterosexual community.

C. INFANTS BORN TO INFECTED MOTHERS

Often, the mother has a drug history, or a sexual partner with an IV drug history.

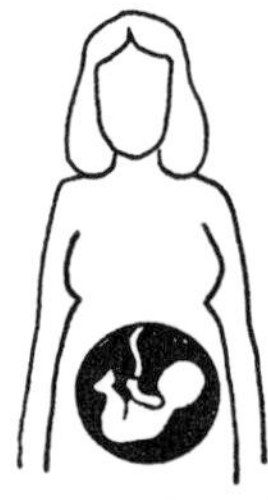

AIDS can be transmitted from:

- mother to fetus during pregnancy through the placenta
- from mother to infant during the birth process
- from mother's milk to infant during breastfeeding

B. SEXUAL CONTACT WITH SOMEONE INFECTED WITH THE VIRUS

Sexual intercourse, vaginal intercourse, anal intercourse, and oral-genital sex with a partner who was a past or present IV drug user may transmit the virus.

Women of childbearing age must know their child could be infected if the mother has been infected.

D. PERSONS WHO HAVE HAD TRANSFUSIONS OF INFECTED BLOOD OR BLOOD PRODUCTS

The risk of contracting this disease from blood products has been greatly reduced.

There is no danger in *donating* blood.

Appendix 3A-3

AIDS TESTING

1. The ELISA test (enzyme-linked immunosorbent assay) is used to check for AIDS *antibodies*. It is relatively simple, inexpensive, and highly sensitive.
   - If the test is positive, it is repeated again to assure the results of the first test. If that too is positive, the Western Blot test, which is more sensitive and technically more difficult, confirms the presence of AIDS virus antibodies.
2. If the antibody is *absent*, the test is *negative*, and it can mean:

   a. The person has not been infected with the virus.

   OR

   b. The person has been infected by the virus but has not yet produced antibodies. Research indicates that some people will produce antibodies within 2 to 12 weeks after infection.
      - *Most* people show antibodies from 12 to 16 weeks.
      - Some people will take 6 months to show antibodies.
3. If the test shows that the antibody is *present*, the test is *positive* and it means:

   a. A person has antibodies to HIV in his/her blood.
   b. A person has been infected by HIV at some point in time.
   c. A person is probably able to transmit the infection to another person.

   (The Screening does not indicate a person has AIDS or ARC.)
4. Babies of HIV positive mothers, have antibodies at birth. Not until they are 18 months old will an antibody test tell if the *child* is HIV positive.

Appendix 3A-4

STAGES
HIV INFECTION

A person infected with HIV can have:

1. *No Symptoms:* This person can be a *carrier* who can transmit the virus to others.

> "It can be spread by people with no outward symptoms. You cannot tell by knowing them well, by liking them, or by respecting them, that they are not infected." (Dr. Molly Coyle, former Commissioner of Health for the State of New Jersey)

2. *ARC* (AIDS-Related Complex): Some symptoms are evident. (*Chronic* swollen glands in the neck, armpits, and/or groin. *Chronic* diarrhea and weight loss; night sweats, fever, and fatigue; loss of appetite; fungus infections of the mouth.)
   - The symptoms can be mild to severe.
3. *AIDS.* A diagnosis of AIDS can be made by finding: a. a positive test result that shows damage to the immune system, b. a positive result on a test for the HIV virus, and c. the symptoms presented in ARC, *as well as* the presence of opportunistic diseases.
   - The two most common of these diseases are (1) Kaposi's Sarcoma (a rare cancer) and (2) Pneumocystis Carini Pneumonia (a parasitic infection of the lungs).
4. Death often occurs within *30 months* after diagnosis, for *men,* and *30 weeks* after diagnosis, *for women.*

Appendix 3A-5

AIDS PREVENTION

1. There is no cure for AIDS. We *do* know how it is spread. Therefore, the best defense we have against it is education about how to avoid exposure to the virus that causes it.

> "The risk of becoming infected with HIV can virtually be eliminated by not engaging in sexual activities and by not using illegal IV drugs."
> (MMWR [*Morbidity & Mortality Weekly Report*]-Supplement. January 29, 199/Vol 37/NaS-2 pg. 4. - Center for Disease Control)

2. School systems should encourage young people who *have not* engaged in sexual intercourse and who *have not* used illicit drugs to continue to—
   a. Abstain from sexual intercourse until they are ready to establish a mutually monogamous relationship within the context of marriage;
   b. Refrain from using or injecting illicit drugs.
3. For young people who *have* engaged in sexual intercourse or who *have* injected illicit drugs, school programs should encourage them to:
   a. Stop engaging in sexual intercourse until they are ready to establish a mutually monogamous relationship within the context of marriage.
   b. Stop using or injecting illicit drugs.
4. Despite all efforts some young people may remain unwilling to adopt behavior that would virtually eliminate their risk of becoming infected. Therefore, school systems, in consultation with parents and health officials, should provide AIDS education programs that address preventive types of behavior that should be practiced by persons with an increased risk of acquiring HIV infection. These include:
   a. Avoid sexual intercourse with anyone who is known to be infected, who is at risk of being infected, or whose HIV infection status is not known.
   b. Use a latex condom with spermicide if engaging in sexual intercourse.
   c. Seek treatment if addicted to drugs.
   d. Do not share needles or other injection equipment.
   e. Seek HIV counseling and testing if HIV infection is suspected.

5. New information keeps being made available. To keep up-to-date:
   a. Read new material.
   b. Request information from:

U.S. Department of Health and Human Services Public Health Service— Centers for Disease Control— Center for Health Promotion and Education— Atlanta, Georgia 30333

   c. Invite specially trained AIDS educators to speak to your students.
6. Avoid the abuse of all mood-altering substances. They can
   a. impair judgement and cause a person to do things he/she would not normally do,
   b. impair the immune system, causing a person to be more susceptible to many infections, including HIV infections.

Appendix 4-A

THE COMMUNITY PARTNERSHIP

Families, schools, and communities must join together in a major cooperative effort. Prevention efforts must include:

- Teachers
- Students
- Parents
- Law Enforcement — Justice System
- Corporations/Small Businesses
- Mass Media
- Advertising and Public Relations
- Celebrities, Entertainers, and Athletes
- Clergy
- Professional Athletic Teams
- City, County, and State Government
- Community Service Organizations
- Military
- Medical Community
- Rehabilitation/Treatment Facilities
- Youth Organizations

To provide:

(1) Opportunities for young people to use their time constructively and increase their self-esteem. (Examples of four successful projects initiated within the community appear in Appendices: 4B, 4C, 4D, and 4E.

(2) Consistent messages that:
  (a) intoxication by any substance is unacceptable,
  (b) there are people who care and who are available to offer help and direction,
  (c) you are each capable of learning *constructive* ways to meet your needs,
  (d) you can learn and practice these skills.

Appendix 4-B

THE POETRY MAN OF THE INNER CITY

Half a dozen young people gathered in a small room at the back of the Flint Street Recreation Center in Rochester, New York. The group of young men ranging in age from 13 to 18 years of age, are absorbed in a world of imagination—writing poems.

Ross Talarico, a writer-in-residence in his hometown, has published five books of prose and poetry. He began to operate writing programs five years ago under the auspices of the city recreation department.

"When you walk into a tough neighborhood, and you want to start a group of kids writing poems—they look at you funny." Talarico challenged anyone he could beat him at pingpong to try the program. Other times, he would reserve the gym for the workshop, so that kids who wanted to play basketball had to try their hand at poetry first.

The results surprised even Talarico.... A collection of writing from the workshops, called "Rochester Voices: Uncommon Writing from Common People," will be used as a textbook in the Rochester public schools next year.

When Talarico reads their poems out loud, the joking stops, and everyone listens. His constant theme in the group is—respect for what you have created. Now, as the young writers read the poems they and their friends have written, poetry stops being something that other people do.

"For many of the kids it's the first time that their own expressions are taken seriously by anyone," Talarico says. "That for me is the essence of the program. I'm not trying to make poets out of anyone—I'm trying to make people feel better about themselves through what they feel inside and through what they're able to express."

Ross Talarico

Appendix 4-C

MARATHON HOUSE

The high school students in Wayne, New Jersey began the many hours of planning for the first Basketball Marathon to aid the Mentally Retarded in 1974. With the approval of the administration and the Board of Education, they collected enough food for over 150 hungry players and an equal amount for other volunteers who would take part in this 40-hour program. Resting areas, custodian assistance, police and teacher supervision were arranged. It was a success! Now, a tradition was established that would continue for many years.

One of the young men who initiated this project, Joe Mannelo, hoped that one day these monies could be used to open a home for retarded adults in town. By 1977, the dream had come true. In the spring of that year, a home—appropriately named Marathon House—opened. At that time it was only the fourth residential home for retarded adults in New Jersey and it was *the first in the country* opened by high school students.

In the late 1970s, a second home opened with money raised by Wayne Valley High School. This time the site was in Sussex County in New Jersey. The marathons continued—the funds were poured into more projects—including another home residence opened by the Bergen Passaic Association for Retarded Citizens, in Wayne.

In November, 1986, the ARC awarded Wayne Valley High School the Humanitarian Award for Community Service. The young people had become involved in an on-going project that was a source of pride, used their time and energy to accomplish real goals, and produced long-lasting effects on the lives of others.

Vicki Menetti

Bob Silbernagel

Appendix 4-D

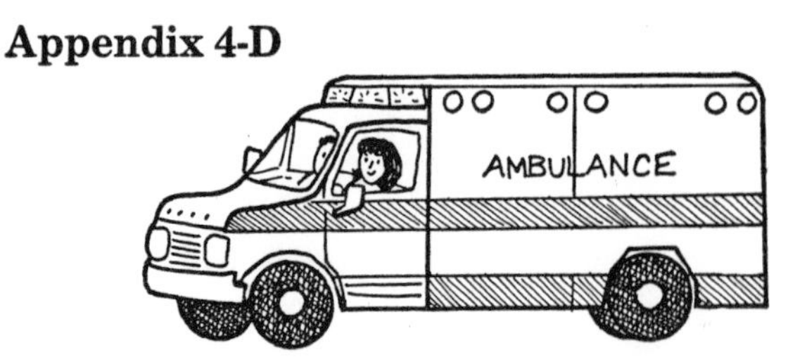

TEENAGE EMERGENCY MEDICAL TECHNICIANS

Broken bones, accidents, and heart attacks are routine for some high school students in the affluent community of Darien, Connecticut, where the only ambulance service is operated around the clock by teenage volunteers. (The teens also bought two of their three ambulances with some money raised at an annual Memorial Day Tag Sale.) They have many work-fun fund-raising activities. They work and earn as much as they can before they ask others for help.

Explorer Post 53 is made up of about 50 teenagers. Each teen is on duty at least twice a month. The qualifications to make the post are *tough*! Students must have at least a C average in school and they are required to take 50 hours of first aid classes and 120 hours of emergency medical technician training. They are carefully screened, and must pass a 90-day probation. "It's the most prestigious organization in Darien and the only one like it in the country," John Doble said. There is a waiting list to join!

Community volunteers, including parents of the teens, staff the service on a first-response basis, while the teenagers are in school. A group of adult volunteers trained in advanced life support also take turns meeting the teen ambulance at every scene, because people under 18 years of age are not allowed by state law to administer invasive medical care.

John Doble said he created the post, which is affiliated with the Boy Scouts Explorer Program, because "the drug thing was rearing its ugly head," and he wanted the young people to learn responsibility, along with the dangers of abuse of alcohol and other drugs from actual experience with its results, rather than by lecture, lecture, lecture. Their compassion is real. When they kneel down next to someone and say, 'I'm here to help you,' they mean it." It offers these young people an opportunity for success as they grow in their sense of trust, compassion, and competence.

John E. Doble

Appendix 4-E

THE INNER CITY ENSEMBLE

Over a dozen years ago, Ralph Gomez put his theater education to work for inner city children by creating the Paterson's Inner City Ensemble Theatre and Dance Company. Its initial purpose was to enhance the identity of the inner-city child. Mr. Gomez encouraged the young people to keep diaries about their feelings and to discuss their fears and problems—in fact, just about anything in their lives—at workshop sessions. And, he taught them to use improvisational stage techniques for self-expression. The ensemble grew to become an accredited arts school with 50 teenagers in its highly selective theater and dance program, as well as a community arts school, for which auditions were not required.

Several "graduates" have gone on to performing as professionals. Nicholas Rodriguez, an Inner City Ensemble alumnus, is currently artistic director of DanceCompass, one of New Jersey's most celebrated modern dance companies. The troupe includes other alumni of the dance program, Daniel Sanchez and Charlton Boyd. In addition to extensive touring throughout the northeast and abroad, DanceCompass is keeping the dream of Ralph Gomez alive through educational programs in the Paterson Community.

The "Graffiti in Control" project, another brainchild of Mr. Gomez, was a concerted effort to get graffiti off the streets of Paterson and into a constructive medium. The participants all signed a contract agreeing not to deface any public property. In return, they entered the mainstream culture. They got studio space and art materials (supplied with money they helped to raise themselves). They had "come in out of the cold." They were in a program doing good work—even exhibiting their works at town malls. In a pediatric ward of St. Joseph's Hospital in Paterson, they painted the name of each child on a canvas board. But, now instead of using spray cans, the *artists* were using an air brush.

Ms. Sharon Stephens, the Executive Director of Dance Compass, co-directed the Inner City Ensemble Theatre and Dance Company for five years.

Sharon Stephens

P.O. Box 43115
Montclair, NJ 07043

Appendix 5

SELF-HELP GROUPS

Here is information on various self-help groups:

Parents of Adolescents

TOUGH LOVE: Parent support groups for dealing with teenagers' unacceptable behavior. Help in starting groups, self-help manual, parent support network. Newsletter. TOUGH LOVE information line: (215) 348-7090, 9-5 p.m. (Eastern time). Write: TOUGH LOVE, Box 1069, Doylestown, PA 18901

Alcoholism

ALCOHOLICS ANONYMOUS: Fellowship sharing experiences, strengths, and hopes with each other so they may solve common problems and help each other recover from alcoholism. Bimonthly newsletter "Loners Internationalist" includes networking by mail. Write: Box 459, Grand Central Station, New York, NY 10163. Call: (212) 686-1100.

AL-ANON FAMILY GROUP: Provides help for family members and friends of problem drinkers by offering comfort, hope, and friendship through shared experiences. "Lone Member Letterbox" newsletter. "Al-Anon Speaks Out" newsletter for professionals. Guidelines for developing new groups. Write: Al-Anon Family Groups, Inc., World Service Office, P.O. Box 862, Midtown Station, New York, NY 10018-0862. Public Information: (800) 356-9996. Contact: Public Information Officer.

ALATEEN: For younger family members who live in an alcoholic family situation to learn effective ways to cope with problems. Helps members achieve detachment from alcoholic family member. Newsletter, pen pal, "Loner's Service." Chapter development kit. Write: Al-Anon Family Groups, Inc., World Service Office, P.O. Box 862, Midtown Station, New York, NY 10018-0862. Public Information: (800) 356-9996. Contact: Public Information Officer.

NATIONAL ASSOCIATION FOR CHILDREN OF ALCOHOLICS: Support and information for children of alcoholics of all ages and those in a position to help them. Write: NACOA, P.O. Box 421691, San Francisco, CA 94142.

Drug Abuse

NARCOTICS ANONYMOUS: Fellowship of recovering addicts meeting to "stay clean of all drugs." Write: Narcotics Anonymous, P.O. Box 9999, Van Nuys, CA 91409. Call: (818) 780-3951.

FAMILIES ANONYMOUS: For relatives and friends concerned about the use of drugs and alcohol or related behavioral problems. Referrals to local groups. Guidelines for developing groups. Newsletter "12-Step Rag." Write: P.O. Box 528, Van Nuys, CA 91408. Call: (818) 989-7841.

NAR-ANON FAMILY GROUPS: Fellowship of relatives and friends of drug abusers. Follows the 12-step program adapted from Alcoholics Anonymous and Al-Anon. Helps members learn to achieve peace of mind and gain hope for the future. Write: Nar-Anon Family Group Headquarters, P.O. Box 2562, Palos Verdes, CA 90274-0119. Call: (213) 547-5800.

NATIONAL FEDERATION OF PARENTS FOR DRUG-FREE YOUTH: Information, networking, newsletter, and guidelines for parents forming groups to address drug abuse problems among adolescents. Write: National Federation of Parents for Drug-Free youth (NFP), Communications Center, 1423 N. Jefferson, Springfield, MO 65802. Call: (417) 836-3709. (Headquarters), National Red Ribbon Campaign, 4600 Eisenhower Avenue, Alexandria, VA 22304.

Appendix 6A

FEDERAL GOVERNMENT AGENCIES FOR DRUG/ALCOHOL & AIDS INFORMATION

The National Clearinghouse for Alcohol and Drug Information (NCADI)

Description

NCADI is a communications service of the Office for Substance Abuse Prevention (OSAP) and is the Nation's primary source for information about alcohol and other drug (AOD) abuse. Located in Rockville, MD, NCADI provides information to thousands of requestors on the latest research results, popular press and scholarly journal articles, prevention and education resources, and prevention programs. Most of NCADI's materials and services are free. In the AOD field, NCADI is known as a "one stop shop" for all information needs.

Audiovisuals—NCADI maintains a free Audiovisual Loan Program that works just like a local library. The Clearinghouse can provide a list of current titles in its collection, which includes NIDA's Drugs in Work Series, prevention programs for grades K-12, and an array of television public service announcements (PSAs).

Prevention Pipeline: An Alcohol and Drug Awareness Service—For a $15 annual handling fee, anyone can receive this bimonthly news service for the AOD field.

Contact

To obtain NCADI materials or services, or to find out more about NCADI operations, write or call: The National Clearinghouse for Alcohol and Drug Information, P.O. Box 2345, Rockville, Maryland 20852, (301) 468-2600

National Institute on Alcohol Abuse & Alcoholism Prevention, Research Branch 16C-03 Parklawn Building, 5600 Fishers Lane, Rockville, MD 20857. Tel. (301) 443-3885

The National AIDS Information Clearinghouse (NAIC)

Description

The National AIDS Information Clearinghouse (NAIC) provides services and educational resources to assist in the development and management of AIDS information and education programs. Operated by the Centers for Disease Control (CDC), NAIC provides services to assist users to:

Audience and services

- identify organizations, such as clinics, hospitals, extended care facilities, public health departments, commercial enterprises, and religious groups whose work is related to AIDS;
- locate and obtain single copies of hard-to-find educational materials such as brochures, pamphlets, curricula, State reports, posters, and audiovisuals;
- order single or bulk copies of key publications that are the primary tools used by CDC in its national AIDS education effort.

NAIC maintains two online information data bases. One lists organizations that provide AIDS-related services and the other describes AIDS educational materials. Information specialists search these data bases to provide information on resources and educational materials related to user needs.

NAIC can supply citizens with single and bulk copies of important publications from the Public Health Service. They address key topics such as AIDS and the workplace, the connection between AIDS and drug abuse, and the safety of the Nation's blood supply.

Contact

To respond to the general public's need for AIDS information, CDC maintains a national AIDS Hotline as part of its overall information and education program. The toll-free Hotline provides 24-hour service to answer questions about AIDS and to offer referrals to appropriate services. The number is (800) 342-AIDS (English) and (800) 344-SIDA (Spanish).

Appendix 6B

STATE GOVERNMENT AGENCIES FOR DRUG/ALCOHOL INFORMATION AND TREATMENT REFERRALS

Alabama

Prevention Coordinator
Alabama Department of Mental Health and Mental Retardation
200 Interstate Park Avenue
Montgomery, AL 36193-5001
(205) 271-1294

Treatment referral:
If you or someone you know is having problems with alcohol or other drugs, the number to call in ALABAMA for referral to a helping agency is (205) 270-4650 or your community mental health center.

Alaska

State Coordinator
State Office of Alcoholism and Drug Abuse
P.O. Box H-05F
Juneau, AK 99811-0607
(907) 586-6201

Treatment referral:
If you or someone you know is having problems with alcohol or other drugs, the number to call in Alaska for referral to a helping agency is (907) 561-4213.

Arkansas

Prevention Coordinator
Director of Governor's Partnership in Substance Abuse Prevention
DADAP, P.O. Box 1437
Little Rock, AR 72203-1437
(501) 682-6656

Treatment referral:
If you or someone you know is having problems with alcohol or other drugs, the number to call in ARKANSAS for referral to a helping agency is (501) 682-6656.

Arizona

Prevention Program Representative
Office of Community Behavioral Health Services
411 North 24th Street
Phoenix, AZ 85008
(602) 220-6478, 220-6502 FAX

Treatment referral:
If you or someone you know is having problems with alcohol or other drugs, the number to call in ARIZONA for referral to a helping agency is (602) 220-6478.

California

State Prevention Coordinator
California Department of Alcohol
and Drug Programs
111 Capitol Mall
Sacramento, CA 95814
(916) 445-1125

> *Treatment referral:*
> *If you or someone you know is having problems with alcohol or other drugs, the number to call in CALIFORNIA for referral to a helping agency is (916) 445-0834. You may also contact your county alcohol or drug program administrator.*

Colorado

Prevention Programs Director
Alcohol and Drug Abuse Division
Colorado Department of Health
4210 East 11th Avenue
Denver, CO 80220
(303) 331-8201

> *Treatment referral:*
> *If you or someone you know is having problems with alcohol or other drugs, the number to call in COLORADO for referral to a helping agency is (303) 331-8201, Monday through Friday, 8 a.m. to 5 p.m.*

Connecticut

Prevention Coordinator
Connecticut Alcohol and Drug
Abuse Commission
Prevention Division
999 Asylum Avenue
Hartford, CT 06105
(203) 566-7458

> *Treatment referral:*
> *If you or someone you know is having problems with alcohol or other drugs, the number to call in CONNECTICUT for referral to a helping agency is (203) 566-4145.*

Delaware

Division of Alcoholism, Drug
Abuse, and Mental Health
Director of Training
1901 North DuPont Highway
New Castle, DE 19720
(302) 421-6550

> *Treatment referral:*
> *If you or someone you know is having problems with alcohol or other drugs, the number to call in DELAWARE for referral to a helping agency is (302) 571-6975.*

District of Columbia

Prevention Coordinator
Office of Health Planning and
Development
1600 L Street, NW
Suite 715-16
Washington, DC 20036
(202) 724-5637

> *Treatment referral:*
> *If you or someone you know is having problems with alcohol or other drugs, the number to call in the DISTRICT OF COLUMBIA for referral to a helping agency is the local Health Department at (202) 727-0660 or the WACADA Hotline (202) 783-1300.*

Florida

Prevention Coordinator
Department of Health and
Rehabilitative Services
1317 Winewood Blvd.
Tallahassee, FL 32399-0700
(904) 488-0900

> *Treatment referral:*
> *If you or someone you know is having problems with alcohol or other drugs, the number to call in FLORIDA for referral to a helping agency is (904) 488-0900.*

Georgia

Prevention Coordinator
Division of Mental Health, Mental
Retardation, and Substance
Abuse Prevention Resource
Center
Suite 319
878 Peachtree Street, NE
Atlanta, GA 30309
(404) 894-4785

> *Treatment referral:*
> *If you or someone you know is having problems with alcohol or other drugs, the number to call in GEORGIA for referral to a helping agency is the Drug Abuse Helpline at (800) 338-6745, 24 hours a day.*

Guam

Department of Mental Health and
Substance Abuse
Drug and Alcohol Unit Supervisor
P.O. Box 9400
Tamuning, Guam 96911
(671) 646-9261 through 9269
(671) 649-6948 FAX

> *Treatment referral:*
> *If you or someone you know is having problems with alcohol or other drugs, the number to call in GUAM for referral to a helping agency is (671) 646-9261 through 9269.*

Hawaii

Alcohol and Drub Abuse Division
Department of Health
Prevention Program Specialist
P.O. Box 3378
Honolulu, HI 96801-9984
(808) 548-4280

Treatment referral:
If you or someone you know is having problems with alcohol or other drugs, the number to call in HAWAII for referral to a helping agency is the Substance Abuse Hotline at (808) 537-1678.

Idaho

State Prevention Coordinator
Substance Abuse Program
Division of Family and Children's Services
Idaho Department of Health and Welfare
450 West State
Boise, ID 83720
(208) 334-5934

Treatment referral:
If you or someone you know is having problems with alcohol or other drugs, the number to call in for referral to a helping agency in IDAHO is (208) 334-5935.

Illinois

Prevention Coordinator
DASA
Division of Prevention
100 West Randolph, Suite 5-600
Chicago, IL 60601
(312) 917-6400

Treatment referral:
If you or someone you know is having problems with alcohol or other drugs, the number to call in ILLINOIS for referral to a helping agency is (312) 782-0686 in downtown Chicago, or (312) 917-3840 in the Chicago area, Monday through Friday, 9 a.m. to 5 p.m.

Indiana

Director, Prevention and Planning
Indiana Department of Mental Health
117 E. Washington Street
Indianapolis, IN 46204
(317) 232-7919

Treatment referral:
If you or someone you know is having problems with alcohol or other drugs, the number to call in INDIANA for referral to a helping agency is (317) 232-7818.

Iowa

Prevention Coordinator
Bureau of Prevention and Training
Division of Substance Abuse and Health Promotion
Department of Public Health
Bureau Chief
Lucas State Office Building 4th Floor
Des Moines, IA 50319
(515) 281-4640

> *Treatment referral:*
> *If you or someone you know is having problems with alcohol or other drugs, the number to call in IOWA for referral to a helping agency is (515) 281-3641, Monday through Friday, 8:00 a.m. to 4:30 p.m.*

Kansas

Alcohol and Drug Abuse Services
Program Development Director
300 SW Oakley, Biddle Building
Topeka, KS 66606
(913) 296-3925

> *Treatment referral:*
> *If you or someone you know is having problems with alcohol or other drugs, the number to call in KANSAS for referral to a helping agency is (913) 296-3925.*

Kentucky

Prevention Coordinator
Division of Substance Abuse
Department for Mental Health and Mental Retardation Services
275 East Main Street
Frankfort, KY 40621
(502) 564-2880

> *Treatment referral:*
> *If you or someone you know is having problems with alcohol or other drugs, the toll-free number to call in KENTUCKY for referral to a helping agency is (800) 432-9337, Monday through Friday, 8 a.m. to 4:30 p.m.*

Louisiana

Prevention Coordinator
Division of Alcohol and Drug Abuse
1201 Capitol Access Road
P.O. Box 3868
Baton Rouge, LA 70802
(504) 342-9351

> *Treatment referral:*
> *If you or someone you know is having problems with alcohol or other drugs, the number to call in LOUISIANA for referral to a helping agency is (504) 342-9350, Monday through Friday, 8 a.m. to 4:30 p.m.*

Maine

Prevention Coordinator
Office of Alcoholism and Drug Abuse Prevention
State of Maine
Department of Human Services
State House Station #11
Augusta, ME 04333
(207) 289-2781

> *Treatment referral:*
> *If you or someone you know is having problems with alcohol or other drugs, the number to call in MAINE for referral to a helping agency is (800) 322-5004, Monday through Friday, 8 a.m. to 5 p.m. You may also call your local regional alcohol and drug abuse council.*

Maryland

Prevention Coordinator
Alcohol and Drug Abuse Administration's Prevention Services
201 West Preston Street
4th Floor
Baltimore, MD 21201
(301) 225-6543

> *Treatment referral:*
> *If you or someone you know is having problems with alcohol or other drugs, the number to call in MARYLAND for referral to a helping agency is (301) 225-6873. You may also call your local health department.*

Massachusetts

State Prevention Coordinator
Division of Substance Abuse Services
Massachusetts Department of Public Health
150 Tremont Street
Sixth Floor
Boston, MA 02111
(617) 727-1960

> *Treatment referral:*
> *If you or someone you know is having problems with alcohol or other drugs, the number to call in MASSACHUSETTS for referral to a helping agency is (800) 327-5050.*

Michigan

Prevention Coordinator
Office of Substance Abuse Services
2150 Apollo Drive
P.O. Box 30206
Lansing, MI 48909
(517) 335-8831

> *Treatment referral:*
> *If you or someone you know is having problems with alcohol or other drugs, the number to call in MICHIGAN for referral to a helping agency is the regional coordinating agency that serves your county. Call one of the numbers listed below during normal working hours.*

Minnesota

Prevention Coordinator
Chemical Dependency Program
Division
Department of Human Services
444 Lafayette Road
St. Paul, MN 55155-3823
(612) 296-4711

Treatment referral:
If you or someone you know is having problems with alcohol or other drugs, the number to call in MINNESOTA for referral to a helping agency is (612) 296-3991.

Mississippi

Prevention Coordinator
Department of Mental Health
Division of Alcohol and Drug
Abuse
1101 Robert E. Lee Bldg.
239 North Lamar Street
Jackson, MS 39201
(610) 359-1288

Treatment referral:
If you or someone you know is having problems with alcohol or other drugs, the number to call in MISSISSIPPI for referral to a helping agency is (601) 359-1288, Monday through Friday, from 8 a.m. to 5 p.m.

Missouri

Prevention Coordinator
Department of Mental Health
Division of Alcohol and Drug
Abuse
P.O. Box 687
Jefferson City, MO 65102
(314) 751-4942, 751-7814 FAX

Treatment referral:
If you or someone you know is having problems with alcohol or other drugs, the number to call in MISSOURI for referral to a helping agency is (314) 751-4942.

Montana

Prevention Coordinator
Department of Institutions
1539 11th Avenue
Helena, MT 59620
(406) 444-2878

Treatment referral:
If you or someone you know is having problems with alcohol or other drugs, the number to call in MONTANA for referral to a helping agency is (406) 444-2827, Monday through Friday, 8 a.m. to 5 p.m.

Nebraska

Prevention Coordinator
Division on Alcoholism and Drug Abuse
Department of Public Institutions
P.O. Box 94728
Lincoln, NE 68509-4728
(402) 471-2851

> *Treatment referral:*
> *If you or someone you know is having problems with alcohol or other drugs, the number to call in NEBRASKA for referral to a helping agency is (402) 471-2851*

Nevada

Prevention Coordinator
Department of Human Resources
505 East King Street, Room 500
Carson City, NV 89710
(702) 885-4790

> *Treatment referral:*
> *If you or someone you know is having problems with alcohol or other drugs, the number to call in NEVADA for referral to a helping agency is (702) 885-4790 in northern Nevada and (702) 486-5250 elsewhere in Nevada, 8 a.m. to 5 p.m. Monday through Friday.*

New Hampshire

Prevention Coordinator
New Hampshire Office of Alcohol and Drug Abuse
Prevention
6 Hazen Drive
Concord, NH 03301
(800) 852-3345, ext. 4628 (toll free)
(603) 271-4628

> *Treatment referral:*
> *If you or someone you know is having problems with alcohol or other drugs, the number to call in NEW HAMPSHIRE for a complete resource guide of statewide treatment services is (800) 852-3345 ext. 4628 (toll free) or (603) 271-4628.*

New Jersey

Prevention Coordinator
New Jersey Department of Health
Division of Alcoholism and Drug Abuse
CN 362
Trenton, NJ 08620-0362
(609) 292-4414

> *Treatment referral:*
> *If you or someone you know is having problems with alcohol or other drugs, the number to call in NEW JERSEY for referral to a helping agency is (609) 292-7232 or (800) 322-5525 (toll free).*

Toll-free hotline number
New Jersey Department of Health: (800) 367-6543
New Jersey Drug Hotline: (800) 225-0196
Alcohol Hotline: (800) 322-5525
AIDS Hotline: (800) 624-2377
COCAINE Hotline: (800) COCAINE [(800 262-2463]
Narcotics Anonymous: (800) 992-0401
New Jersey Self-Help Clearing-house: (800) 452-9790

New Mexico

State Prevention Coordinator
HED/BHSD/Substance Abuse Bureau
1190 St. Francis Drive
Santa Fe, NM 87503
(505) 827-2589

Treatment referral:
If you or someone you know is having problems with alcohol or other drugs, the number to call in NEW MEXICO for referral to a helping agency is (505) 256-8300, Monday through Friday, 8 a.m. to 5 p.m.

New York

New York State Division of Alcoholism and Alcohol Abuse
Deputy Director for Prevention and Intervention
194 Washington Avenue
Albany, NY 12210
(518) 474-3377

New York State Division of Substance Abuse Services
Deputy Director for Substance Abuse Prevention
Executive Park South
Box 8200
Albany, NY 12203
(518) 457-2963

Treatment referral:
If you or someone you know is having problems with alcohol or other drugs, the number to call in NEW YORK is (800) 252-2557. For drugs other than alcohol, call (800) 522-5353 (toll free).

North Carolina

Prevention Coordinator
North Carolina Department of
Human Resources
Division of Mental Health, Mental
Retardation, and Substance
Abuse Services
Prevention Coordinator
Albermarle, NC 27611
(919) 733-4670

Treatment referral:
If you or someone you know is having problems with alcohol or other drugs, the number to call in NORTH CAROLINA for referral to a helping agency is (919) 733-4670, Monday through Friday, 8 a.m. to 5 p.m.

North Dakota

Prevention Coordinator
Division of Alcoholism & Drug
Abuse
Department of Human Services
1839 E. Capitol Avenue
Bismarck, ND 58501
(701) 224-2769
(800) 642-6042 (toll free; ND only)
ND Prevention Resource Center
Division of Alcoholism and Drug
Abuse
1839 E. Capitol Avenue
Bismark, ND 58501
(701) 224-3603
(800) 642-6744 (Toll Free; ND only)

Treatment referral:
If you or someone you know is having problems with alcohol or other drugs, the number to call in NORTH DAKOTA for referral to a helping agency is (800) 642-6042, Monday through Friday, 8 a.m. to 5 p.m.

Ohio

Prevention Coordinator
Ohio Department of Health
Department of Alcohol and Drug
Addiction
170 North High Street
Columbus, OH 43215
(614) 466-3445

Treatment referral:
If you or someone you know is having problems with alcohol or other drugs, the number to call in OHIO for referral to a helping agency are (614) 466-3445, and (614) 466-7893, Monday through Friday, 8 a.m. to 5 p.m.

Oklahoma

Director of Prevention Services
Oklahoma Department of Mental Health and Substance Abuse Services
P.O. Box 53277
Oklahoma City, OK 73152-3277
(405) 271-8755

Treatment referral:
If you or someone you know is having problems with alcohol or other drugs, the number to call in OKLAHOMA for referral to a helping agency is (800) 522-9054, 24 hours a day. From out of State, call (405) 271-8755 during regular business hours.

Oregon

Prevention Manager
Office of Alcohol and Drug Abuse Programs
1178 Chemeketa Street, NE
Salem, OR 97310
(503) 378-2163

Treatment referral:
If you or someone you know is having problems with alcohol or other drugs, the number to call in OREGON for referral to a helping agency is (800) 621-1646. In Portland, call (503) 232-8083.

Pennsylvania

Prevention Coordinator
Division of Prevention and Intervention Services
P.O. Box 90, Room 929
Health and Welfare Building
Harrisburg, PA 17108
(717) 783-8200

Treatment referral:
If you or someone you know is having problems with alcohol or other drugs, the number to call in PENNSYLVANIA for referral to a helping agency is (800) 932-0912, Monday through Friday, 7:30 a.m. to 4:00 p.m.

Puerto Rico

Prevention Coordinator
Department of Anti-Addiction Services
Assistant Secretary for Prevention
Barbosa Avenue #414
Rio Piedras, PR 00928
(809) 763-7575, ext. 2224
763-3133

Treatment referral:
If you or someone you know is having problems with alcohol or other drugs, the number to call in PUERTO RICO for referral to a helping agency are (809) 758-7211, 751-5565, 751-5965 and, toll free, (800) 462-4495 or (800) 462-4405, seven days a week from 7 a.m. to 11 p.m.

Rhode Island

Prevention Coordinator
Department of Mental Health, Retardation, and Hospitals
Division of Substance Abuse
P.O. Box 20363
Cranston, RI 02920
(401) 464-2336 (TDD); (401) 464-2191

> *Treatment referral:*
> *If you or someone you know is having problems with alcohol or other drugs, the number to call in RHODE ISLAND for referral to a helping agency is (800) 622-722.*

South Carolina

Prevention Coordinator
Director of Programs and Services
SCCADA
700 Forest Drive
Suite 300
Columbia, SC 25204
(803) 734-9520

> *Treatment referral:*
> *If you or someone you know is having problems with alcohol or other drugs, the number to call in SOUTH CAROLINA for referral to a helping agency is (800) 942-DIAL [(800) 942-3425]. You may also call your county AOD abuse authority.*

South Dakota

Prevention Coordinator
South Dakota Department of Human Services
Division of Alcohol and Drug Abuse
523 East Capitol
Pierre, SD 57501
(605) 773-3123

> *Treatment referral:*
> *If you or someone you know is having problems with alcohol or other drugs, the number to call in SOUTH DAKOTA for referral to a helping agency is (605) 773-3123, 8 a.m. to 5 p.m., Monday through Friday.*

Tennessee

Prevention Coordinator
Department of Mental Health
Division of Alcohol and Drug Abuse Services
706 Church Street, 4th Floor
Nashville, TN 37219
(615) 741-3862

> *Treatment referral:*
> *If you or someone you know is having problems with alcohol or other drugs, the number to call in TENNESSEE for referral to a helping agency is (800) 635-DRUG [(800) 635-3784].*

Texas

Statewide Prevention Coordinator
Texas Commission on Alcohol and Drug Abuse
1705 Guadaloupe Street
Austin, TX 78701-1214
(512) 463-5510

Treatment referral:
If you or someone you know is having problems with alcohol or other drugs, the number to call in TEXAS for referral to a helping agency is (512) 463-5510, Monday through Friday, 8 a.m. to 5 p.m.

Utah

Prevention Representative
Alcohol and Drug Abuse Clinic
50 North Medical Drive
P.O. Box 2500
Salt Lake City, UT 84132
(801) 581-6228

Treatment referral:
If you or someone you know is having problems with alcohol or other drugs, the number to call in UTAH for referral to a helping agency is (801) 538-3939. You may also call one of the regional groups listed below.

Vermont

Prevention Unit
Office of Alcohol and Drug Abuse Programs
Chief of Substance Abuse Prevention
103 South Main Street
Waterbury, VT 05676
(802) 241-2170

Treatment referral:
If you or someone you know is having problems with alcohol or other drugs, the number to call in VERMONT for referral to a helping agency is (802) 241-2170.

Virginia

Substance Abuse Prevention Coordinator
Office of Prevention, Promotion, and Library Services
Department of Mental Health, Mental Retardation, and Substance Abuse Services
P.O. Box 1797
Richmond, VA 23214
(804) 786-1530

Treatment referral:
If you or someone you know is having problems with alcohol or other drugs, the toll-free number to call in VIRGINIA for referral to a helping agency is (800) 451-5544, Monday through Friday, 9 a.m. to 6 p.m.

U.S. Virgin Islands

Prevention Coordinator/RADAR Center
Mental Health, Alcoholism, and Drug Dependency Services
#6 and 7 Estate Ruby, Christiansted
St. Croix, U.S. VI 00820
(809) 773-8443

> *Treatment referral:*
> *If you or someone you know is having problems with alcohol or other drugs, the number to call in the U.S. VIRGIN ISLANDS is (800) 773-4869, 24 hours a day, 7 days a week.*

Washington

Prevention/Early Intervention Administrator
Division of Alcohol and Substance Abuse
M.S. OB-44W
Olympia, WA 98504
(206) 753-3203

> *Treatment referral:*
> *If you or someone you know is having problems with alcohol or other drugs, the toll-free number to call in WASHINGTON for referral to a helping agency is (800) 572-1240.*

West Virginia

Prevention Coordinator
Division on Alcoholism and Drug Abuse
West Virginia Department of Health and Human Resources
State Capitol Complex
Building 3, Room 402
Charleston, WV 25305
(304) 348-2276

> *Treatment referral:*
> *If you or someone you know is having problems with alcohol or other drugs, the number to call in WEST VIRGINIA for referral to a helping agency is (304) 348-2276. You may also call your local community behavioral health center.*

Wisconsin

Office of Alcohol and Other Drug Abuse
Prevention Specialist
1 West Wilson Street, Room 434
Madison, WI 53707
(608) 266-9485

> *Treatment referral:*
> *If you or someone you know is having difficulty with alcohol or other drugs, the number to call in WISCONSIN for referral to a helping agency is (608) 266-2717.*

Wyoming

Prevention Coordinator
Division of Community Programs
Office of Substance Abuse
Hathaway Building
Cheyenne, WY 82002
(307) 777-7115

Treatment referral:
If you or someone you know is having problems with alcohol or other drugs, the number to call in WYOMING for referral to a helping agency is (307) 777-7115, Monday through Friday 9 a.m. to 5 p.m.

HUMAN PRETZEL: 1) SELECT A MEMBER OF THE GROUP WHO LIKES TO SOLVE PUZZLES AND SEND THAT PERSON OUT OF THE ROOM. THE REST OF THE GROUP JOINS HANDS IN A CIRCLE. WITHOUT BREAKING THE HAND CONTACT, THEY TANGLE THEMSELVES UP BY GOING UNDER, OVER, IN, AND OUT OF EACH OTHERS' ARMS. THE MEMBER COMES BACK IN AND GIVES THEM INSTRUCTIONS ON HOW TO UNTANGLE THEMSELVES.

2) HAVE ALL THE KIDS IN THE GROUP FORM A CIRCLE AND REACH ACROSS THE CIRCLE WITH THEIR RIGHT HAND AND GRAB A DIFFERENT Person's LEFT HAND. THE OBJECT IS NOW TO UNTANGLE THE PRETZEL WITHOUT LETTING GO OF ANYONE'S HAND. (TEAMWORK AND COOPERATION)

CEREAL MADNESS: MIX SEVERAL DIFFERENT KINDS OF DRY CEREAL IN A BOWL CHOOSE KINDS WITH DISTINCT SHAPES. GIVE EACH GROUP A BOWL OF THE CEREAL AND A BUNCH OF SPOONS. USING THE SPOONS ONLY, HAVE THEM DIVIDE THEIR CEREAL INTO LIKE KINDS. THE FIRST TEAM TO SUCCESSFULLY SEPARATE THE CEREAL WINS. (TEAMWORK)

JELLY BEANS: GIVE EACH STUDENT AN ENVELOPE CONTAINING JELLY BEANS OF DIFFERENT COLORS. THE OBJECT OF THE GAME IS TO GET NINE JELLY BEANS OF THE SAME COLOR IN YOUR ENVELOPE. ASK OTHER PEOPLE FOR THE COLOR JELLY BEAN THAT YOU WANT AND TRADE THEM FOR ONE OF YOURS. YOU MAY ONLY TRADE ONE JELLY BEAN AT A TIME. THE FIRST PERSON TO GET NINE JELLY BEANS OF THE SAME COLOR IS THE WINNER.

TRY NOT TO YAWN:ASK TWO KIDS TO COME TO THE FRONT. TELL EVERYONE YOU'RE GOING TO HAVE A CONTEST. HAVE THE TWO PEOPLE YAWN AND STRETCH AS MUCH AS POSSIBLE--TRYING TO GET THE OTHERS TO YAWN. HAVE OTHERS WATCH THEM AND TRY NOT TO YAWN. AS PEOPLE BREAK DOWN AND YAWN, HAVE THEM JOIN THE YAWNERS AT THE FRONT. AFTER A MINUTE OR SO, HAVE EVERYONE STRETCH, YAWN, OPEN AND SHUT EYES, AND ROLL AND SHRUG SHOULDERS.

BALLOON SHENANIGANS: FORM PAIRS AND GIVE EACH PERSON A BALLOON. HAVE THE PAIRS PLACE THE BALLOON ON THE FLOOR.
PICK UP THE BALLOON WITH THEIR ELBOWS.....
PICK UP THE BALLOON WITH THEIR BACKS......
RUN RELAYS WITH THE BALLOONS BETWEEN THEIR HEADS---THEIR HIPS

STYLE SHOW: DIVIDE INTO GROUPS OF 5 / EACH GROUP NEEDS A MODEL, 2 DESIGNERS, A NARRATOR, AND A WRITER. THEY WILL DESIGN, CREATE, DRESS THE MODEL, WRITE SCRIPT, MODEL, NARRATE FOR THE STYLE SHOW WHICH WILL FOLLOW.

DESIGN THE FOLLOWING WEAR FOR THE YEAR 2050:
SCHOOL, EVENING, SPORTS, WORK, PROM

SUPPLIES: SARAN WRAP, ALUMINUM FOIL, GARBAGE BAGS, TRASH CAN BAGS, STRING, RUBBER BANDS, ETC.

VARIATION: BRIDAL WEAR USING TOILET PAPER, PAPER TOWELS, ETC.

ROWDIE RECIPES: BEFORE THE MEETING WRITE THE FOLLOWING FOODS ON INDEX CARDS: EGGS, CHEESE, BREAD, TOMATO SAUCE, PICKLES, BOLOGNA, MUSTARD, KETCHUP, MAYONNAISE, TUNA, PEPPERONI, TOMATO, LETTUCE, HAMBURGER, BACON.
INSTRUCTION: LEADER CALLS OUT A DISH OR A MEAL, AND ALL THE INGREDIENTS MUST RUN TO THE CENTER OF THE ROOM TO ANSWER A QUESTION FOR THE REST OF THE GROUP. QUESTIONS COULD RELATE TO ANY TOPIC, OR COULD BE GETTING TO KNOW YOU IN NATURE. QUESTIONS COULD RELATE TO FOOD.

CALL OUT THE FOLLOWING: **BLT SANDWICH, OMELETTE, TUNA SANDWICH, BREAKFAST, PIZZA, CASSEROLE, CHEF'S SALAD, SUBMARINE SANDWICH, CHEESEBURGER.**

MARSHMALLOW ON A STRING: GIVE PAIRS TWO MARSHMALLOWS AND A PIECE OF STRING 3-4 FEET LONG. INSTRUCT THEM TO TIE THE MARSHMALLOW ON BOTH ENDS. ON PARTNER PUT THE MARSHMALLOW IN HIS,HER MOUTH. OBJECT IS TO SWING THE MARSHMALLOW WITH HIS HEAD TO GET IT INTO HIS PARTNERS MOUTH. NO HANDS MAY BE USED.

ORGANIZED ORCHESTRA: DIVIDE INTO 3 GROUPS. THE FIRST GROUP CLAPS THE BEAT--THE SECOND GROUP STOMPS (DOUBLE TIME) -- THE THIRD GROUP SINGS OR WHISTLES THE SONG THE RHYTHM OF THE OTHER GROUPS. SONGS: **LEAN ON ME, SCHOOL SONG, ROW, ROW, ROW YOUR BOAT, ETC.INCREASE AND DECREASE VOLUME.**

FUN ACTIVITIES FOR RETREAT

TOWER BUILDERS:
GIVE EVERY TWO PEOPLE A HANDFUL OF MARSHMALLOWS AND SEVERAL TOOTHPICKS. HAVE A RACE TO SEE WHICH PAIR CAN BUILD THE TALLEST TOWER--CAPABLE OF STANDING BY ITSELF. REWARD WITH LEFT OVER MARSHMALLOWS. (TALK ABOUT WORKING TOGETHER, BUILDING A STRONG FOUNDATION, ETC.)

IMPROMPTU SPEECHES: *OBSERVE THE PARTICIPANT FOR EASE OF PRESENTATION, EYE CONTACT, VOICE PROJECTION, ETC.*

PEOPLE SEARCH

COMPLIMENT TOSS: HAVE EVERYONE SIT IN A CIRCLE. USING A BALL, BEANBAG, OR OTHER TOSSIBLE ITEM, TOSS EACH OTHER COMPLIMENTS. HAVE THE PERSON HOLDING THE BEANBAG TOSS IT TO SOMEONE ACROSS THE CIRCLE, AND AS HE OR SHE DOES, GIVE THAT PERSON A COMPLIMENT. EMPHASIZE THAT THESE ARE TO BE PERSONALITY TRAITS, NOT PHYSICAL TRAITS. TO REALLY KEEP THINGS MOVING, HAVE THE ENTIRE GROUP CLAPPING A BEAT THAT THE TOSSES MUST FOLLOW. AS THE COMPLIMENTS ARE FLYING, BE SURE TO SEE THAT EVERYONE RECEIVES THE BAG AT LEAST ONCE.

MUSICAL PAPER PLATES: YOU WILL NEED A PAPER PLATE FOR EACH PERSON EXCEPT ONE AND SOME MUSIC. SAY: GET UP, STAND UP AND MOVE AROUND. IT'S PAPER-PLATE-PUSHING TIME.
DISTRIBUTE THE PAPER PLATES. ONE PERSON WON'T GET ONE. HAVE KIDS PLACE THE PAPER PLATES IN A LARGE CIRCLE ON THE FLOOR.
INSTRUCTIONS WE'RE GOING TO PLAY MUSICAL PAPER PLATES. WALK CLOCKWISE AROUND THE CIRCLE WHILE THE MUSIC IS PLAYING. WHEN THE MUSIC STOPS, SIT ON A PLATE. IF YOU Don't GET A PLATE, YOU'RE NO OUT. INSTEAD, SIT ON THE LAP OF A PERSON WHO'S SITTING ON A PLATE.
REMOVE A PLATE FOR EACH TIME YOU STOP THE MUSIC. THE KIDS ARE NEVER OUT, THEY JUST KEEP PILING UP ON THE REMAINING PLATES AND PEOPLE. CONTINUE UNTIL EVERYONE IS PILED UP ON ONE PLATE.